This book is extremely powerful in providing insights on the way entrepreneurship offers tools for understanding how an entrepreneurial firm can succeed in international business. It deals with the essential theoretical concepts and strategic actions, and delves into the social and environmental dimensions with such dedication as no other book in the market does. After reading the book, you will have many new inspiring research ideas and wisdom about international entrepreneurship.

Mika Gabrielsson,
Professor of International Business,
University of Eastern Finland

Contemporary Entrepreneurship Issues in International Business

EMERGING ISSUES IN INTERNATIONAL BUSINESS AND GLOBAL STRATEGY

ISSN: 2661-4901

Series Editor: Hussain G Rammal *(University of Technology Sydney, Australia)*

Published

Vol. 1 *Contemporary Entrepreneurship Issues in International Business*
edited by Pavlina Jasovska, Danielle Logue and Hussain G Rammal

Emerging Issues in International Business and Global Strategy – **Volume 1**

Contemporary Entrepreneurship Issues in International Business

Editors

Pavlina Jasovska
Danielle Logue
Hussain G Rammal

University of Technology Sydney, Australia

World Scientific

NEW JERSEY • LONDON • SINGAPORE • BEIJING • SHANGHAI • HONG KONG • TAIPEI • CHENNAI • TOKYO

Published by

World Scientific Publishing Co. Pte. Ltd.
5 Toh Tuck Link, Singapore 596224
USA office: 27 Warren Street, Suite 401-402, Hackensack, NJ 07601
UK office: 57 Shelton Street, Covent Garden, London WC2H 9HE

Library of Congress Cataloging-in-Publication Data
Names: Jasovska, Pavlina, editor. | Logue, Danielle, editor. | Rammal, Hussain, editor.
Title: Contemporary entrepreneurship issues in international business / edited by Pavlina Jasovska, Danielle Logue, Hussain G Rammal, University of Technology Sydney, Australia.
Description: New Jersey : World Scientific, 2021. | Series: Emerging issues in international business and global strategy, 2661-4901 ; volume 1 | Includes bibliographical references and index.
Identifiers: LCCN 2020044705 (print) | LCCN 2020044706 (ebook) | ISBN 9789811228438 (v. 1 ; hardcover) | ISBN 9789811228445 (v. 1 ; ebook for institutions) | ISBN 9789811228452 (v. 1 ; ebook for individuals)
Subjects: LCSH: Entrepreneurship. | International business enterprises.
Classification: LCC HB615 .C64785 2021 (print) | LCC HB615 (ebook) | DDC 338.8/8--dc23
LC record available at https://lccn.loc.gov/2020044705
LC ebook record available at https://lccn.loc.gov/2020044706

British Library Cataloguing-in-Publication Data
A catalogue record for this book is available from the British Library.

For any available supplementary material, please visit
https://www.worldscientific.com/worldscibooks/10.1142/12045#t=suppl

Desk Editors: Aanand Jayaraman/Sandhya Venkatesh

Typeset by Stallion Press
Email: enquiries@stallionpress.com

https://doi.org/10.1142/9789811228445_fmatter

About the Editors

Pavlina Jasovska is Lecturer of International Business and Strategy at the University of Technology Sydney, Australia. Her research interests are in the internationalisation of both small and large firms with a specific focus on entrepreneurship and institutional embeddedness across borders. Pavlina's research appears in journals such as *Journal of World Business* and *Journal of Knowledge Management.*

Danielle Logue is Associate Professor of Innovation, Entrepreneurship and Strategy at the University of Technology Sydney, Australia. Her research interests include the emergence of new markets and fields, social innovation and processes of social, digital and cultural entrepreneurship. Danielle's research has been published in journals such as *Strategic Management Journal, Academy of Management Annals, Organization Studies, Human Relations* and *Journal of Management Inquiry*, where she also serves on the editorial board.

Hussain G. Rammal is Associate Professor of International Business and Strategy at the University of Technology Sydney, Australia. Hussain is co-editor-in-chief of the *Review of International Business and Strategy* journal published by Emerald and the founding editor of the book series *Emerging Issues in International Business and Global Strategy*, published by World Scientific. He is the Real Impact Editor (Oceania) for the *Journal of Knowledge Management* and serves on the editorial boards of leading journals, including *International Business Review and Accounting, Auditing and Accountability Journal*. Hussain's research has been published in journals such as *Journal of World Business, International Business Review*, *Journal of Business Ethics*, *Journal of Knowledge Management,* and *Accounting, Auditing and Accountability Journal*. His research interests include the inter- and intra-organisational transfer of knowledge, trade in services and the role of the state in firms' internationalisation process.

https://doi.org/10.1142/9789811228445_fmatter

Contents

https://doi.org/10.1142/9789811228445_fmatter

Introduction — The Evolution of Entrepreneurship Studies in the International Business Literature: Trends and Direction for Future Research

Pavlina Jasovska*, Danielle Logue†, Hussain G. Rammal‡

University of Technology Sydney, Australia

**pavlina.jasovska@uts.edu.au*

†danielle.logue@uts.edu.au

‡hussain.rammal@uts.edu.au

Abstract

The field of international entrepreneurship (IE) has withstood significant challenges to gain legitimacy and establish itself as a valid area of research. Historically, IE literature has focused on the rapid and early internationalisation of new ventures and start-ups. However, over time, researchers have acknowledged that it is the identification and capture of international opportunities that represents an act of entrepreneurship in disrupting and creating markets in foreign countries. By applying this broader definition of IE, researchers can study activities by entrepreneurs and their start-ups solving social, cultural and environmental challenges in foreign markets. In this chapter, we review the development of IE, introduce the chapters in this book and highlight some important insights and avenues for future research.

Keywords: International entrepreneurship; International new ventures; Born globals; International opportunity.

International Entrepreneurship

The role of entrepreneurship in international business has evolved since the 1990s. Until then, international business was mainly a domain of large and established firms forming subsidiaries all over the world. However, since the 1990s, small and medium-sized enterprises and entrepreneurial start-ups have started to grow beyond their domestic markets in large numbers. This growth was facilitated by globalisation, falling national trade barriers, liberalisation of markets and developments in transport and information technology (Knight, 2001). As an immediate response, interest in this research, labelled as international entrepreneurship, has surged among both practitioners (Rennie, 1993) and academic scholars (Knight and Cavusgil, 1996; McDougall, 1989; Oviatt and McDougall, 1994). Indeed, international entrepreneurship has become one of the most dynamic and debated research domains. Our motivation for this edited book is, therefore, to contribute to and extend the most recent debates with studies covering diverse geographies, contexts and research questions that all meaningfully provide a novel perspective on the latest state of international entrepreneurship.

We structure this introduction into three parts. In the first part, we provide a brief overview of international entrepreneurship and its development since the early 1990s. We describe three stages — each of them covering a distinct definition of international entrepreneurship. We look at these definitions as important building blocks to determine the boundaries of the international entrepreneurship domain and explain why they were central to researchers and theorists at that time. We also highlight why definitions shifted over time, and hence, how international entrepreneurship moved along the three stages which we describe. In the second part, we provide an overview of the chapters in this edited book. The final part presents the insights and contributions of this book and outlines areas of future research inquiry.

First Stage: Fascination with a New Phenomenon: 1994–2005

At the beginning of the domain development, international entrepreneurship scholars were fascinated by the changes in the global arena, such as falling national trade barriers and advancements in technologies and transport that enabled smaller and resource-poor firms to internationalise early and rapidly after their inception. We regard this era of early research on international entrepreneurship as phenomenon driven. Although such rapid and early internationalisation was noted in academic literature even earlier (Hedlund and Kverneland, 1985), the work on internationalising start-ups and small firms, and specifically on early and rapid cross-border venturing, can be traced back to seminal articles of Oviatt and McDougall (1994) and Knight and Cavusgil (1996). These authors introduced to the academic audience the concepts of *International New Ventures* (INVs) (Oviatt and McDougall, 1994) and *Born Globals* (BGs) (Knight and Cavusgil, 1996). Both articles later received the Decade Award of the *Journal of International Business Studies*.

Oviatt and McDougall (1994) define international new venture as follows:

> … a business organisation that, from inception, seeks to derive significant competitive advantage from the use of resources and the sale of outputs in multiple countries. (p. 49)

Knight and Cavusgil (1996) refer to born global firms as follows:

> … small, technology oriented companies that operate in international markets from the earliest days of their establishment. (p. 11)

Evident from the above definitions, BGs are extreme and narrow cases of rapid and early internationalisation and can be characterised as a subset of new international ventures (Coviello, 2015). Nevertheless, both INVs and BGs share major commonalities, such as both are young firms that internationalise rapidly after their inception.

The reason for studying these "new" types of firms went beyond simple interest. Researchers at that time believed that their internationalisation pattern contradicted traditional internationalisation frameworks emphasising gradual and staged internationalisation (Bilkey and Tesar,

1977; Johanson and Wiedersheim-Paul, 1975) and the necessity of internationalising firms to possess firm-specific advantages (Buckley and Casson, 1976/1991; Dunning, 1980). In particular, the liabilities present during internationalisation, such as liability of foreignness (Hymer, 1960/1976; Zaheer, 1995), were expected to discourage small and young firms from internationalising. Established models in international business predicted that successful internationalisation can start after firms gain resources, experience, knowledge, legitimacy and reputation in their home markets and then they would internationalise to countries that are similar to their home countries. These assumptions were refuted by the internationalisation patterns of INVs and BGs.

During this first stage, the domain of international entrepreneurship slowly gained a considerable amount of legitimacy and recognition among researchers within but also outside of the international business discipline, for example a Special Research Forum published in the *Academy of Management Journal* (McDougall and Oviatt, 2000). Moreover, in 2003, the *Journal of International Entrepreneurship* was established, and *International Entrepreneurship and Management Journal's* first issue was published in 2005. Scholars who attempted to refine and extend international entrepreneurship research did not significantly challenge existing concepts of *International New Ventures* and *Born Globals* (Reuber *et al.*, 2017). Researchers rather played with different aspects of time, age and speed, such as in the cases of instant internationals (McAuley, 1999), born-again globals (Bell *et al.*, 2001) or born graduals (Moen and Servais, 2002). Thus, a strong focus on firm-level characteristics persisted.

Second Stage: From Broadening the Scope to Reconciliation: 2005–2014

While in the first stage authors mostly stayed in the circle of firm-level variables (time, age and speed), in the following years, the international entrepreneurship domain started to refocus away from simply seeing international entrepreneurship as rapid and early internationalisation. In this second era, scholars attempted to go back to the original roots of this domain: entrepreneurship and international business. Researchers realised that constricting the discipline of international entrepreneurship only to young and rapidly internationalising firms is quite limiting and also not consistent with the founding theories. In particular, in their core, entrepreneurship and international business are not restricted to age or speed of firm activities (Keupp and Gassmann, 2009). Entrepreneurship is about creating new end means in products and services (Shane and Venkataraman, 2000) or new markets and categories (Santos and Eisenhardt, 2009; Wry *et al.*, 2011). Despite entrepreneurship scholars exploring why some opportunities get created and acted on, many early studies on international entrepreneurship did not account for frameworks grounded in general entrepreneurship research.

The reconciliation of the field's core elements and focus on theoretical grounding led to several revisions of international entrepreneurship definitions — see Keupp and Gassmann (2009) for an overview. The most significant update was the one incorporating the notion of opportunity development (Oviatt and McDougall, 2005). Hence, international entrepreneurship went beyond being only about early and rapid internationalisation to covering the following:

> ... the discovery, enactment, evaluation, and exploitation of opportunities — across national borders — to create future goods and services. (p. 7)

Opportunities, as a core concept of entrepreneurship, are about market imperfections identified and exploited by an entrepreneur who connects unstructured information and its flow with resources to generate an innovation (Casson, 2003). In a single-country scenario, such market imperfections are about taking advantage of bounded rationality of market actors to create new products, services or markets. On the contrary, in international business, such market imperfections are defined by different geographies. Therefore, international entrepreneurship is about opportunities to create new markets in foreign countries (Johanson and Vahlne, 2009; Mainela *et al.*, 2014). Such opportunities can be part of exchanges between the focal firm and its international business partner (Ellis, 2011). Moreover, the extent to which international entrepreneurs can see and act upon opportunities is determined by their attitude towards desirability and feasibility (Muzychenko and Liesch, 2015).

This new perspective brought to the fore "individual-level factors related to the recognition and pursuit of opportunities, the institutional- and industry-level factors which enable or constrain the pursuit of opportunities, and the post-entry processes and outcomes through which the pursuit of opportunity is enacted" (Reuber *et al.*, 2018, p. 396). Focus on entrepreneurial opportunities has not only broadened the perspective on entrepreneurial activities across the borders but also helped uncover factors and outcomes which were not visible before. For example, the researchers were able to study why some opportunities can be identified but not exploited or why some individuals and not others can see the opportunities as attractive and feasible to pursue.

Third Stage: Going Back to the Core: 2014–Present

The current era is characterised by international entrepreneurship scholars continuing to search for theoretical grounds at the intersection of international business and entrepreneurship. However, this time by not only centring on the entrepreneurial or opportunity side but also on the features of cross-border entry. While there were several influential articles during this time, we consider a review article by Mainela *et al.* (2014) as the starting point. In their paper, Mainela *et al.* (2014) provide a fine-grained overview of the concept of international opportunities, which they define as follows:

> … a situation that both spans and integrates elements from multiple national contexts in which entrepreneurial action and interaction transform the manifestations of economic activity. (p. 120)

In their definition, the authors highlight that tensions and interactions arising from the multiplicity of cross-border settings are the ultimate drivers of international opportunities (Mainela *et al.*, 2014). Hence, they focus on contextual differences — a unique element of international business studies.

International entrepreneurship research has, in recent years, recognised the importance of contextual embeddedness. While the latest decade of research on international entrepreneurship has largely focused on the notion of international opportunity and market-making, Reuber *et al.* (2018) importantly note that researching the definition of opportunity is meaningless without including the context. Hence, while the creative destruction and pursuit of opportunity across borders have remained central, researchers started to look at further possibilities to describe various situations, contexts, types of actors and also different stages of opportunity development (Reuber *et al.*, 2017). Institutions in home countries and host countries both enable and constrain entrepreneurial action. Contextualisation is an important element in both international business studies and international entrepreneurship (Mainela *et al.*, 2014). It provides a fruitful perspective on studying, for instance immigrant entrepreneurs (Elo *et al.*, 2018), the role of home country institutions in social entrepreneurship across borders (Chen *et al.*, 2018) or entrepreneurs in third-world countries such as those in Africa (Dana and Ratten, 2017).

We see this final stage also as an attempt for going back to traditional international business theories and finding overlaps with international entrepreneurship. For example, the authors of the Uppsala internationalisation model did see the internationalisation process as initiated by "knowledge of opportunities or problems" (Johanson and Vahlne, 1977, p. 27). Hence, it is meaningful to explore the processual nature of international opportunity development, such as what happens with start-ups beyond their early years of life (Reuber *et al.*, 2017; Zander *et al.*, 2015) or before they are incorporated (Hewerdine and Welch, 2013). Furthermore, describing the opportunity process as a market-making activity and "resource recombination ... mirrors resource bundling to craft [firm-specific advantages] in IB theory" (Verbeke and Ciravegna, 2018, p. 389). Verbeke and Ciravegna (2018) illustrate this recombination with an example of Uber, which internationalised rapidly because of the nature of the services they provide, but also due to their ability to recombine their distinct resources: unique product and the ability to rapidly expand their labour base. Finally, Reuber *et al.* (2018) see international entrepreneurs as operating in a "global ecosystem" formed by suppliers, distributors or contractors and link to the notion of "global factory", which was initially developed to understand multinational enterprises and their complex value chains.

In this edited book, we aim to contribute to this third stage of international entrepreneurship. In particular, we wanted to open the door to research topics and areas that are not traditionally covered in academic journals, but are promising topics for the field and interesting ideas to be read by both entrepreneurship and international business scholars. We specified it in our call for chapters that our understanding of international entrepreneurship is not restricted to early and rapid internationalisation. We welcome that authors responding to our call looked at various novel contexts and took different perspectives. With this edited book, we envision to provide further avenues for contributions to international entrepreneurship, which includes drawing from various concepts and theories outside of international business and entrepreneurship.

Overview of Chapters in this Volume

This book is structured in three parts and includes 10 chapters. The first part of the book focuses on "New Concepts and Theorising", and consists of four chapters.

Chapter 1, titled "Effectuation Theory and International Business Research: A Bibliometric Overview" by Gil-Barragan, Aguilera-Castillo and Amaya, highlights the research themes and trends found in the literature on effectuation theory. The authors perform a bibliometric analysis and bibliographic coupling technique to analyse 328 relevant articles. Three areas for future research are identified in the chapter: the need for a deeper understanding of the effectuation principles; analysing the importance of the context of the firm; and researching the relationship between effectuation and international performance of the firm.

Chapter 2 by Jasovska and Liesch titled "Entrepreneurial Market-Making Across Borders: The Case of Cultural and Technological Innovation", answers the question of how entrepreneurial firms can manage the tension between uniqueness and similarity in cross-border situations when the innovation in the firm can be technological or cultural. The authors introduce the four strategies of assembling, disseminating, sharpening and delimitating that define the content of strategies that entrepreneurs might be expected to employ when internationalising.

In Chapter 3, "Effect of International Entrepreneurial Orientation on the Organisational Performance of Brazilian Exporting Companies", Guerra and Farinha measure the strength of the dimensions of innovativeness, proactivity and risk-taking in relation to growth in sales and profitability of companies located in Brazil. The authors find support for the majority of the hypothesised relationships and suggest directions for future research.

Chapter 4, titled "Piecing Together a Jigsaw Puzzle on Intermittent Internationalisation" by Shahid and Hallo, focuses on how global disruptions force international firms to move in and out of markets. Drawing on the internationalisation models, network theory, knowledge-based view and entrepreneurial psychology, the authors demonstrate how the phenomenon of intermittent internationalisation should be explored from multi-theoretical perspectives.

The second part of the book entitled "International Entrepreneurship in Action", consists of the following three chapters.

Kayacı in Chapter 5 titled "Entrepreneurship in Cross-border Investments: Cases of Emerging Multinationals' Strategic Asset-seeking Internationalisation" undertakes a comparative analysis of three cases of Turkish infant multinationals to understand how entrepreneurial internationalisation works in emerging market contexts. The study finds that the success of these firms is based on the founding entrepreneur's ability to manage the underdeveloped institutional context.

In Chapter 6, "Internationalisation and Competitive Strategies of Enterprises", Zapletalová focuses on the relationship between competitive strategy and international activities of entrepreneurial enterprises. Using primary data collected from enterprises from the Czech Republic, the author found that these companies in international markets used the differentiation and differentiation focus strategies. The selection of the appropriate competitive strategy is affected by several variables: industry, resources and knowledge of international markets.

Chapter 7, titled "The Value of Talent Management to Entrepreneurial Spinoff Teams" by Kriz, Moeller, Russo and Liesch, draws on Garnsey's *Theory of the Early Growth of the Firm*, Harper's *Theory of Entrepreneurial Teams* and Timmons' *Model of New Venture Creation* to highlight the value of talent management in supporting entrepreneurial founders and their teams to develop an early stage innovation for domestic and global markets. The authors propose that by understanding complex talent dynamics during the incubation journey, spinoffs can be more effectively managed and technology commercialisation success achieved.

The last part of the book comprises the remaining three chapters that focus on "Social and Environmental Characteristics of International Entrepreneurship".

Chapter 8, titled "Importance of Green Investment and Entrepreneurship for Economic Development" by Djukic and Ilic, discusses the issue of green investment, green finance and green bonds for entrepreneurial activities. The authors compare Malaysia, as a country with a higher level of sustainable development, to Serbia, Northern Macedonia and Bosnia and Herzegovina, as countries that are in the process of transition to a more sustainable investment system. The study highlights best practices of green investment and provides suggestions for how these practices could be adopted in less developed economies.

Chapter 9 by Okyireh and Okyireh reviews published studies on international entrepreneurship in West Africa. The study, titled "The State of Enterprises in West Africa: Psychological, Managerial and Environmental Perspectives", identifies motives for why people engage in entrepreneurial activities in West Africa. The authors suggest that the success of entrepreneurial ventures depends on the entrepreneur, their family and government policies, and classify them into psychological, managerial and environmental factors.

The final chapter, titled "What Causes Social Entrepreneurship at a Societal Level? Emancipation theory as an explanatory framework" by Sena and Pasquini, describes the emergence of social entrepreneurship as an emancipatory phenomenon. The authors identify action resources, emancipative values and civic entitlements as elements of the human empowerment process that drives social entrepreneurship.

Future Research Directions

This volume comes together at an interesting time where we are living through what future generations might refer to as an external shock, leading to major global economic and societal transformation. The interconnectedness of global markets and value chains is disrupted; rapid digital transformation is necessarily occurring and intensifying the fourth industrial revolution (Chalmers *et al.*, 2020). At the same time, countries turn inward to manage public health by closing borders and refocusing on national value chains and resources (Hwang and Höllerer, 2020). The pace of globalisation has weakened, perhaps momentarily, and the taken-for-granted features of international business are challenged, with new entrepreneurial opportunities emerging as entire industries and workforces are displaced, reconfigured and transformed. In this context, the chapters presented in this volume provide several promising and necessary areas for future research.

IE and Entrepreneurial Ecosystems

Several of the chapters point to the role of networks and knowledge systems in understanding how entrepreneurial action and interaction span multiple national contexts, assisting in the identification of opportunities. This holistic standpoint reflects growing attention in entrepreneurial research more broadly to the role of entrepreneurial eco-systems (Jacobides *et al.*, 2018), that we argue is also generative for scholars of international entrepreneurship (Reuber *et al.*, 2017). It is a different way of conceiving international business constellations as compared to markets, alliances or hierarchically managed supply chains. An ecosystem is a "community of organizations, institutions, and individuals that impact the enterprise and the enterprise's customers and supplies" (Teece, 2007, p. 1325). This economic community of interacting actors considers all actors beyond the boundaries of a single industry, providing insights into the environment that a firm or entrepreneur must monitor and react. An eco-system approach to international entrepreneurship highlights multilateral dependencies, modularity or complementarity of activities amongst different actors in an ecosystem and so interactions that may generate entrepreneurial opportunity. While theoretically valuable, the concept is empirically useful as beyond international entrepreneurs having particular personal characteristics or attitudes (Muzychenko and Liesch, 2015). Increasingly important is their ability to understand and conceptualise an entrepreneurial ecosystem, their position within it and opportunities for development, connection or expansion.

IE and Processes of (Open) Innovation

Scholars of international entrepreneurship are being attentive to sources and processes of innovation that generate entrepreneurial opportunities. For example, in Chapter 2 by Jasovska and Liesch, the authors importantly highlight how processes of innovation can be both technological and also cultural. By adopting a more comprehensive definition of innovation and understanding of innovation processes, international entrepreneurship scholars open up a line of inquiry into the impact of how novel processes of innovation, such as open innovation, may transcend and operate across national boundaries. Open innovation has become a significant way for organisations to leverage external sources of innovation through the exchange of knowledge beyond organisational and also national boundaries (Chesbrough, 2003; Chesbrough and Bogers, 2014; Randhawa *et al.*, 2017). In using open innovation processes, firms engage with communities of users or consumers across national settings as co-creators of knowledge and innovation (Bogers *et al.*, 2010). This is increasingly enabled by either internal units or innovation intermediaries that host online, web-based platforms where firms collaborate with internal or external stakeholders (Boudreau and Lakhani, 2009). For international entrepreneurship scholars, this raises questions as to how such sources and changes in knowledge flows and networks of interaction, and the incorporation of local institutional knowledge, enable or constrain opportunity identification and development.

IE and Diffusion, Translation and Institutional Entrepreneurship

Many studies in IE have demonstrated the important role of a country's institutional context in understanding and identifying entrepreneurial opportunities and enabling or constraining their pursuit (see for example Chapter 5). What is less considered, however, is how international entrepreneurship is often a process of institutional entrepreneurship, as theorised in neo-institutional literature, whereby actors diffuse new idea and models, translate them into local contexts and try to foster embeddedness in local institutional contexts (Battilana *et al.*, 2009). Institutional entrepreneurship refers to "the activities of actors who have an interest in particular institutional arrangements and who leverage resources to create new institutions or transform existing ones" (Maguire *et al.*, 2004, p. 657; Hardy and Maguire, 2017). There is by now a large and supportive literature for IE scholars that investigates the global spread of organisational forms and strategies, models, templates and ideas (Dobbin *et al.*, 2007; Djelic and Sahlin-Andersson 2006). It takes the position that institutional entrepreneurs are often carriers of ideas, concepts, practices or business models from one (national) context to another. As they diffuse these ideas, they engage in the process of local translation.

Translation "involves the combination of locally available principles and practices with new ones originating elsewhere" (Campbell 2004, p. 65), with recipients enacting them in different ways, depending on the local institutional context that some describe as a process of "glocalisation" (Drori *et al.*, 2013). We see processes of institutional entrepreneurship and the difficulties of translation in cross-national industries such as accounting (Greenwood and Suddaby, 2006), chemical industry (Hoffman,

1999), forestry (Zietsma and Lawrence, 2010), technology start-ups (Zilber, 2006) and management consulting (David *et al.*, 2013), amongst many others. What this more sociological lens offers is an emphasis on how values, norms and social structures are also part of the entrepreneurship process when attempting to enter markets in new countries or create opportunities.

IE, Social Innovation and Sustainable Development

Increasingly, we are observing scholars examine IE in settings whereby social and sustainable development and innovation are both a drastic need and an opportunity (for example, see Chapters 8, 9 and 10 in particular). Theoretically and empirically, this is an important area of research to further explore. Grand challenges such as inequality, climate change and poverty are both national and cross-national problems requiring international collaboration, collective effort and sharing and translation of knowledge across borders. In doing so, it raises questions as to the role of IE in processes of social innovation that are attempting to address these challenges. Social innovation is a form of social value creation, capture and distribution (Logue, 2019), and often requires cross-sector collaborations to be achieved. As such, international entrepreneurs can simultaneously be social entrepreneurs, when introducing new ventures or models of social innovation from one context to another, contributing to local institutional change (Tracey and Stott, 2017). For IE, social innovation and sustainable development also bring to the fore the importance of IE research to examine a diversity of national contexts and markets, in different stages of development, as we see in this volume from the insights shared from Africa and South America.

In considering how international entrepreneurship as a concept and line of research inquiry has evolved, we again find ourselves at a dramatic moment in time which will no doubt bring substantive theoretical and empirical challenges and also opportunities.

References

Battilana, J., B. Leca, and E. Boxenbaum (2009). 2 how actors change institutions: Towards a theory of institutional entrepreneurship. *Academy of Management Annals*, 3(1), 65–107.

Bell, J., R. McNaughton, and Young, S. (2001). 'Born-again global' firms: An extension to the 'born global' phenomenon. *Journal of International Management*, *7*, 173–189.

Bilkey, W. J. and Tesar, G. (1977). The export behavior of smaller-sized wisconsin manufacturing firms. *Journal of International Business Studies*, 8(1), 93–98.

Bogers, M., A. Afuah, and B. Bastian (2010). Users as innovators: A review, critique, and future research directions. *Journal of Management*, 36(4), 857–875.

Boudreau, K. and K. Lakhani (2009). How to manage outside innovation. *MIT Sloan Management Review*, 50(4), 69–76.

Buckley, P. J. and M. Casson (1976/1991). *The Future of Multinational Enterprise* (2nd ed.). London: The Macmillan Press.

Campbell, J.L. (2004). *Institutional change and globalization.* USA, Princeton University Press.

Casson, M. (2003). *The entrepreneur: An economic theory* (2nd ed.). Cheltenham, UK: Edward Elgar.

Chalmers, D., N. G. MacKenzie, and S. Carter (2020). Artificial Intelligence and Entrepreneurship: Implications for Venture Creation in the Fourth Industrial Revolution. *Entrepreneurship Theory and Practice*, https://doi.org/10.1177/1042258720934581.

Chen, J., Saarenketo, S., and K. Puumalainen (2018). Home country institutions, social value orientation, and the internationalization of ventures. *International Business Review*, 27(2), 443–454.

Chesbrough, H. (2003). *Open Innovation: The New Imperative for Creating and Profiting from Technology*. Harvard Business School Press, Boston, MA.

Chesbrough, H. and M. Bogers (2014). "Explicating open innovation: Clarifying an emerging paradigm for understanding innovation", New Frontiers in Open Innovation, Oxford University Press, Oxford.

Coviello, N. (2015). Re-thinking research on born globals. *Journal of International Business Studies*, 46(1), 17–26.

Dana, L.-P. and Ratten, V. (2017). International entrepreneurship in resource-rich landlocked African countries. *Journal of International Entrepreneurship*, 15(4), 416–435.

David, R. J., W.D. Sine, and H.A. Haveman (2013). Seizing opportunity in emerging fields: How institutional entrepreneurs legitimated the professional form of management consulting. *Organization Science*, 24(2), 356–377.

Djelic, M. L. and K. Sahlin-Andersson (eds.) (2006). *Transnational Governance: Institutional Dynamics of Regulation.* Cambridge University Press.

Dobbin, F., B. Simmons, and G. Garrett (2007). The global diffusion of public policies: Social construction, coercion, competition, or learning? *Annual Review of Sociology*, 33, 449–472.

Drori, G. S., M. A. Höllerer, and P. Walgenbach (eds.). (2013). *Global Themes and Local Variations in Organization and Management: Perspectives on Glocalization*. Routledge.

Dunning, J. H. (1980). Toward an eclectic theory of international production: Some empirical tests. *Journal of International Business Studies*, 11(1), 9–31.

Ellis, P. D. (2011). Social ties and international entrepreneurship: Opportunities and constraints affecting firm internationalization. *Journal of International Business Studies*, 42(1), 99–127.

Elo, M., Sandberg, S., Servais, P., Basco, R., Cruz, A. D., Riddle, L., and F. Täube (2018). Advancing the views on migrant and diaspora entrepreneurs in international entrepreneurship. *Journal of International Entrepreneurship*, 16(2), 119–133.

Greenwood, R. and R. Suddaby (2006). Institutional entrepreneurship in mature fields: The big five accounting firms. *Academy of Management Journal*, 49(1), 27–48.

Hardy, C. and S. Maguire (2017). Institutional entrepreneurship and change in fields. In Greenwood, R., C. Oliver, T. Lawrence, and R. Meyer (eds.). *The Sage Handbook of Organizational Institutionalism*, UK, Sage: 261–280.

Hedlund, G. and Kverneland, A. (1985). Are Strategies for Foreign Markets Changing? The case of Swedish investment in Japan. *International Studies of Management & Organization*, 15(2), 41–59.

Hewerdine, L. and Welch, C. (2013). Are International New Ventures Really New?: A process study of organizational emergence and internationalization. *Journal of World Business*, 48(4), 466–477.

Hoffman, A. J. (1999). Institutional evolution and change: Environmentalism and the US chemical industry. *Academy of Management Journal*, 42(4): 351-371.

Hymer, S. H. (1960/1976). *The International Operations of National Firms: A Study of Direct Foreign Investment*. Cambridge, MA: MIT Press.

Jacobides, M. G., C. Cennamo, and A. Gawer (2018). Towards a theory of ecosystems. *Strategic Management Journal*, 39(8), 2255–2276.

Johanson, J. and J. –E. Vahlne (1977). The internationalization process of the firm: A model of knowledge development and increasing foreign market commitments. *Journal of International Business Studies*, 8(1), 23–32.

Johanson, J. and J. –E. Vahlne (2009). The uppsala internationalization process model revisited: From liability of foreignness to liability of outsidership. *Journal of International Business Studies*, 40(9), 1411–1431.

Johanson, J. and F. Wiedersheim-Paul (1975). The internationalization of the firm: Four Swedish cases. *Journal of Management Studies*, 12(3), 305–323.

Keupp, M. M. and O. Gassmann (2009). The past and the future of international entrepreneurship: A review and suggestions for developing the field. *Journal of Management*, 35(3), 600–633.

Knight, G. A. (2001). Entrepreneurship and strategy in the international SME. *Journal of International Management*, 7(3), 155–171.

Knight, G. A. and S. T. Cavusgil (1996). The Born Global Firm: A Challenge to Traditional Internationalization Theory. In S. T. Cavusgil, and T. K. Madsen (Eds.), *Advances in International Marketing* (pp. 11–26). Bingley, UK: JAI Press.

Logue, D. (2019). *Theories of social innovation*. UK, Edward Elgar Publishing.

Mainela, T., Puhakka, V., and P. Servais (2014). The concept of international opportunity in international entrepreneurship: A review and a research agenda. *International Journal of Management Reviews*, 16(1), 105–129.

McAuley, A. (1999). Entrepreneurial instant exporters in the Scottish arts and crafts Sector. *Journal of International Marketing*, 7(4), 67–82.

McDougall, P. P. (1989). International versus domestic entrepreneurship: New venture strategic behaviour and industry structure. *Journal of Business Venturing*, 4, 387–400.

McDougall, P. P. and B. M. Oviatt (2000). International entrepreneurship: The intersection of two research paths. *Academy of Management Journal*, 43(5), 902–906.

Moen, Ø. and P. Servais (2002). Born global or gradual global? Examining the export behavior of small and medium-sized enterprises. *Journal of International Marketing* 10(3), 49–72.

Muzychenko, O. and P. W. Liesch (2015). International opportunity identification in the internationalisation of the firm. *Journal of World Business*, 50(4), 704–717.

Oviatt, B. M. and P. P. McDougall (1994). Toward a theory of international new ventures. *Journal of International Business Studies*, 25(1), 45–64.

Oviatt, B. M. and P. P. McDougall (2005). The internationalization of entrepreneurship. *Journal of International Business Studies*, 36(1), 2–8.

Randhawa, K., E. Josserand, J. Schweitzer, and D. Logue (2017). Knowledge collaboration between organizations and online communities: The role of open innovation intermediaries. *Journal of Knowledge Management*, 21(6), 1293–1318.

Rennie, M. W. (1993). Global Competitiveness: Born Global. *McKinsey Quarterly*, (4), 45–52.

Reuber, A. R., P. Dimitratos, and O. Kuivalainen (2017). Beyond categorization: New directions for theory development about entrepreneurial internationalization. *Journal of International Business Studies*, 48(4), 411–422.

Reuber, A. R., G. A. Knight, P. W. Liesch, and L. Zhou (2018). International entrepreneurship: The pursuit of entrepreneurial opportunities across national borders. *Journal of International Business Studies*, 49(4), 395–406.

Santos, F. M. and K. M. Eisenhardt (2009). Constructing markets and shaping boundaries: Entrepreneurial power in nascent fields. *Academy of Management Journal*, 52(4), 643–671.

Shane, S. and S. Venkataraman (2000). The promise of entrepreneurship as a field of research. *Academy of Management Review*, 25(1), 217–226.

Teece, D.J. (2007). Explicating dynamic capabilities: The nature and microfoundations of (sustainable) enterprise performance. *Strategic Management Journal*, 28(13), 1319–1350.

Tracey, P. and N. Stott (2017). Social innovation: a window on alternative ways of organizing and innovating. *Innovation*, 19(1), 51–60.

Verbeke, A. and L. Ciravegna (2018). International entrepreneurship research versus international business research: A false dichotomy? *Journal of International Business Studies*, 49(4), 387–394.

Wry, T., M. Lounsbury, and M. A. Glynn (2011). Legitimating nascent collective identities: Coordinating cultural entrepreneurship. *Organization Science*, 22(2), 449–463.

Zaheer, S. (1995). Overcoming the Liability of Foreignness. *Academy of Management Journal*, 38(2), 341–363.

Zander, I., P. McDougall-Covin, and E. L. Rose (2015). Born globals and international business: Evolution of a field of research. *Journal of International Business Studies*, 46(1), 27–35.

Zietsma, C. and T. B. Lawrence (2010). Institutional work in the transformation of an organizational field: The interplay of boundary work and practice work. *Administrative Science Quarterly*, 55(2), 189–221.

Zilber, T.B. (2006). The work of the symbolic in institutional processes: Translations of rational myths in Israeli high tech. *Academy of Management Journal*, 49(2), 281–303.

Part 1

New Concepts and Theorising

https://doi.org/10.1142/9789811228445_0001

Chapter 1

Effectuation Theory and International Business Research: A Bibliometric Overview

Juan M. Gil-Barragan[*,‡], Andrés Aguilera-Castillo[†,§] and Sergio Andres Salas Amaya[*,¶]

[*]*Universidad EAN, Bogotá, Cundinamarca, Colombia*

[†]*University of Urbino, Urbino, Italy*

[‡]*jmgilbar@universidadean.edu.co*

[§]*a.aguileracastillo@campus.uniurb.it*

[¶]*sasalas@universidadean.edu.co*

Abstract

This chapter aims to provide a better understanding of effectuation theory by analysing 328 articles collected from the Scopus database. For this purpose, a bibliometric analysis and a bibliographic coupling were performed. Despite the growing interest of effectuation theory in international entrepreneurship research, the development of this research remains in a nascent stage. Therefore, the aim of this chapter is to identify the main research themes, the intellectual structure and the main trends of this academic field to guide international business researchers in possible areas of future research.

Keywords: Effectuation; Entrepreneurship; Bibliometric analysis; Co-citation analysis; Intellectual structure.

Introduction

The traditional body of international entrepreneurship research is based on rational decision-making models, called causation (Sarasvathy, 2001). Causation is a goal-driven approach in which the future is predictable; therefore, it usually involves actions such as analysing long-run opportunities and selecting the ones that might deliver the best returns; designing a strategy to take advantage of resources and capabilities; developing business plans; doing market research; analysing the competitor's environment; and implementing and controlling the process to achieve these goals (Chandler *et al.*, 2011).

In contrast, effectuation is a means-driven approach in which the future is unpredictable (Sarasvathy, 2001). Effectuation logic is a decision-making process which consists of mobilising resources and capacities within the control of their network to co-create the future (Sarasvathy *et al.*, 2014). It also focuses on opportunity development and on taking advantage of unexpected outcomes (Chetty *et al.*, 2015; Sarasvathy and Dew, 2005b). The effectual approach is based on the following principles: (1) available means, including who I am, what I know and whom I know; (2) experimentation, which means trying different approaches before starting the venture; (3) affordable loss, which refers to estimating how much loss is affordable rather than calculating expected returns; (4) flexibility to explore new opportunities; and (5) pre-commitments within the network to control the future (Sarasvathy, 2008). From a practical point of view, effectuation is appropriate in contexts of uncertainty (Gil-Barragan *et al.*, 2020b; Sarasvathy and Dew, 2005b). Therefore, effectuation theory has been used to explain how firms are created (Sarasvathy, 2001), how entrepreneurs identify international opportunities (Mainela *et al.*, 2014; Reuber *et al.*, 2016, 2018), how the decision-making process is affected by uncertainty (Dew *et al.*, 2009) and how entrepreneurs successfully create international ventures (Andersson, 2011; Galkina and Chetty, 2015; Harms and Schiele, 2012; Sarasvathy *et al.*, 2014; Schweizer *et al.*, 2010).

Since Sarasvathy's (2001) seminal article, effectuation has become one of the dominant theories in entrepreneurship (Alvarez *et al.*, 2016), and has garnered considerable scholarly attention over the last 20 years in international entrepreneurship studies and opportunity development (Karami *et al.*, 2019; Kujala and Törnroos, 2018; Perry *et al.*, 2012; Read *et al.*, 2016). An explanation of the growing attention is that effectuation theory recognises uncertainty as inherent to the internationalisation process (Sarasvathy, 2001), which is largely ignored in the causation approach (Sarasvathy, 2008). Consequently, effectuation has been connected to the Uppsala model and the Born Global theories (Harms and Schiele, 2012; Jones *et al.*, 2011; Schweizer *et al.*, 2010). However, this research field is still in a nascent stage (Perry *et al.*, 2012, Gil-barragan *et al.*, 2020a). It means that theory development is characterised by open-ended research questions, mainly addressed by qualitative methods (Edmondson and McManus, 2007). Therefore, a better understanding of the effectuation theory will contribute to the development of international entrepreneurship research (Karami *et al.*, 2019).

To our knowledge, two literature reviews have documented the development of this field (Matalamäki, 2017; Perry *et al.*, 2012). In the first review, using classification systems, Perry *et al.* (2012) analysed 29 articles to identify the relevance of effectuation to explain entrepreneurs' behaviour. Matalamäki (2017) complemented this literature review by increasing the analysed articles to 81. However, there is a lack of bibliometric literature review. Bibliometric methods complement traditional literatures reviews by applying statistical methods to determine quantitative and qualitative changes in a given scientific research topic, to establish the profile of publications on the topic and to detect tendencies within a discipline (Tranfield *et al.*, 2003; Zupic and Čater, 2015). Therefore, the aim of this chapter is to identify the structure and development of the effectuation theory over time, to determine its structure and key trends. This chapter presents a review of the literature on the theory of effectuation theory by analysing 328 articles collected from the Scopus database. The references were obtained considering all the documents published between 2001 and 2019 in the journals indexed in Scopus, which has broader coverage than the Web of Science (WOS) database (Zupic and Čater, 2015).

Using Bibexcel, VOSviewer, Pajek and Tree of Science to analyse the data, we applied mathematical and statistical methods to classify the literature and identify its structure and key trends. The results of the bibliometric analysis are based on the evaluation of the most influential authors, articles and journals. The impact of the articles was evaluated, and the structure of the research field was identified. This methodology is based on two approaches (Cobo *et al.*, 2015). The first approach is to use a series of indicators to evaluate the impact of the articles in a given field of study. The second approach is to identify the structure and dynamic aspects of the research field. This approach entails performing bibliographic coupling and co-citation analysis. Bibliographic coupling consists of studying the citing documents, whereas co-citation analysis consists of exploring the cited documents (Van Eck and Waltman, 2014). This chapter is organised as follows: First, we describe the state of the art of the theory of effectuation. Second, the method is described, and a brief description of bibliometric methods is given. Third, the results of the bibliometric analysis are presented, and the conceptual structure of the literature is explained. Finally, conclusions, limitations and research opportunities are presented.

Method

Bibliometric analysis is a quantitative and qualitative research methodology that allows the evaluation of the development of a particular research field and its influence on the development of knowledge (Leeuwen, 2006). This methodology also permits us to identify the impact of the citations of the actors in this area and connections within the research field (Cobo *et al.*, 2015). Bibliometric analysis is a methodology that complements the traditional structured literature review (Zupic and Čater, 2015). Its main contribution is analysis and science mapping, which allows the evaluation of the research and reveals the structure and dynamics of the scientific field (Cobo *et al.*, 2015), supporting a qualitative method to identify current research, analysing the various research questions and evaluating the future research questions. Moreover, it is based on statistical methods to analyse data from an objective and quantitative perspective (Merigó *et al.*, 2015). The bibliometric methodology utilises co-citation analysis of a research field. This analysis contributes to identify the cited documents that received the highest number of citations from a third document. In other words, if most of the documents cite a specific article, it means that this article has been influential on the development of the research field.

The publications analysed in this paper were gathered from the Scopus database because it contains a large number of high-impact and academically relevant documents (Mongeon and Paul-Hus, 2016). To select the relevant literature, we searched for the keywords "effectuation", "effectual", "causation" and "effectuation theory" in the topic (i.e. title, abstract or keywords) of published documents and then studied the abstracts to select only those that were directly related to the subject of this study (Leeuwen, 2006). Moreover, the year 2001 was selected as the starting year because the seminal article that gave basis to formulate the effectuation theory was published in that year (Perry *et al.*, 2012). The study selected 298 articles, 23 book chapters and 7 books; in total, 328 documents were obtained. The search process in Scopus was limited to research that was published between 2001 and 2019.

Results of the Bibliographic Analysis

General Results

Table 1 shows a summary of the general results of the bibliometric analysis. The H index shows that among the analysed documents, 43 had been cited at least 43 times, which reflects the importance of a specific group of articles (Martínez *et al.*, 2014). On average, the 328 documents have been cited almost 16 times.

According to Figures 1 and 2, since the publication of Sarasvathy's (2001) seminal article, research on effectuation has increased significantly. Particularly, the number of publications per year shows that the authors' productivity has increased significantly since 2007. However, most of the documents have been published in the last five years (67%). Similarly, the influence of this research area has grown more in the last 5 years. The number of citations shows that there have been an increasing number of international researchers who study the phenomena (Merigó *et al.*, 2016).

Most Influential Documents

Table 2 shows the top-ranking influential documents. To select these documents, a co-citation analysis of the 328 documents from Scopus was

Table 1: Overall Summary of Results

Criteria	Quantity/Scopus
Number of published articles	328
Total times cited	5.230
Average citations per item	15.95
H index	43
Number of authors	501

Source: Compiled by the authors based on Scopus data.

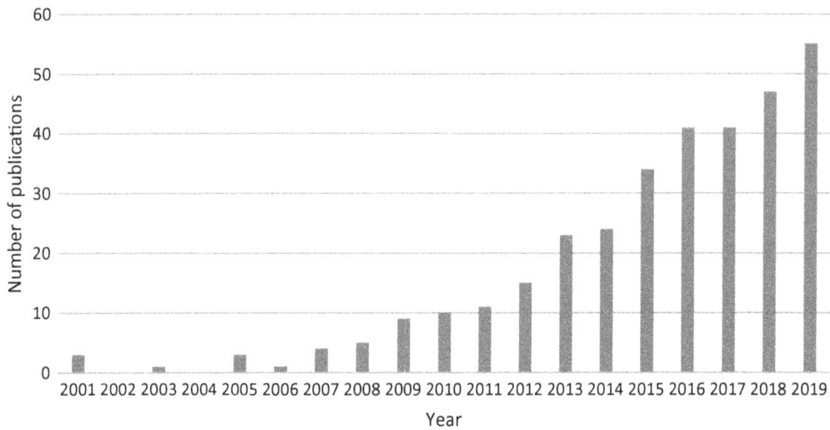

Figure 1: Number of Publications Per Year

Source: Compiled by the authors based on WoS data.

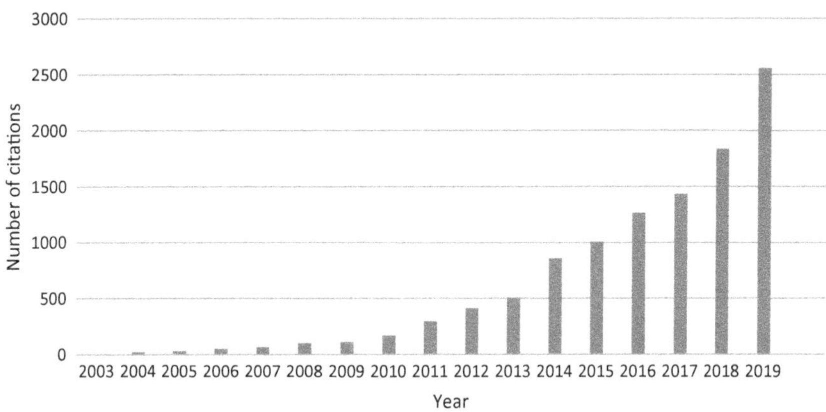

Figure 2: Number of Citations Per Year

Source: Compiled by the authors based on WoS data.

performed. Table 2 displays the documents with the highest number of citations among the 328 analysed documents. The article "Causation And Effectuation: Toward A Theoretical Shift From Economic Inevitability To Entrepreneurial Contingency" (Sarasvathy, 2001) is the most cited article in the collection, with 263 citations. This study introduces the framework that defines the principles of effectuation logic. Dew, Read,

Table 2: Most Influential Documents

No.	Authors	Title of the Article	Citations by the 328 Documents from Scopus	Total Citations Scopus
1	Sarasvathy (2001)	Causation and effectuation: Toward a theoretical shift from economic inevitability to entrepreneurial contingency	263	1.895
2	Dew *et al.* (2009)	Effectual versus predictive logics in entrepreneurial decision-making: Differences between experts and novices	98	276
3	Chandler *et al.* (2011)	Causation and effectuation processes: A validation study	97	243
4	Sarasvathy and Dew (2005b)	New market creation through transformation	95	221
5	Fisher (2012)	Effectuation, causation, and bricolage: A behavioural comparison of emerging theories in entrepreneurship research	80	244
6	Perry *et al.* (2012)	Entrepreneurial effectuation: A review and suggestions for future research	78	162
7	Read *et al.* (2009)	Meta-analytic review of effectuation and venture performance	77	169
8	Yin (2003)	Case study research: Design and methods	71	
9	Wiltbank *et al.* (2006)	What to do next? The case for non-predictive strategy	68	266
10	Eisenhardt (1989)	Building theories from case study research	67	n/a
11	Wiltbank *et al.* (2009)	Prediction and control under uncertainty: Outcomes in angel investing	63	167
12	Read and Sarasvathy (2005)	Knowing what to do and doing what you know: Effectuation as a form of entrepreneurial expertise	60	n/a
13	Brettel *et al.* (2012)	Corporate effectuation: Entrepreneurial action and its impact on R&D project performance	60	137
14	Shane and Venkataraman (2000)	The promise of entrepreneurship as a field of research	60	5.012
15	Baker and Nelson (2005)	Creating something from nothing: Resource construction through entrepreneurial bricolage	59	1.251

Source: Authors' elaborations based on WOS database.

Sarasvathy and Wiltbank are the authors of the second-most influential document, "Effectual Versus Predictive Logics in Entrepreneurial Decision-Making: Differences Between Experts and Novices", with 98 citations. In this article, Dew *et al.* (2009) demonstrate that expert entrepreneurs make decisions using effectuation logic, while novice entrepreneurs tend to use causation logic. The third most influential document is "Causation and Effectuation Processes: A Validation Study", accounting 97 citations. In this study, Chandler *et al.* (2011) develop and validate measures of causation and effectuation. The fourth most cited article, "New Market Creation Through Transformation", proposes that new market creation is a dynamic process that includes effectual thinking and networks (Sarasvathy and Dew, 2005b). The article "Effectuation, Causation, And Bricolage: A Behavioural Comparison of Emerging Theories in Entrepreneurship Research" sheds light on the contrast and similarities among effectuation, bricolage and causation frameworks (Fisher, 2012).

Most Influential Authors

There are 501 single authors in the sample of articles analysed. Table 3 reveals the top-ranking influential authors. In order to classify and understand their importance, we ranked them based on the total number of citations. According to the data, Sarasvathy, Dew, Read and Wiltbank are the most influential authors, with 1.094, 631, 552 and 420 citations, respectively. Sarasvathy is the author of the article "Causation and effectuation: Toward a theoretical shift from economic inevitability to entrepreneurial contingency", considered the seminal work of this theory (Arend *et al.*, 2015). Moreover, Sarasvathy S. and Dew N. are the co-authors of the articles "New market creation through transformation" (Sarasvathy and Dew, 2005b); "Entrepreneurial logics for a technology of foolishness" (Sarasvathy and Dew, 2005a); and "Innovations, stakeholders & entrepreneurship" (Dew and Sarasvathy, 2007). Likewise, Sarasvathy, Dew, Read and Wiltbank are co-authors of the following influential articles: "Effectual versus predictive logics in entrepreneurial decision-making: Differences between experts and novices" (Dew *et al.*, 2009); "What to do next? The case for non-predictive strategy" (Wiltbank *et al.*, 2006); "Marketing under uncertainty: The logic of an effectual approach" (Read *et al.*, 2009); "Prediction and control under uncertainty: Outcomes in angel investing" (Wiltbank *et al.*, 2009); "Designing organizations that design environments: Lessons from entrepreneurial

Table 3: Most Influential Authors

Rank	Authors	Citations Among the Analysed Documents	Documents	Average Citation Per Document
1	Sarasvathy S	1094	35	31.3
2	Dew N	631	21	30.0
3	Read S	552	16	34.5
4	Wiltbank R	420	15	28.0
5	Chandler G	213	7	30.4
6	Mauer R	163	10	16.3
7	Shane S	162	6	27.0
8	Venkataraman S	160	7	22.9
9	Song M	145	3	48.3
10	Mckelvie A	141	5	28.2
11	Detienne D	130	5	26.0
12	Eisenhardt K	125	8	15.6
13	Barney J	121	6	20.2
14	Mumford T	112	2	56.0
15	Coviello N	106	10	10.6
16	Simon H	106	7	15.1
17	Brettel M	105	5	21.0
18	March J	85	5	17.0
19	Baker T	81	3	27.0
20	Fisher G	80	1	80.0

Source: Authors' elaborations based on WOS database.

expertise" (Sarasvathy *et al.*, 2008); and "Outlines of a behavioural theory of the entrepreneurial firm" (Dew *et al.*, 2008). It means that the main most influential authors developed research together, especially between the years 2005 and 2009. Finally, Sarasvathy, Dew, Read and Wiltbank are also the most productive authors with the publication of 35, 21, 16 and 15 documents, respectively.

In relation to the number of documents by an author, we observed that Sarasvathy and Dew are the most productive authors, with 35 and 21 documents each, respectively. However, when reviewing the average citation per document, Mumford and Song have the higher average.

The average citation per document of Mumford corresponds to the articles "Issues of research design and construct measurement in entrepreneurship research: the past decade" (Chandler *et al.*, 2007) and "Causation and effectuation processes: A validation study" (Chandler *et al.*, 2011). The documents with the higher number of citations of Song are "Marketing under uncertainty: The logic of an effectual approach" (Read *et al.*, 2009) and "A meta-analytic review of effectuation and venture performance" (Read *et al.*, 2009). In both articles, Read is the main author.

Most-cited References

To identify the co-occurrence relationship of the 328 documents included in the sample, a co-citation analysis was performed. The network of co-cited articles shows the grouping of different articles in four clusters. Each cluster includes both articles on effectuation and articles from other disciplines that have had a profound impact on the development of the effectuation theory. As Figure 3 shows, the first cluster — red colour — consists of articles related to international entrepreneurship

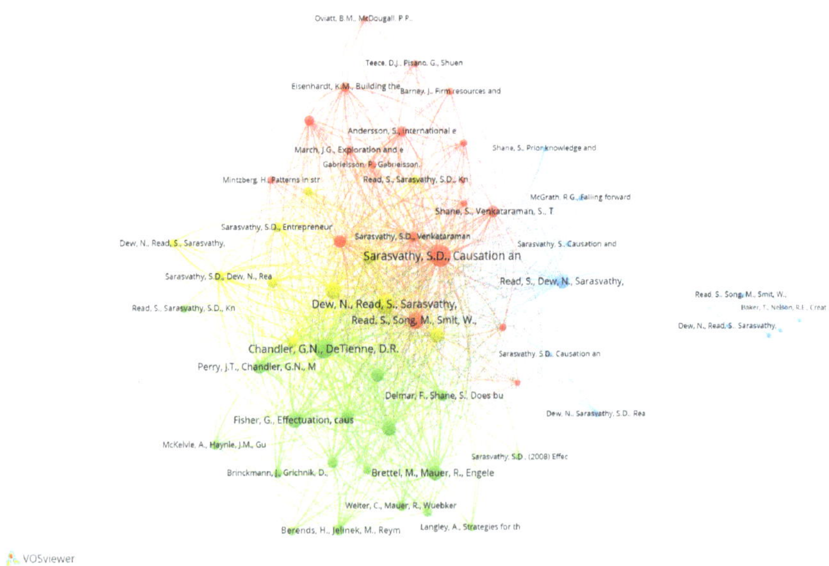

Figure 3: Network of Co-citation of Articles

Source: VOSviewer based on Scopus data.

(e.g. Andersson, 2011; Gabrielsson and Gabrielsson, 2013; Oviatt and McDougal, 1994). The second cluster — blue colour — comprises articles about marketing and innovation (e.g. Baker and Nelson, 2005; Read *et al.*, 2009; Sarasvathy and Dew, 2005). The third cluster — green colour — consists of theoretical reviews (e.g. Fisher, 2012; Perry *et al.*, 2012) Finally, the fourth cluster — yellow — consists of the development of uncertainty (e.g. Mcmullen and Shepherd, 2006; Wiltbank *et al.*, 2006, 2009).

Figure 3 also shows that the seminal article "Causation and effectuation: Toward a theoretical shift from economic inevitability to entrepreneurial contingency" (Sarasvathy, 2001) has the greater number of connections with and within the clusters. Moreover, the articles of Sarasvathy, Dew, Read and Wiltbank are points of departure of the clusters.

Figure 4 shows the citation relationship of the most cited authors. Cluster 1 — red colour — reveals the authors that question the systematic planning view of different theories. For instance, the studies of Knight (1921), Weick (1979), March (1982, 1991), March and Simon (1958),

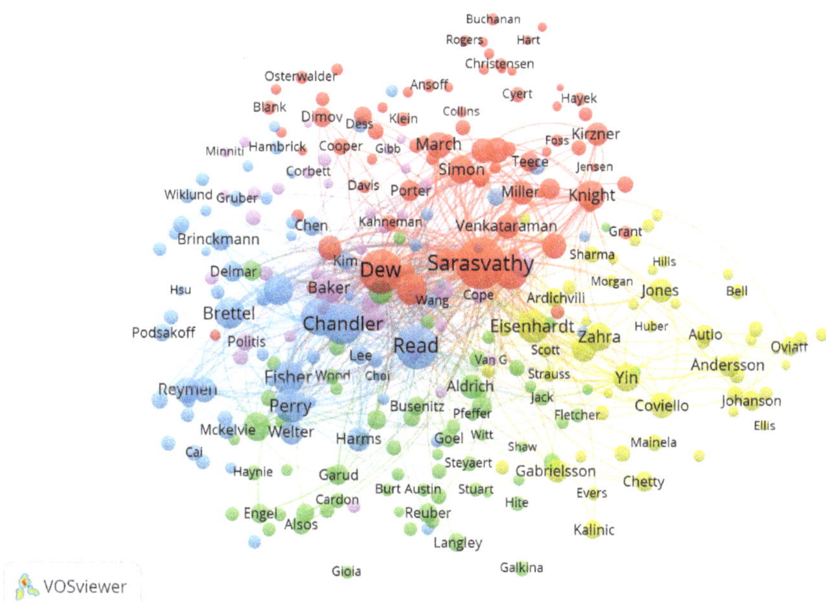

Figure 4: Network of Co-cited Authors

Source: VOSviewer based on Scopus data.

Mintzberg (1978), Mintzberg and McHugh (1985) and Sarasvathy (2001) are well known for proposing different approaches to the systematic planning. Authors in the second cluster — yellow — are scholars from international entrepreneurship (e.g. Coviello, Oviatt, Ellis, Chetty, Gabrielsson and Zahra). The third cluster — green colour — comprises authors who debate the effectuation theory. For instance, Goel and Karri (2006) argue that effectuation supposes over-trust. Arend *et al.* (2015) state that effectuation theory has an unsatisfactory level of testability. Finally, Garud and Gehman (2016) explain that effectuation theory lacks unanimous framework. The fourth cluster — blue colour — comprises authors who study entrepreneurial behaviour (e.g. Chandler, Read, Fisher, Perry).

Conceptual Structure

Based on the analysed data from Scopus, we were able to identify the conceptual structure of the theory of effectuation. For this purpose, and following Robledo *et al.* (2014), we constructed the tree of science of effectuation theory (Figure 5). This tree has three categories. The first one

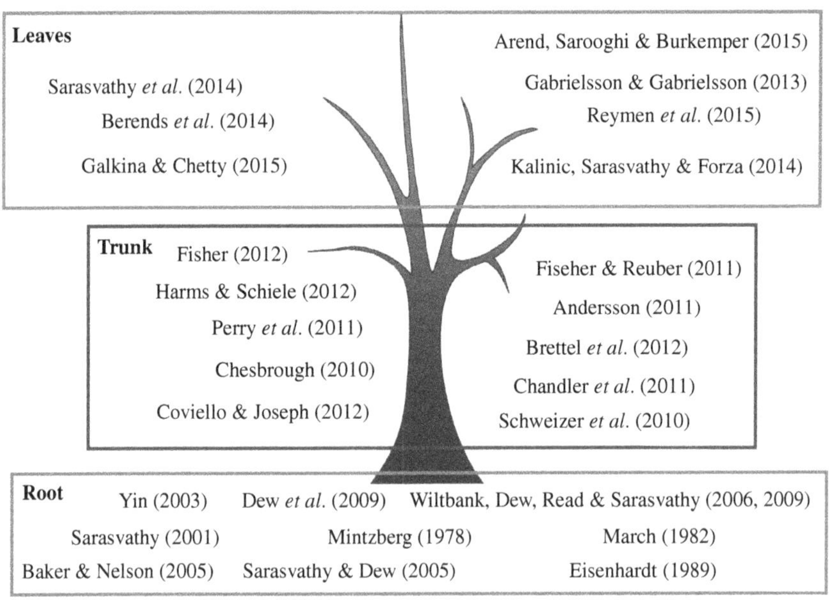

Figure 5: Tree of Science of Effectuation Theory

Source: Tree of Science based on Scopus data.

is the root, which contains the articles that provide the theoretical and conceptual foundations for this area of research. This category shows that effectuation theory is based on the non-systematic planning approach (March, 1982; Mintzberg, 1978; Sarasvathy, 2001); on the explanation of the effectuation principles, such as uncertainty (Dew *et al.*, 2009; Sarasvathy and Dew, 2005b; Wiltbank *et al.*, 2006, 2009); on entrepreneurial bricolage (Baker and Nelson, 2005); and on case study methodology (Eisenhardt, 1989; Yin, 2003). Regarding international entrepreneurship research, the root also includes the Uppsala model (Johanson and Vahlne, 1977) and the Born Global theory (Oviatt and McDougal, 1994).

The second category is the trunk, which contains the articles that have developed this area of research. These are classified into four areas. The first area consists of articles that use effectuation theory to investigate marketing and innovation (Brettel *et al.*, 2012; Chesbrough, 2010; Coviello and Joseph, 2012). The second area uses effectuation theory to investigate SMEs' internationalisation process (Andersson, 2011; Harms and Schiele, 2012; Schweizer *et al.*, 2010). This area has been developed through five sub-areas: (1) decision-making process (Chetty *et al.*, 2015; Kalinic *et al.*, 2014); (2) international entrepreneurship (Nowiński and Rialp, 2013; Sarasvathy *et al.*, 2014); (3) marketing (Evers *et al.*, 2012; Mort *et al.*, 2012); (4) networks and recognition of international opportunities (Evers and O'Gorman, 2011; Fuerst and Zettinig, 2015; Galkina and Chetty, 2015); and (5) survival in International Business (Gabrielsson and Gabrielsson, 2013).

The third area uses effectuation theory to investigate entrepreneurial bricolage (Fisher, 2012). The fourth area comprises articles that advance the literature review and measurement instruments (Chandler *et al.*, 2011; Perry *et al.*, 2012).

The third category is the leaves, which consist of the most recent influential articles. These articles show that effectuation is being oriented towards furthering research in marketing and innovation (Berends *et al.*, 2014), venture creation (Reymen *et al.*, 2015) and a deeper research on SMEs' internationalisation process. An interesting aspect to observe is the influence of the international entrepreneurship researchers. Kalinic *et al.* (2014) research the decision-making process of entrepreneurs during internationalisation. Galkina and Chetty (2015) explore the impact of effectuation on knowledge acquisition, identification of international opportunities and networking. Gabrielsson and Gabrielsson (2013) study growth and survival of SMEs in international markets. Finally, Sarasvathy *et al.* (2014) propose recommendations for future research at the intersection of IE and effectuation research. Note that these articles represent 60% of the articles in the leaves category. This indicates the importance of the effectuation theory in this research field. It also shows that the development of research on effectuation theory might be driven by answering the questions how and why SMEs use effectual logic (Ahi *et al.*, 2017; Crick and Crick, 2016; Laine and Galkina, 2017); how the capabilities of the firm affect this process (Kujala and Törnroos, 2018; Nemkova, 2017); and the identification of the effects of effectual logic on the enterprise (Chandra, 2017; Chandra *et al.*, 2015; Deligianni *et al.*, 2017; Ripollés and Blesa, 2017; Yang and Gabrielsson, 2017).

Conclusion and Research Opportunities

By employing bibliometric analysis, this study presents a comprehensive view of the effectuation theory. Considering the co-citation analysis, the graphic mapping and the tree of science, effectuation theory is analysed from different points of view. From an overall perspective, the results show that IE research has had a significant growing interest. The bibliometric analysis of 328 effectuation research documents gathered from the Scopus database shows that the formulation of the effectuation theory is based on criticisms about the systematic planning approach, entrepreneurial bricolage and case studies. It also shows that the disciplines that have had a profound impact on the development of the effectuation theory are international entrepreneurship, venture creation, marketing and innovation. The most recent articles are oriented towards furthering research in these categories. However, among them, international entrepreneurship seems to be most prolific.

Our review reveals three areas for further research (see Table 4). The first one is related to a need for a deeper understanding of the effectuation principles. Effectuation theory is based on the following five principles: the bird-in-hand principle which is confirmed by means of "Who I am", "What I know" and "Who I know"; the affordable loss principle that consists of evaluating opportunities based on whether the downside is acceptable, rather than on the attractiveness of the predicted upside; the crazy quilt principle which is about forming partnerships to jointly co-create the future; the lemonade principle that consists of embracing surprises that arise from uncertain situations; and the pilot-in-plane principle which explains that the future is created rather than predicted (Sarasvathy, 2008). However most of the research has mainly focused on the bird-in-hand and crazy quilt principles (Read *et al.*, 2016). Therefore, further research might provide a deeper understanding about how and why SMEs implement the neglected effectuation principles (Ahi *et al.*, 2017; Crick and Crick, 2016; Laine and Galkina, 2017).

The second area for further research is related to the analysis of the context of the firm. On the one hand, it is well know that institutions can influence firm behaviour (Mesquita and Lazzarini, 2008; North, 1990; Wright *et al.*, 2005; Yamakawa *et al.*, 2008) and the internationalising SMEs' networking activities (Laine and Galkina, 2017). Hence, it would be interesting to use the lens of Institutional theory to advance research on effectuation. On the other hand, the main unit of analysis of effectuation theory is entrepreneurs or SMEs. Therefore, applying effectuation theory to explain the decision-making process of larger firms seems to be promising. This comparison may help to comprehend how the differences in the capabilities of the firm affect the effectual logic (Kujala and Törnroos, 2018; Nemkova, 2017). Moreover, studies that address the differences between developed and emerging economies are needed. For instance, recent literature shows that the internationalisation process of SMEs differs in developed and emerging economies (Ellis, 2011; Musteen *et al.*, 2010). Similarly, when firms face cultural differences, an adapted strategy might be more appropriate (Audretsch *et al.*, 2017; Chung *et al.*, 2012; Dimitratos *et al.*, 2012). These areas may provide important steps to our understanding of how the effectuation decision-making process changes according to the specific context of the firm (Karami, Wooliscroft, and McNeill, 2019).

Finally, future research should consider the effects of effectuation theory on the international performance of the firm. Although international entrepreneurship research has made great advances in measuring firm performance (Brouthers *et al.*, 2015; Gerschewski *et al.*, 2015; Stoian *et al.*, 2017), there is scant research on the effects of effectuation theory on firm performance. Indeed, recent articles are taking the first steps to identify foreign market entry performance (Andersson, 2011); growth and survival (Gabrielsson and Gabrielsson, 2013); marketing performance (Yang and Gabrielsson, 2017); diversification and performance (Deligianni *et al.*, 2017); and overall firm performance (Ahi *et al.*, 2017; Laine and Galkina, 2017).

Table 4: Promising Theoretical Areas for Future Research

Future Directions		
To have a deeper understanding of the effectuation principles	To analyse the importance of context	To identify the effects on the international performance
1. The bird-in-hand principle	1. Institutional theory	1. Product performance
2. The affordable-loss principle	2. Larger firms	2. Financial performance
3. The crazy-quilt principle	3. Contextual difference between developed and emerging economies	3. Growth and survival
4. The lemonade principle	4. Cultural differences	4. Foreign market entry performance
5. The pilot-in-plane principle		5. Marketing performance
		6. Diversification and performance

Source: Authors' elaborations.

Limitation of the Study

This study is restricted to the use of only one database as a source of data collection. This leaves the results valid within this scope, but not necessarily within a larger database. Further studies might extend the research by including other databases such as Google Scholar. Another drawback is the nature of the bibliometric approach, which assumes that authors cite works that they consider important (Leeuwen, 2006), ignoring the complex nature of citing behaviour. Finally, future researchers can also use different types of meta-analytic techniques to analyse the literature.

References

Ahi, A., G. Baronchelli, O. Kuivalainen, and M. Piantoni (2017). International market entry: How do small and medium-sized enterprises make decisions? *Journal of International Marketing*, 25(1), 1–21.

Alvarez, S. A., D. Audretsch, and A. N. Link (2016). Advancing our understanding of theory in entrepreneurship. *Strategic Entrepreneurship Journal*, 10(1), 3–4, https://doi/abs/10.1002/sej.1216.

Andersson, S. (2011). International entrepreneurship, born globals and the theory of effectuation. *Journal of Small Business and Enterprise Development*, 18(3), 627–643, https://doi.org/10.1108/14626001111155745.

Arend, R. J., H. Sarooghi, and A. Burkemper (2015). Effectuation as ineffectual? Applying the 3E theory-assessment framework to a proposed new theory of entrepreneurship. *Academy of Management Review*, 40(4), 630–651, https://doi.org/10.5465/amr.2014.0455.

Audretsch, D. B., M. Obschonka, S. D. Gosling, and J. Potter (2017). A new perspective on entrepreneurial regions: Linking cultural identity with latent and manifest entrepreneurship. *Small Business Economics*, 48(3), 681–697, https://doi.org/10.1007/s11187-016-9787-9.

Baker, T. and R. E. Nelson (2005). Creating something from nothing: Resource construction through entrepreneurial bricolage. *Administrative Science Quarterly*, 50(3), 329–366.

Berends, H., M. Jelinek, I. Reymen, and R. Stultiëns (2014). Product innovation processes in small firms: Combining entrepreneurial effectuation and managerial causation. *The Journal of Product Innovation Management*, 31(3), 616–635, https://doi.org/10.1111/jpim.12117.

Brettel, M., R. Mauer, A. Engelen, and D. Küpper (2012). Corporate effectuation: Entrepreneurial action and its impact on R&D project performance. *Journal of Business Venturing*, 27(2), 167–184, https://doi.org/10.1016/j.jbusvent.2011.01.001.

Brouthers, K. D., G. Nakos, and P. Dimitratos (2015). SME entrepreneurial orientation, international performance, and the moderating role of strategic alliances. *Entrepreneurship: Theory and Practice*, 39(5), 1161–1187, https://doi.org/10.1111/etap.12101.

Chandler, G., D. DeTienne, and T. Mumford (2007). Causation and effectuation: Measure development and theoretical implications. In A. Z. S. Alvarez, P. Davidsson, J. Fiet, G. George, D. F. Kuratko, C. Mason, M. Maula, M. Minniti, S. Sarasvathy, D. A. Shepherd, P. Westhead, J. Wiklund, M. Wright, and S. A. Zahra (ed.), *Frontiers of Entrepreneurship Research*. Wellesley.

Chandler, G. N., D. R. DeTienne, A. McKelvie, and T. V. Mumford (2011). Causation and effectuation processes: A validation study. *Journal of Business Venturing*, 26(3), 375–390, https://doi.org/10.1016/j.jbusvent.2009.10.006.

Chandra, Y. (2017). A time-based process model of international entrepreneurial opportunity evaluation. *Journal of International Business Studies*, 48(4), 423–451, https://doi.org/10.1057/s41267-017-0068-x.

Chandra, Y., C. Styles, and I. F. Wilkinson (2015). Opportunity portfolio: Moving beyond single opportunity explanations in international entrepreneurship research. *Asia Pacific Journal of Management*, 32(1), 199–228, https://doi.org/10.1007/s10490-014-9400-1.

Chesbrough, H. (2010). Business model innovation: Opportunities and barriers. *Long Range Planning*, 43(2–3), 354–363, https://doi.org/10.1016/j.lrp.2009.07.010.

Chetty, S., A. Ojala, and T. Leppäaho (2015). Effectuation and foreign market entry of entrepreneurial firms. *European Journal of Marketing*, 49(9–10), 1436–1459, https://doi.org/10.1108/EJM-11-2013-0630.

Chung, H. F. L., C. L. Wang, and P.-H. Huang (2012). A contingency approach to international marketing strategy and decision-making structure among exporting firms. *International Marketing Review*, 29(1), 54–87, https://doi.org/10.1108/02651331211201543.

Cobo, M. J., M. A. Martínez, M. Gutiérrez-Salcedo, H. Fujita, and E. Herrera-Viedma (2015). 25 years at knowledge-based systems: A bibliometric analysis. *Knowledge-Based Systems*, 80, 3–13, https://doi.org/10.1016/j.knosys.2014.12.035.

Coviello, N. E. and R. M. Joseph (2012). Creating major innovations with customers: Insights from small and young technology firms. *Journal of Marketing*, 76(6), 87–104, https://doi.org/10.1509/jm.10.0418.

Crick, D. and J. Crick (2016). The first export order: A marketing innovation revisited. *Journal of Strategic Marketing*, 24(2), 77–89, https://doi.org/10.1080/0965254X.2014.1001870.

Deligianni, I., I. Voudouris, and S. Lioukas (2017). Do effectuation processes shape the relationship between product diversification and performance in new ventures?. *Entrepreneurship: Theory and Practice*, 41(3), 1–29, https://doi.org/10.1111/etap.12210.

Dew, N., S. Read, S. D. Sarasvathy, and R. Wiltbank (2008). Outlines of a behavioral theory of the entrepreneurial firm. *Journal of Economic Behavior and Organization*, 66(1), 37–59, https://doi.org/10.1016/j.jebo.2006.10.008.

Dew, N., S. Read, S. D. Sarasvathy, and R. Wiltbank (2009). Effectual versus predictive logics in entrepreneurial decision-making: Differences between experts and novices. *Journal of Business Venturing*, 24(4), 287–309, https://doi.org/10.1016/j.jbusvent.2008.02.002.

Dew, N. and S. D. Sarasvathy (2007). Innovations, stakeholders & entrepreneurship. *Journal of Business Ethics*, 74(3), 267–283, https://doi.org/10.1007/s10551-006-9234-y.

Dimitratos, P., I. Voudouris, E. Plakoyiannaki, and G. Nakos (2012). International entrepreneurial culture-Toward a comprehensive opportunity-based operationalization of international entrepreneurship. *International Business Review*, 21(4), 708–721, https://doi.org/10.1016/j.ibusrev.2011.08.001.

Edmondson, A. C. and S. E. McManus (2007). Methodological fit in management field research. *Academy of Management Review*, 32(4), 1155–1179, https://doi.org/10.5465/AMR.2007.26586086.

Eisenhardt, K. M. (1989). Building theories from case study research. *The Academy of Management Review*, 14(4), 532–550.

Ellis, P. D. (2011). Social ties and international entrepreneurship: Opportunities and constraints affecting firm internationalization. *Journal of International Business Studies*, 42(1), 99–127, https://doi.org/10.1057/jibs.2010.20.

Evers, N., S. Andersson, and M. Hannibal (2012). Stakeholders and marketing capabilities in international new ventures: Evidence from Ireland, Sweden and Denmark. *Journal of International Marketing*, 20(4), 46–71, https://doi.org/10.1509/jim.12.0077.

Evers, N. and C. O'Gorman (2011). Improvised internationalization in new ventures: The role of prior knowledge and networks. *Entrepreneurship and Regional Development*, 23(7–8), 549–574, https://doi.org/10.1080/08985621003690299.

Fisher, G. (2012). Effectuation, causation, and bricolage: A behavioral comparison of emerging theories in entrepreneurship research. *Entrepreneurship: Theory and Practice*, 36(5), 1019–1051, https://doi.org/10.1111/j.1540-6520.2012.00537.x.

Fuerst, S. and P. Zettinig (2015). Knowledge creation dynamics within the international new venture. *European Business Review*, 27(2), 182–213, https://doi.org/10.1108/EBR-03-2013-0036.

Gabrielsson, P. and M. Gabrielsson (2013). A dynamic model of growth phases and survival in international business-to-business new ventures: The moderating effect of decision-making logic. *Industrial Marketing Management*, 42(8), 1357–1373, https://doi.org/10.1016/j.indmarman.2013.07.011.

Galkina, T. and S. Chetty (2015). Effectuation and networking of internationalizing SMEs. *Management International Review*, 55(5), 647–676, https://doi.org/10.1007/s11575-015-0251-x.

Garud, R. and J. Gehman (2016). Theory evaluation, entrepreneurial processes, and performativity. *Academy of Management Review*, 41(3), 544–549, https://doi.org/10.5465/amr.2015.0407.

Gerschewski, S., E. L. Rose, and V. J. Lindsay (2015). Understanding the drivers of international performance for born global firms: An integrated perspective. *Journal of World Business*, 50(3), 558–575, https://doi.org/10.1016/j.jwb.2014.09.001.

Gil-barragan, J. M., J. A. Belso-Martínez, and F. Mas-Verdú (2020a). Bibliometric analysis of the theory of effectuation and the internationalisation of small and medium-sized enterprises. *European Journal of International Management*, *in-press*.

Gil-barragan, J. M., J. A. Belso-Martínez, and F. Mas-Verdú (2020b). When do domestic networks cause accelerated internationalization under different decision-making logic? Evidence from weak institutional environment. *European Business Review*, 32(2), 227–255, https://doi.org/10.1108/EBR-11-2018-0191.

Goel, S. and R. Karri (2006). Entrepreneurs, effectual logic, and over-trust. *Entrepreneurship Theory and Practice*, 30(4), 477–493, https://doi.org/10.1111/j.1540-6520.2006.00131.x.

Harms, R. and H. Schiele (2012). Antecedents and consequences of effectuation and causation in the international new venture creation process. *Journal of*

International Entrepreneurship, 10(2), 95–116, https://doi.org/10.1007/s10843-012-0089-2.

Johanson, J. and J. E. Vahlne (1977). The internationalization process of the firm: A model knowledge development and increasing foreign market commitments. *Journal of International Business Studies*, 8(1), 23–32, https://doi.org/10.2307/254397.

Jones, M. V., N. E. Coviello, and Y. K. Tang (2011). International entrepreneurship research (1989–2009): A domain ontology and thematic analysis. *Journal of Business Venturing*, 26(6), 632–659, https://doi.org/10.1016/j.jbusvent.2011.04.001.

Kalinic, I., S. D. Sarasvathy, and C. Forza (2014). "Expect the unexpected": Implications of effectual logic on the internationalization process. *International Business Review*, 23(3), 635–647, https://doi.org/10.1016/j.ibusrev.2013.11.004.

Karami, M., B. Wooliscroft, and L. McNeill (2019). Effectuation and internationalisation: A review and agenda for future research. In *Small Business Economics*. Springer New York LLC, https://doi.org/10.1007/s11187-019-00183-4.

Knight, F. H. (1921). *Risk, Uncertainty, and Profit*. Houghton Mifflin.

Kujala, I. and J. Å. Törnroos (2018). Internationalizing through networks from emerging to developed markets with a case study from Ghana to the U.S.A. *Industrial Marketing Management*, 69, 98–109, https://doi.org/10.1016/j.indmarman.2018.01.015.

Laine, I. and T. Galkina (2017). The interplay of effectuation and causation in decision making: Russian SMEs under institutional uncertainty. *International Entrepreneurship and Management Journal*, 13(3), 905–941, https://doi.org/10.1007/s11365-016-0423-6.

Leeuwen, T. V. (2006). The application of bibliometric analyses in the evaluation of social science research. Who benefits from it, and why it is still feasible. *Scientometrics*, 66(1), 133–154.

Mainela, T., V. Puhakka, and P. Servais (2014). The concept of international opportunity in international entrepreneurship: A review and a research agenda. *International Journal of Management Reviews*, 16(1), 105–129, https://doi.org/10.1111/ijmr.12011.

March, J. G. (1982). Theories of choice and making decisions. *Society*, 20(1), 29–39, https://doi.org/10.1007/BF02694989.

March, J. G. (1991). Exploration and exploitation in. *Organization Science*, 2(1), 71–87, https://doi.org/10.1287/orsc.2.1.71.

March, J. and H. Simon (1958). *Organizations*. Wiley.

Martínez, M. A., M. Herrera, J. López-Gijón, and E. Herrera-Viedma (2014). H-Classics: Characterizing the concept of citation classics through H-index. *Scientometrics*, 98(3), 1971–1983, https://doi.org/10.1007/s11192-013-1155-9.

Matalamäki, M. J. (2017). Effectuation, an emerging theory of entrepreneurship — towards a mature stage of the development. *Journal of Small Business and Enterprise Development*, 24(4), 928–949, https://doi.org/https://doi.org/10.1108/JSBED-02-2017-0030.

Mcmullen, J. S. and D. A. Shepherd (2006). Entrepreneurial action and the role of uncertainty in the theory of the entrepreneur. *Academy of Management Review*, 31(1), 3–23, https://doi.org/10.4337/9781783479801.00007.

Merigó, J. M., A. M. Gil-Lafuente, and R. R. Yager (2015). An overview of fuzzy research with bibliometric indicators. *Applied Soft Computing Journal*, *27*, 420–433, https://doi.org/10.1016/j.asoc.2014.10.035.

Merigo, M. and D. Urbano (2016). *Academic Research in Innovation: A Country Analysis*, https://doi.org/10.1007/s11192-016-1984-4.

Mesquita, L. F. and S. G. Lazzarini (2008). Horizontal and vertical relationships in developing economies: Implications for SMEs' access to global markets. *Academy of Management Journal*, 51(2), 359–380, https://doi.org/10.5465/AMJ.2008.31767280.

Mintzberg, H. (1978). Patterns in strategy formation. *Management Science*, 24(9), 934–948, https://doi.org/10.1287/mnsc.24.9.934.

Mintzberg, H. and A. McHugh (1985). Strategy formation in an adhocracy. *Administrative Science Quarterly*, 30(2), 160–197, https://doi.org/10.2307/2393104.

Mongeon, P. and A. Paul-Hus (2016). The journal coverage of web of science and scopus: A comparative analysis. *Scientometrics*, 106(1), 213–228, https://doi.org/10.1007/s11192-015-1765-5.

Mort, G. S., J. Weerawardena, and P. Liesch (2012). Advancing entrepreneurial marketing: Evidence from born global firms. *European Journal of Marketing*, 46(3–4), 542–561, https://doi.org/10.1108/03090561211202602.

Musteen, M., J. Francis, and D. K. Datta (2010). The influence of international networks on internationalization speed and performance: A study of Czech SMEs. *Journal of World Business*, 45(3), 197–205, https://doi.org/10.1016/j.jwb.2009.12.003.

Nemkova, E. (2017). The impact of agility on the market performance of born-global firms: An exploratory study of the 'Tech City' innovation cluster. *Journal of Business Research*, 80, 257–265, https://doi.org/10.1016/j.jbusres.2017.04.017.

North, D. C. (1990). *Institutions, Institutional Change and Economic Performance.* Harvard University Press.

Nowiński, W. and A. Rialp (2013). Drivers and strategies of international new ventures from a Central European transition economy. *Journal of East European Management Studies*, 18(2), 191–231.

Oviatt, B. M. and P. P. McDougal (1994). Toward a theory of international new ventures. *Journal of International Business Studies*, 25(1), 45–64.

Perry, J. T., G. N. Chandler, and G. Markova (2012). Entrepreneurial effectuation: A review and suggestions for future research. *Entrepreneurship: Theory and Practice*, 36(4), 837–861, https://doi.org/10.1111/j.1540-6520.2010.00435.x.

Read, S. and S. D. Sarasvathy (2005). Knowing what to do and doing what you know. *The Journal of Private Equity*, 9(1), 45–62, https://doi.org/10.3905/jpe.2005.605370.

Read, S., M. Song, and W. Smit (2009). A meta-analytic review of effectuation and venture performance. *Journal of Business Venturing*, 24(6), 573–587, https://doi.org/10.1016/j.jbusvent.2008.02.005.

Read, S., S. D. Sarasvathy, N. Dew, and W. Robert (2016). Response to Arend, Sarooghi, and Burkemper (2015): Cocreating effectual entrepreneurship research. *Academy of Management Perspectives*, 41(3), 528–536, https://doi.org/10.5465/amr.2015.0180.

Read, S., N. Dew, S. D. Sarasvathy, M. Song, and R. Wiltbank (2009). Marketing under uncertainty: The logic of an effectual approach. *Journal of Marketing*, 73(3), 1–18.

Reuber, A. R., E. Fischer, and N. Coviello (2016). Deepening the dialogue: New directions for the evolution of effectuation theory. *Academy of Management Review*, 41(3), 536–540.

Reuber, A. R., G. A. Knight, P. W. Liesch, and L. Zhou (2018). International entrepreneurship: The pursuit of entrepreneurial opportunities across national borders. *Journal of International Business Studies*, 49(4), 395–406, https://doi.org/10.1057/s41267-018-0149-5.

Reymen, I. M. M. J., P. Andries, H. Berends, R. Mauer, U. T. E. Stephan, and E. V. A. N. Burg (2015). Understanding dynamics of strategic decision making in venture creation: A process study of effectuation and causation. *Strategic Entrepreneurship Journal*, 9(4), 351–379, https://doi/full/10.1002/sej.1201.

Ripollés, M. and A. Blesa (2017). Entry mode choices in the international new ventures context. A study from different theoretical perspectives. *International Entrepreneurship and Management Journal*, 13(2), 465–485, https://doi.org/10.1007/s11365-016-0410-y.

Robledo Giraldo, S., G. A. Osorio Zuluaga, and C. López Espinosa (2014). Networking en pequeña empresa: Una revisión bibliográfica utilizando la teoría de grafos. *Revista Vinculos*, 11(6), 2014.

Sarasvathy, S. D. (2001). Causation and effectuation: Toward a theoretical shift from economic inevitability to entrepreneurial contingency. *The Academy of Management Review*, 26(2), 243–263, https://doi.org/10.2307/259121.

Sarasvathy, S. D. (2008). *Effectuation: Elements of Entrepreneurial Expertise*. Edward Elgar Publishing Limited.

Sarasvathy, S. D. and N. Dew (2005a). Entrepreneurial logics for a technology of foolishness. *Scandinavian Journal of Management*, 21(4 SPEC. ISS.), 385–406, https://doi.org/10.1016/j.scaman.2005.09.009.

Sarasvathy, S. D. and N. Dew (2005b). New market creation through transformation. *Journal of Evolutionary Economics*, 15(5), 533–565, https://doi.org/10.1007/s00191-005-0264-x.

Sarasvathy, S. D., N. Dew, S. Read, and R. Wiltbank (2008). Designing organizations that design environments: Lessons from entrepreneurial expertise. *Organization Studies*, 29(3), 331–350, https://doi.org/10.1177/0170840607088017.

Sarasvathy, S. D., K. Kumar, J. G. York, and S. Bhagavatula (2014). An effectual approach to international entrepreneurship: Overlaps, challenges, and provocative possibilities. *Entrepreneurship Theory and Practice*, 38(1), 71–93, https://doi.org/https://doi.org/10.1111/etap.12088.

Schweizer, R., J. E. Vahlne, and J. Johanson (2010). Internationalization as an entrepreneurial process. *Journal of International Entrepreneurship*, 8(4), 343–370, https://doi.org/10.1007/s10843-010-0064-8.

Shane, S. and S. Venkataraman (2000). The promise of entrepreneurship as a field of research. *Academy of Management Review*, 25(1), 217–226.

Stoian, M. C., J. Rialp, and P. Dimitratos (2017). SME networks and international performance: Unveiling the significance of foreign market entry mode. *Journal of Small Business Management*, 55(1), 128–148, https://doi.org/10.1111/jsbm.12241.

Tranfield, D., D. Denyer, and P. Smart (2003). Towards a methodology for developing evidence-informed management knowledge by means of systematic review. *British Journal of Management*, 14(3), 207–222, https://doi.org/10.1111/1467-8551.00375.

Van Eck, N. J. and L. Waltman (2014). Visualizing bibliometric networks. In Y. Ding, R. Rousseau, and D. Wolfram (Eds.), *Measuring Scholarly Impact: Methods and Practice* (pp. 285–320). Springer International Publishing, https://doi.org/10.1007/978-3-319-10377-8.

Weick, K. (1979). *The Social Psychology of Organizing*. Addison-Wesley, Reading.

Wiltbank, R., N. Dew, S. Read, and S. D. Sarasvathy (2006). What to do next? The case for non-predictive strategy. *Strategic Management Journal*, 27(10), 981–998, https://doi.org/10.1002/smj.555.

Wiltbank, R., S. Read, N. Dew, and S. D. Sarasvathy (2009). Prediction and control under uncertainty: Outcomes in angel investing. *Journal of Business Venturing*, 24(2), 116–133, https://doi.org/10.1016/j.jbusvent.2007.11.004.

Wright, M., I. Filatotchev, R. E. Hoskisson, and M. W. Peng (2005). Strategy research in emerging economies: Challenging the conventional wisdom — Introduction. *Journal of Management Studies*, 42(1), 1–33, https://doi.org/10.1111/j.1467-6486.2005.00487.x.

Yamakawa, Y., M. W. Peng, and D. L. Deeds (2008). What drives new ventures to internationalize from emerging to developed economies? *Entrepreneurship: Theory and Practice*, 32(1), 59–82.

Yang, M. and P. Gabrielsson (2017). Entrepreneurial marketing of international high-tech business-to-business new ventures: A decision-making process perspective. *Industrial Marketing Management*, 64, 147–160, https://doi.org/10.1016/j.indmarman.2017.01.007.

Yin, R. K. (2003). *Case Study Research: Design and Methods* (Sage (ed.)). Thousand Oaks.

Zupic, I. and T. Čater (2015). Bibliometric methods in management and organization. *Organizational Research Methods*, 18(3), 429–472, https://doi.org/10.1177/1094428114562629.

https://doi.org/10.1142/9789811228445_0002

Chapter 2

Entrepreneurial Market-making Across Borders: The Case of Cultural and Technological Innovation

Pavlina Jasovska*,‡ and Peter Liesch†,§

*University of Technology Sydney, Sydney, New South Wales, Australia

†University of Queensland, Brisbane, Queensland, Australia

‡pavlina.jasovska@uts.edu.au

§p.liesch@business.uq.edu.au

Abstract

International entrepreneurship is typified by market-making activities which can be technological or cultural. Technological innovations are created by experimentation, whereas the change through cultural innovation is shaped by the collective endeavours of entrepreneurs. For cultural and technological innovation, we theorise how international entrepreneurs must accommodate the multiplicity of national markets and their diversity to achieve legitimacy, but in doing so, they must also maintain their uniqueness. We identify and elaborate four strategies: assembling, disseminating, sharpening and delimitating. Our contextualisation of cross-border venturing of cultural and technological innovations provides an understanding of how entrepreneurs make markets.

Keywords: Entrepreneurial market-making; Legitimacy; Differentiation; Optimal distinctiveness; Technological innovation; Cultural innovation.

Introduction

A challenge to international entrepreneurs is how the tensions of doing business in foreign markets are overcome. New ventures must adapt to foreign market conditions, as do their rivals, but they also need to offer novelty to gain competitive advantage. For example, in seeking to partner with export firms, foreign distributors must be alert for revelation of the "right" identity in the internationalising firm, the identity that captures their attention. It is reported that new ventures that make markets across borders overcome liabilities in foreign markets by certifying their new technology (Turcan, 2013), forming links with reputable multinational corporations (Nummela *et al.*, 2016), managing organisational identity by incorporation (McGaughey, 2007) or telling convincing stories to stakeholders in a given context (Andersen and Rask, 2014). However, beyond simply overcoming foreign market liabilities, international venturing is challenged by the nature of innovation, be it technological or cultural.

Technological innovation is characterised by ground-breaking novelty, and benefits from original differentiation to drive technological change for market-making such as the Tablet PC introduced by Microsoft, the Walkman produced by Sony or the Internet search introduced by Google (Tushman and Anderson, 1986; Tushman and Murmann, 2002). Entrepreneurs making markets with cultural innovation (Rao *et al.*, 2000), on the contrary, seek collective legitimacy in a constituency to pursue cultural change, such as adventure tourism catering for those who eschew the budget, a packaged holiday inciting a cult-like collective identity of the daring tourist. Early success of technological innovation is strongly defined by competitive pressures for delivering a unique design (Santos and Eisenhardt, 2009) and the foundational years of cultural innovation are characterised by collective action and movement-like endeavours (Rao *et al.*, 2000). When considering ventures operating in multiple geographies, it is less clear whether legitimation is advantageous or whether differentiation would lead to success and survival in foreign markets.

While it has been recognised that international venturing is challenged by various pressures occurring during internationalisation, particularly foreignness and newness (McGaughey, 2007), our understanding of how ventures navigate the tensions specific to the nature of their innovation (technological or cultural) remains limited. We address the dynamics of cross-border venturing in the context of cultural and technological innovation. The literature on optimal distinctiveness of entrepreneurial firms states that both novelty and familiarity are essential for their success (Zimmerman and Zeitz, 2002; Navis and Glynn, 2010; 2011; McKnight and Zietsma, 2018). Crossing diverse geographies brings additional considerations. To illustrate, in the case of internationalising technology entrepreneurs, while liabilities of foreignness and newness and pressures to innovate are present, these ventures might also experience significant technological uncertainty due to the nature of their "new-to-the-world" inventions (Kriz and Welch, 2018). We address the following question: how does the entrepreneurial firm resolve the tension between uniqueness and similarity when innovation in the firm can be technological or cultural?

We introduce four strategies that define the content of strategies that entrepreneurs might be expected to employ when internationalising into new markets: for technological innovation, strategies of *assembling* and *upholding technological market referent*, and for cultural innovation, strategies of *sharpening* and *delimitating within market movement boundaries*. We offer contributions to the literature on international venturing and optimal distinctiveness. We show how entrepreneurial market-making across borders brings the additional complexities of simultaneous presence in diverse and often conflicting environments which can be resolved by well-crafted strategies to achieve optimal distinctiveness. Our treatment of optimal distinctiveness highlights its contextual embeddedness, depending on the innovation and the country (Zhao *et al.*, 2017; see also Haans, 2018). We extend this literature by explicitly addressing the international business context with its unique features such as the liability of foreignness and the multiplicity and diversity of markets in which the firm can operate.

Market-making Entrepreneurs: Technological and Cultural Innovation

While entrepreneurial market-making is characterised by linking the knowledge of entrepreneurs with the resources they can assemble (Casson, 2003), the innovation that unfolds can be driven by technological or cultural change. Entrepreneurs pursuing technological change create groundbreaking innovation "in science and engineering" (Beckman *et al.*, 2012, p. 90) to realise “creative destruction” (Schumpeter, 1942/2003) and become leaders in the industry through taking the position of a “dominant design” (Utterback and Abernathy, 1975), or “cognitive referent” to other industry members (Santos and Eisenhardt, 2009). For example, the design of Segway was considered to be an unprecedented invention:

> The Segway was an engineering marvel, and riding it was a thrill. ‘It was like a magic carpet. It was transformational as a product,’ says Bill Sahlman, the Harvard entrepreneurship professor… (Grant, 2016, p. 51, original quotations).

In this process, several technological designs compete through “experimentation and creative turbulence” (Suárez and Utterback, 1995, p. 418) and “substantial technological rivalry between alternative technological regimes” (Anderson and Tushman, 1990). This rivalry leads to an industry hierarchy. Entrepreneurial firms such as Apple, Google and Microsoft have taken a prime position, even becoming referents for their smartphones, internet search or software industries. This positioning depends on a complex array of factors that include performance, entry timing, efficiency and consumer preferences. In general, the period of experimentation and competition is followed by groundbreaking invention defining the future industry standard and the configuration of followers, with scaling up and economies of scale ultimately being realised.

While we develop our understanding of technology entrepreneurs from the literature that reports on the phenomenon of technology industry life cycles (Utterback and Abernathy, 1975; Anderson and Tushman, 1990; Suárez and Utterback, 1995), we frame this process from a socio-cognitive perspective (Grodal, Gotsopoulos *et al.*, 2015; Suarez *et al.*, 2015). We posit that technology entrepreneurs use symbolic tools and socio-cognitive labels to communicate the nature of their market offerings to relevant stakeholders because “culture is enshrined in technological artefacts” (Lounsbury *et al.*, 2018, p. 6). The following story illustrates how Twitter has transformed how people connect:

> He [founder of Twitter] has also been heralded as the ‘Apparent heir to Steve Jobs’ by GigaOm, thanks to his obsessive and visionary focus on

> product development. He has led Twitter to transform the way people communicate over the media, it has changed the communication of entertainment, politics and almost everyone (Srikanth, 2018, original quotation).

Entrepreneurs pursuing cultural innovation are, on the contrary, characterised by social movement-inspired behaviours where their market-making is "a political project involving collective action" (Rao *et al.*, 2000, p. 238). A social movement is "a set of opinions and beliefs in a population which represents preferences for changing some elements of the social structure and/or reward distribution of a society" (McCarthy and Zald, 1977, p. 1217). Thus, to maintain the activist spirit, the market-making by entrepreneurs is defined by mass action and resource mobilisation of movement members as opposed to competition (Swaminathan and Wade 2001; Lounsbury *et al.*, 2003). Mobilisation happens through fans, geeks, enthusiasts gathering at forums, social media and specialised events to build traction and visibility, as happened in the craft beer industry:

> [T]he social movement–like character of the segment means that craft producers and consumers constitute a self-conscious community…. Information flows rapidly and pervasively through this network, which revolves around the many brewpubs, tap houses, beer clubs (many with selective incentives), organized trips, brewers' guilds, festivals, magazines, and newsletters found in the 'microbrewery' segment (Carroll and Swaminathan, 2000, p. 731, original quotations).

Rather than challenging technological inefficiencies, entrepreneurs introducing cultural innovations address social problems by bringing justice or by developing opposition to the existing *status quo* (e.g. mass production) and its cultural meanings, frames, lifestyles and practices (Rao *et al.*, 2003). Indisputably, technological innovations might also change people's behaviour, for example Google transforming the Internet search, or as shown in the earlier quote of Twitter. However, we have seen how non-technology innovations formed by collective action, instead of experimentation by individual market actors, have led to the renewal of craft brewing (Swaminathan and Wade, 2001), the formation of industry bodies (Rao *et al.*, 2000) or the adoption of nouvelle French cuisine by elite chefs (Rao *et al.*, 2003). Cultural innovations have led to the creation of new markets with, for example temporary accommodation no longer the domain of the large standardised multinational hotel chains, following the revolutionary movement inspired by Airbnb, with technology being a supporting dimension only. We have markets for organic, vegan and other foods following shared collectives identifying with perceptions of "good", healthy and sustainable living, as illustrated by the following:

> 'Bonjour Baguette' is beginning to offer breakfast delivery around San Francisco, complete with flavourful food in tastefully-decorated boxes. Although the food is nothing new, the approach the company is taking is innovative, as an all-encompassing service offering not only delicious food but also an enjoyable experience (Boulard, 2018, original quotations).

Both technological and cultural market-making are driven by environmental opportunities such as changes in technology, policies, lifestyles and consumer tastes (Swaminathan and Wade, 2001). Moreover, both types of entrepreneurial endeavours are characterised by early ambiguity, unclear structures and vague definitions of their market categories (Aldrich and Fiol, 1994; Santos and Eisenhardt, 2009). However, market actors in these two entrepreneurial categories are likely to have different trajectories when crossing national boundaries, at least in part due to their differing needs for optimal distinctiveness.

Optimal Distinctiveness During Cross-border Venturing

Optimal distinctiveness is defined as the need for differentiation from others while also striving for market assimilation (Zhao *et al.*, 2017). Entrepreneurship focuses on uniqueness for competitive advantage (Schumpeter, 1942/2003; Casson, 2003), whereas conformity for legitimacy demands similarity and correspondence for institutional acceptability (Meyer and Rowan, 1977; DiMaggio, 1983). Yet collective efforts combined with entrepreneurial uniqueness lead to legitimacy quests with overarching social rules, norms and beliefs, but within an environment enabling entrepreneurial opportunity creation and exploitation. The following example of the innovative company, Tesla, demonstrates how not only industry characteristics but also personality of an entrepreneur can co-create a persuasive entrepreneurial story:

> I keep bringing up Tesla, and it's partly that Elon Musk named his car company after him, but Tesla was super-idealistic, and most of the things he wanted to create eventually came to fruition, but he didn't get rich off any of them, and a lot of them he didn't even get credit for, at least not until relatively recently (Fox, 2018).

We see the dynamic nature of internationalisation as a growth strategy for the firm to be instrumental in the orchestration of similar and distinctive features that lead to entrepreneurial market-making. The international context presents conditions of uncertainty and ambiguity in the form of multiple, fragmented and sometimes competing environments (Kostova and Zaheer, 1999). Construction and carriage of the identity to foreign partners is demanding because the perception of different stakeholders in foreign markets is shaped by varying institutional contexts, historical legacies and scripts (Brannen, 2004). Simultaneously, internationalising firms need to strive for distinctiveness *vis-à-vis* local and other international firms to successfully compete (Kostova *et al.*, 2008). Meanings, labels and stories, which invite interpretation and are open to social construction, define negation and sense-making purposes under the challenging conditions of different geographies (Vaara and Tienari, 2010; Haley and Boje, 2014) with their liabilities of foreignness (Zaheer, 1995), of newness (McGaughey, 2007) and of outsidership (Johanson and Vahlne, 2009).

That entrepreneurs might have different needs for achieving optimal distinctiveness, and how such endeavours can be challenged by conditions unique to cross-border venturing (Zhao *et al.*, 2017; Haans, 2018; Tracey *et al.*, 2018), has not been adequately addressed. We argue that well-crafted strategies that navigate optimal distinctiveness are an essential vehicle for integrating these similar but distinctive features that enable the entrepreneur, be they technological or cultural, to make markets internationally.

Strategies to Achieve Optimal Distinctiveness During International Venturing

We frame our response to how the entrepreneurial firm makes markets across borders, when innovation can be technological or cultural, around the orchestration of an optimally distinctive entrepreneurial identity (Navis and Glynn, 2010). International entrepreneurs strive to convince relevant stakeholders abroad, such as export/import distributors, joint venture partners and foreign market customers to win their attention by constructing shared understanding around differentiation and legitimation. Table 1 displays a typology of the strategies of international entrepreneurs who make markets across national borders.

In Table 1, we analyse cross-border venturing from two perspectives: technological versus cultural innovation, and nascent versus established foreign market. First, entrepreneurs employ strategies to establish a single unique *technological market referent* (technological innovation) and mobilise collective action to shape *market movement boundaries* (cultural innovation). Second, both entrepreneurs, introducing technological and cultural innovation, can operate in nascent or established markets. By markets, we refer to fields, industries or socio-cognitive market categories in which similar organisations operate and compete (Porac and Thomas, 1990). A nascent market is characterised by unstable conditions, unclear structures and practices such as the case of the nascent microbrewery movement (Carroll and Swaminathan, 2000), clean-tech start-ups (McKnight and Zietsma, 2018) or a new wave of satellite radios (Navis and Glynn, 2010). The established phase occurs when standardisation and economies of scale are achieved and when social change has taken place.

Through the interplay of these dimensions, four theoretical possibilities emerge: Technological innovation entering a nascent or established market in a foreign country, and cultural innovation entering a nascent or established market in a foreign country. These possibilities represent contextual environments and determine four types of strategies employed the entrepreneur: strategies of *assembling* and of *upholding* a technological market referent in the case of technological innovation, and strategies of *sharpening* and of *delimitating* within market movement boundaries in the case of cultural innovation, with illustrative examples of real ventures presented in Table 2.

Assembling Technological Market Referent

The success of technology entrepreneurs is driven by the availability of resources and the timing of their entry (Anderson and Tushman, 1990; Suarez, Grodal *et al.*, 2015). Technology entrepreneurs bring to the world

Table 1: Framework for Orchestrating Optimal Distinctiveness in Foreign Markets

	Nascent Foreign Market	Established Foreign Market
Technological innovation	**(1) Assembling technological market referent** **Differentiation:** – Forces: Competitive forces to form new market referent – Strategy: o Transfer venture's technological innovation into a foreign country o Distil novel features from venture's technological innovation **Legitimation:** – Forces: Liability of newness and foreignness; technological uncertainties – Strategy: o Implement familiar elements of foreign market context into venture's technological innovation o Enact foreign market support	**(2) Upholding technological market referent** **Legitimation:** – Forces: Liability of foreignness – Strategy: o Orient venture's technological innovation towards market referent in a foreign country o Negotiate linking venture's technological innovation with market referent in a foreign country **Differentiation:** – Forces: Competitive forces within a saturated market from domestic and other foreign entrants – Strategy: o Foreground novelty of venture's technological innovation towards market referent in a foreign country o Mediate for a novelty of venture's technological innovation in a foreign country

(*Continued*)

Table 1: (*Continued*)

	Nascent Foreign Market	Established Foreign Market
Cultural innovation	**(3) Sharpening market movement boundaries** **Legitimation:** – Forces: Liability of newness and foreignness; movement-like uncertainties – Strategy: ○ Construct venture's cultural innovation to co-form market movement boundaries in a foreign market ○ Replot venture's cultural innovation to co-form new market movement boundaries in a foreign market **Differentiation:** – Forces: Competitive forces from imitators outside of market movement boundaries – Strategy: ○ Relate venture's novel elements of cultural innovation to foreign market context ○ Reinforce venture's cultural innovation highlighting novelty within a foreign market context	**(4) Delimitating within market movement boundaries** **Differentiation:** – Forces: Competitive forces within the market movement boundaries – Strategy: ○ Exploit novelty of venture's cultural innovation to stretch market movement boundaries in a foreign country ○ Recombine venture's cultural innovation to stretch formed market movement boundaries in a foreign country **Legitimation:** – Forces: Liability of foreignness – Strategy: ○ Espouse venture's novel cultural innovation within formed market movement boundaries in a foreign country ○ Navigate venture's cultural innovation within market movement boundaries in a foreign country

Table 2: Examples of Strategies

		Example 1	Example 2
Technological innovation	**Assembling technological market referent** (Nascent host market)	*Transferring a novel product — an invention with unique features targeted towards the needs of people in developing world:* "Frugal Digital's Clock Sense, designed in Copenhagen after research in India, uses an analogue alarm clock body to measure the amount of oxygenated haemoglobin in the blood. With help of two LEDs and a simple light sensor, the device can provide a simple reading of the overall health of a patient". (Pareek, 2013)	*Forming link with local audience by establishing centre for local entrepreneurs to assimilate in local environment and enable market entry of a unique product:* "After building a successful software solutions company in the US, Rebecca Enonchong decided to go back to her home country, Cameroon, to set up another branch of her business…Although she arrived in Cameroon with high spirits, she soon faced many challenges…She created ActivSpaces — African Centres for Technology, Innovation and Ventures, which are incubators for startups. She also created networks to invest in the startups, and started to develop the ecosystem in Cameroon, and across the continent". (ITU News, 2018)
	Upholding technological market referent (Established host market)	*Highlighting the characteristics of the country of origin contributing to unique features of the product and legitimacy as a quality product:* "'You've built a technology that can work in the toughest conditions…to take it elsewhere is the least problematic (bit),' said Pankit Desai, co-CEO at Mumbai-based cybersecurity startup, Sequretek. 'And our product is fairly domain-insensitive and product-insensitive. We've already taken care of the upfront cost to build our product. The only thing to invest in is go-to-market.'" (Bhattacharya, 2018)	*Explaining the link between user characteristics and developed innovation and portraying it as a unique feature:* "We're getting to the stage where mobile internet usage is set to overtake desktop. In some parts of the world people's first experience of the internet is through their low-cost smartphone. This new way of consuming content is seeing a shift in the way in which companies like Canva work and the ways in which we seek to reach millions of users across the globe". (Psomadelis, 2018)

(*Continued*)

Table 2: (*Continued*)

		Example 1	Example 2
Cultural innovation	**Sharpening market movement boundaries** (Nascent host market)	*Linking brewery to neighbouring industries of Danish fine dining to gain traction but highlighting individual entrepreneurial identity:* "He [Mikkeller's founder] makes house beer for some of the best and most prominent gourmet restaurants in Denmark…Because of Mikkel's inventive and constant development of Mikkeller, he has been called the 'cult', 'rock'n'roll' and 'gypsy'- brewer in the Danish and international press". (Mikkeller, 2015)	*Co-forming a food category with an environmental aspect by bringing in the local traditions (Ayurveda in India):* "'The genesis of Ayurveda is that what you ingest will make a difference to you. Take a look at what we have launched in the South of India,' defends Mehta. 'In foods we are very clear we are going to get into categories where we can make differentiated products…We are going to get into fields which are nutritious, tasty and which will not cost the earth,' he adds". (Shashidhar, 2018)
	Delimitating within market movement boundaries (Established host market)	*Mentioning international accolades to gain reputation in the industry occupied by large incumbents and bringing in a regional story:* "The Pikes 2014 'Traditionale' Riesling won a Gold Medal and Trophy for the Champion International Wine in the recent International Aromatic Wine Competition held in Christchurch NZ [New Zealand]. A great result that underlines the high quality of the 2014 Riesling vintage in Clare". (Pikeswines, 2015)	*Entering growing Chinese "sharing economy" by adjusting labels to local language which both legitimates and creates a point of difference:* "Airbnb began building relationships with the government and built a 60-person product team in Beijing. Once the company began 'localizing' the product, it saw an almost immediate lift in bookings. For example, Airbnb unveiled a new brand name to be used in the country: 'Aibiying' (爱彼迎), which means 'welcome each other with love.' The re-naming was part of a larger effort by the company to expand its visibility and presence in China". (Marinova, 2017)

inventions which might often fail, can be copied by competitors or replaced by better albeit similar designs (Suarez *et al.*, 2015). Thus, their early stages are characterised by significant rivalry (Anderson and Tushman, 1990). In the market space of other firms offering similar products, these entrepreneurs strive to provide to their stakeholders a competency-destroying or competency-enhancing offering, one that is different from their peers (Tushman and Anderson, 1986). For internationalising technology entrepreneurs, while liabilities of foreignness and newness and pressures to innovate are present, they can also experience significant technological uncertainty in foreign markets (Kriz and Welch 2018). These firms, working on "new-to-the-world" inventions, for instance a firm developing new breeds of wheat (Kriz and Welch, 2018), are often pushed to internationalise early while they are still in a scientific exploratory phase. Therefore, without the ability to exploit a well-formed stock of knowledge and expertise, their foreign market activities often result in failure and an inability to attract stakeholders' support.

Differentiate

When going international, technology ventures engage in activities supporting their experimentation and hence participate in the emergence of a new market referent. Thus, strategies driving differentiation in foreign markets will dominate. Technology entrepreneurs can incorporate narratives about, for instance novel technology features, unique patents or distinctiveness from existing products. Santos and Eisenhardt (2009) found in their study of five technology entrepreneurs a tendency to form a cognitive referent to gain a strong leadership position in the market. They revealed that the storytelling and meaning-making of an Internet industry start-up were characterised by building an individual identity of "what you are" formed by "a story about a customer with an unusual need that the founder insisted that Magic [the start-up] satisfy" (Santos and Eisenhardt, 2009, p. 651).

Because entry is more viable into markets with weak structures and unclear rules (Fligstein, 1991; Leblebici *et al.*, 1991), technology entrepreneurs can exploit the ambiguity and technological uncertainty of an emerging (nascent) industry in a foreign market. Hence, these firms distil novel features from their inventions. To illustrate, if necessary, they might selectively emphasise technology elements or functions which are novel in certain markets and de-emphasise those that appear not to be competitive. This suggests transferring well-defined existing innovations across borders rather than experimentation from basic science that involves additional costs. For example, Twitter messages in Western languages are restricted to 140 characters and this rule applies also to Japanese users for whom one character can often equal one word. Twitter corroborated this existing feature to enable and empower Japanese users to anonymously express their views in longer messages (Nussey and Ingram, 2018).

Legitimate

While at the nascent stage when the internationalising technology new ventures are motivated to innovate and compete with other entrepreneurs, they also have to accommodate the socio-cultural context of the foreign market which inherently shapes stakeholders' sense-making activities (Suarez *et al.*, 2015). Therefore, they need to engage in strategies that integrate novel elements into foreign market contexts, but yet they must articulate familiar features. As such, firms might recombine the innovative features of their product with cognitively close vocabularies, which are collectively endorsed in foreign markets. These could be, for example attending to local habits and preferences, such as highlighting the technological functionality needed by people in a local market. An extreme case would be presenting their product as "frugal innovation" — a new-to-the-world invention with reduced complexity and costs designed also to address the needs of people in the developing world, for example. The content of such strategies could be filled by sensible issues, social values or solutions towards sustainability to motivate and empower users in third-world countries.

Support from host country stakeholders for their product or service can be critical. This is achieved by purposively selecting stakeholders who have a strong voice in the market and can facilitate legitimation processes in the foreign market. Technology entrepreneurs might connect with stakeholders such as development agencies or other entrepreneurs to secure credibility and reputation, enhancing legitimacy and competitive advantage (McKnight and Zietsma, 2018) of their technologies. In nascent markets, however, the supporting constituents might not exist. Thus, technology entrepreneurs might create proto-institutions to favour their activities (Zietsma and McKnight, 2009), be of interest to local start-ups and represent a substantial part of their stories (e.g. engage in an establishment of an incubator to support local entrepreneurship in emerging markets).

Overall, we propose that in foreign markets where the respective market is in a nascent stage, differentiation strategies are dominant. Entrant firms bringing technology innovation must account for the possibility that the host market is occupied by other firms also pursuing experimentation for market leadership. Hence, they must provide novelty *vis-à-vis* local competitors, and they must be mindful that their presentation of the offering speaks to a particular foreign context.

Upholding Technological Market Referent (Technological Innovation)

When the market for technology new ventures passes its initial stage in which firms compete for a leading position in the market, it is technologically inefficient to deviate from the established dominant design (Utterback and Abernathy, 1975) or cognitive referent (Santos and Eisenhardt, 2009). Even though the number of firms in the industry is increasing and competition is intensifying (Hannan and Freeman, 1977), differentiation not only creates confusion among stakeholders but it also brings the additional costs of diseconomies of scale (Suárez and Utterback, 1995). For example, the evolution of the commercial aeroplane went through several innovative processes as the design was improved, ultimately moving towards global standardisation (Tushman and Murmann, 2002). Common standards form boundaries within which new technology products emerge. They also enable firms to gain advantages from interconnectivity, such as when information technology firms source parts from one another (Garud *et al.*, 2002). Therefore, instead of differentiation, these firms, as members of an established industry, tend to focus on standardisation and economies of scale (Anderson and Tushman, 1990; Suárez and Utterback, 1995).

Legitimate

Technology entrepreneurs entering an established foreign market are likely to engage in convergence towards a developed industry referent abroad which is already recognised by stakeholders. Because they might experience liabilities of newness (Stinchcombe, 1965), of foreignness

(Zaheer, 1995) and of technological uncertainty (Kriz and Welch, 2018), these firms need to navigate their experiments towards the already established market referent abroad. Complete novelty is likely to be risky, as the audience in the foreign market might not categorise their offerings under familiar concepts. They would not assign them clear meaning due to an already existing market referent with the new ventures not falling within its domain.

Hence, technology entrepreneurs likely incorporate into their strategies the elements of an already established market referent and the existing technology infrastructure, thus demonstrating a form of symbiosis. These overlaps between internationalising ventures entering established markets are important for shaping the legitimacy of new entrants and their successful alignment (Dobrev *et al.*, 2006; McKnight and Zietsma, 2018). Wade (1995) in his study of the microprocessor industry found that the success of this sector was driven by firms imitating already established products and designs, referred to as "technology bandwagons". In the context of clean technology enterprises, McKnight and Zietsma (2018) confirmed that this imitation, or alignment, is directed towards established market leaders. Hence, to manage the liabilities of internationalising technology new ventures, stories are expected to include host context elements, such as sharing a well-known technology platform or promoting collaboration with local firms.

Moreover, amending features of the existing design to align with the developed foreign market can be costly. Entrepreneurs in foreign markets who have already invested resources into the innovation process, or who have committed to mimicking inventors, will be less likely to engage in experimentation and amendments of their product (Suarez *et al.*, 2015). Hence, instead of changing to gain support, which might occur in ventures entering nascent markets, entrepreneurial ventures entering an established market might "negotiate" with local constituents for a link between their own innovation and the existing market referent in the foreign country. Entrepreneurs are likely to educate relevant foreign market stakeholders, such as highlighting the specific functions or explaining how the product or service responds to needs. For instance, Canva, a venture selling software for designers, uses the slogan "Design anything publish anywhere" to not only corroborate flexibility of the program but also to promote the fact that in some countries the mobile phone is the only device for using the Internet (Psomadelis, 2018).

Differentiate

While contributing to a standardised design appears to be crucial, technology entrepreneurs should also account for the saturation of the industry and any barriers to market entry (Suarez *et al.*, 2015). Therefore, it is essential to foreground some elements of novelty in their strategies. McKnight and Zietsma (2018) provided evidence by showing how lobbying activities with policymakers enabled firms to legitimise but at the same time also to develop and market unique products in the area of clean technology. Internationalising ventures need to integrate their legitimation activities with tales about distinctiveness, which in the cross-country context can be represented by the country of origin (its technological advancement or specific conditions) acting as a unique feature. Another feasible option can be to incorporate successful achievements, which in the case of technology entrepreneurs can bestow important credibility on aspirant firms. These firms might also corroborate a successful track record of the individual entrepreneur through narratives of a technology venture, as found by Lounsbury and Glynn (2001).

From our discussion here, upholding a market referent in foreign countries can be challenging, especially when it is an already established dominant design often represented by strong market leaders. New ventures have to negotiate a position in such a market by not only dis-embedding from the existing industry referent in the foreign market but they also need to account for increased competition in established markets and the market power of existing designs.

Sharpening Market Movement Boundaries (Cultural Innovation)

Achieving legitimacy is crucial for entrepreneurs creating cultural innovations which are dependent on a collective endeavour for successful uptake. Cultural innovations are generally formed by social movements and activist groups who motivate cultural change (Rao *et al.*, 2000) or challenge societal *status quo* (Mathias *et al.*, 2018). For example, growth in the craft beer movement has been identified with the assumed proprietorship of beer brewing by large corporations and their aversion to challenge (Carroll and Swaminathan, 2000), small coffee retailers have reintroduced the symbolism of the real coffee experience (Rindova and Fombrun, 2001) and organic food producers have brought back the natural methods of farming that seem lost to large-scale commercialism (Lee *et al.*, 2017). Thus, strengthening the nascent market by collaboration, collective endeavour and convergence is necessary during the early stages of a cultural innovation because of the risks to free-riding entrants and lack of support from stakeholders.

Legitimate

Internationalising entrepreneurs pursuing cultural change might be expected to construct their identity around the market's collective features to focus on similarity and to gain a positive reception from their stakeholders. These entrepreneurs can symbolically collaborate to strengthen the boundaries of the market overseas, such as local activities that reinforce the global community of the microbrewing industry. Thus, strategies are focused predominantly on collective identities, with firms setting out to claim membership in a new market, and seeking legitimacy within it (Navis and Glynn, 2010). To illustrate, microbreweries in the craft beer industry are likely to focus on collective stories around the accepted craft definition of being small, independent and having an innovative or traditional way of brewing (Carroll and Swaminathan, 2000). They might refer to a neighbouring industry of boutique wineries by using common features of authentic location, or claim membership in a larger social movement, such as the "slow food" movement. Nevertheless, they also replot their stories to align with the nuances of the local market to avoid possible penalties and mitigate the uncertainties and risks associated with an emerging industry. For example, lager is traditionally considered to be a craft beer in Germany; however, in the US, it symbolises a product from large mass-beer corporations (Barlow *et al.*, 2018).

Differentiate

While nascent markets for cultural innovation are characterised by convergence towards a collective identity, this also forms a "cost of limited growth and marginality in a market" (Lee *et al.*, 2017, p. 447). Even though legitimation is important for building coherence and opposition to other industries, strategies need to be bolstered with uniqueness, such as growth narratives about the individual practices of ventures (Wry *et al.*, 2011), personal tales about the entrepreneurs (Clegg *et al.*, 2007) or bringing in particular historical events, myths and images that appeal to a foreign audience to weave a story of distinctiveness. To illustrate, Danish craft breweries entering the US market have incorporated old legends about Vikings into beer labels through images, names and product descriptions (Jasovska, 2019).

Other examples include multiplex cinemas, a category already established in the US, entering the European market where the concept was in its infancy (Delmestri and Wezel, 2011), and British retailers introducing the concept of build-it-yourself furniture in Asia (Owens *et al*., 2013). Delmestri and Wezel (2011) found that familiar global values of "modernity" and "progress" enabled multiplex cinemas to enter the European market. Likewise, the study of British furniture retailers entering Asia demonstrated that foreign firms negotiated the local industry characteristics by not changing their own products and design (Owens *et al*., 2013). They successfully introduced a movement of build-it-yourself furniture, which was still only emerging in Asia. The same study also reported that firms used elements, novel in foreign markets, to differentiate themselves from competitors in the furniture retailing sector. Because nascent markets are able to be manipulated and are open to changes (Pontikes and Barnett, 2015), instead of altering material elements, ventures pursuing cultural innovation can exploit ambiguity in the foreign market and amend stakeholders' cognition through frames and labels.

In summary, in the emerging markets for cultural innovation, collective attributes are not deeply embedded. Hence, entrepreneurs entering a nascent market overseas need to carefully choose collective features and adapt these for translation into stories. Legitimation forces are therefore dominant in foreign markets, as the emerging market for the cultural innovation needs to be well defined and articulated, signalling a clear message to its audience. However, such legitimation efforts should be accompanied by differentiation, which will protect the entrepreneur's limited growth thus far and any potential drift to sameness.

Delimiting Within Market Movement Boundaries (Cultural Innovation)

In the case of an established market for cultural innovation, the audience in a foreign country will be familiar with the industry identity. Therefore, the entry into this market is less complicated because the industry boundaries are well articulated, assisting new ventures to navigate their chosen strategies. However, increased competition and saturation that occurs in established markets creates pressures on firms both operating in the field and those attempting to enter it (Navis and Glynn, 2010). Entrepreneurial firms operating in this context of cultural innovation are expected to engage in strategies that lead to the creation of difference from peers such that they might gain a competitive advantage. Navis and Glynn (2010) examined the evolution of the satellite radio industry which emerged as an opposition to corporate radio chains. They reported that after a period of legitimation, firms framed their identity around distinctiveness using labels such as "premium", "only service" and "uncompromised" (Navis and Glynn, 2010, p. 453).

Differentiate

Internationalising ventures that enter an established market with cultural innovation are expected to focus on strategies to highlight their distinctiveness. The space within the established market becomes occupied by many firms competing for the same consumer. Firms can compete if they focus on unique features and distinguish themselves from domestic and foreign competitors in the crowded space such that the market becomes theirs only. As they already are international firms, turning a liability of foreignness, or a distinctiveness of the product, into an opportunity can represent a feasible strategy of differentiation (Regnér and Edman, 2014). Lamb *et al.* (2011) identified a storytelling strategy adopted by newly internationalising winemakers in Australia who focused on pursuing distinctive niche strategies in markets populated by large established incumbents. In their study, small wineries described their wines as being "different and distinctive; it is a regional story" (Lamb *et al.*, 2011, p. 683), which conveys local meaning to a wider audience looking for romanticism. Besides exploiting novelty, firms also signalled their link to cultural codes familiar to the foreign market audience (e.g. Australian wine alongside quality food products).

Entrepreneurs emphasise uniqueness to withstand competitive pressures in the foreign market while at the same time retaining their original identity as established in the home market. Thus, ventures pursuing cultural innovation should engage in crafting strategies which enable them to recombine the established elements in a distinct way. Beverland (2005) reported that producers of traditional and centuries-known wines responded to the influx of industrial brands by retaining historical legacies but at the same time exploiting them to form a distinctive authenticity such as the notions of terroir. Terroir, defined by the location of the vineyard and winemaker's aura, represented not only a unique feature but also categorised wines as being boutique (Beverland, 2005). While this stable market could be saturated with similar firms, the clear membership attributes of wineries provided guidance on how much a firm might differentiate itself from other industry members.

Legitimate

While delimitation, that is demarcation, symbolises gaining a unique positioning, it also means that it should not significantly deviate from existing collective market boundaries. To portray and reinforce familiarity, internationally recognised ranking systems, relationships with reputable market members and collective symbols endorsed by stakeholders illuminate important features of the organisation and convey a clear market membership that not only avoids direct competition with new entrants and hostile free riders (Aldrich and Fiol, 1994) but also facilitates entry into markets where the entrant is a foreigner (Kodeih and Greenwood, 2014). Kodeih and Greenwood (2014) reported that French tertiary colleges needed to self-categorise under a global label of "International Business School" (IBS), a label well established in foreign markets. When considering internationalisation into markets where the French university was unknown, collective stories around being an IBS was essential. However, to avoid any unwanted deviations from the orthodoxy that could be sanctioned, unique features should, where possible, refer to elements endorsed by local stakeholders. McDonald's restaurants do adapt their well-practised traditional menu to the different dining habits in some target markets (Haley and Boje, 2014). Nonetheless, these ventures engage in strategies that replicate, in large part, the collective features of the existing industry in their home countries.

To summarise, the market delimitation that entrepreneurs of cultural innovation can engage in is characterised by differentiation, however bounded by the existing industry norms in the foreign market. Even though distinctiveness forces are crucial as the competition within the established market in the foreign country requires unique offerings, too great a deviation will be detrimental.

Discussion, Limitations and Conclusion

Model

We set out to understand how new ventures of cultural and technological innovation make markets internationally. Motivated by the tension that has been captured in "the challenge of optimal distinctiveness; how different can and should firms be?" (McKnight and Zietsma, 2018, p. 493), we posed the following question: how does the entrepreneurial firm resolve the tension between uniqueness and similarity when innovation in the firm can be technological or cultural? To address this puzzle, we theorised the strategies entrepreneurs employ in order to position their firms and to be understood in foreign countries as optimally distinctive.

We assert that optimal distinctiveness in entrepreneurial ventures can successfully facilitate the creation of international opportunities. Entrepreneurs need to address the similarity demands of market membership, but they must also conceive stories that are unique and provide differentiation for competitive advantage. We introduce four strategies that entrepreneurs might be expected to employ during internationalising into new markets: for technological innovation, strategies of *assembling* and *upholding technological market referent*, and for cultural innovation, strategies of *sharpening* and *delimitating within market movement boundaries* (Table 1). Each strategy assists in lessening the negative consequences of environmental uncertainty in foreign markets, as well as alleviating some of the pressures in business relationships and in competition.

We do not see the forces of similarity and uniqueness as completely exclusionary, and the final strategies as attempts to form a stable threshold (Farjoun, 2010; Zhao *et al.*, 2017; McKnight and Zietsma, 2018). On the contrary, we consider these forces as complementary and entrepreneurs as actors purposely managing their orchestration and mutual coherence under a specific combination of foreign and home market conditions. Our framework offers evidence on contextually embedded optimal distinctiveness, which is not a predefined rationally devised endpoint ventures are heading to but rather refers to their continuous endeavour of navigating how their offerings are understood in foreign countries.

The novelty of our model is in highlighting that cross-border venturing is fuelled by non-material resources available to entrepreneurs under specific multiple conditions. For instance, entrepreneurs could draw narratives by using a positive country-of-origin image (e.g. Danish craft breweries using legends about Vikings) and they might recombine them with the specific symbols of a specific host market (e.g. not offering lager beer, perceived as a product from large breweries, in the US). As such, attending to a given socio-cognitive context of markets and resources available within in it can form a competitive advantage for the internationalising firm. This also highlights how instrumental the multiplicity of such conditions is. Strategies of entrepreneurs are not shaped only by their immediate context, but industry legacies formed at home (and embedded in venture's identity) assist in navigating the content of their strategies.

We provide an understanding of how the context of new ventures influences their strategies. Hence, the balance between similarity and uniqueness is inevitably formed by the conditions in which the new venture operates, and as such, it is not necessarily stable in time and space. In our framework, we depicted these conditions as a stage of industry life cycle (nascent and established), the nature of the entrepreneurial innovation (cultural and technological). Therefore, we assume that the optimal distinctiveness threshold of the enterprise not only evolves over time but it is also shaped by the context within which the firm operates at a given time. For example, due to a new global ranking system, French business schools replotted their identity and became not only traditional in the domestic market but also internationally recognised institutions (Kodeih and Greenwood, 2014).

Contributions

We offer contributions to the literature on international entrepreneurship and optimal distinctiveness. Our framework speaks to international business research identifying internationalisation as entrepreneurial market-making and opportunity development (Johanson and Vahlne, 2009: Mainela *et al.*, 2014; Muzychenko and Liesch, 2015; Reuber *et al.*, 2018). The question of how firms capture international opportunities and make markets across national boundaries can be considered from the perspective of optimal distinctiveness. Thus, internationalisation need not only be seen as an exercise of managing risks and uncertainties in foreign markets (Liesch *et al.*, 2011), but rather, it can also be seen as an activity embedded in multiple and socially constructed environments.

Further, our four-strategy framework offers research opportunity beyond the often-accepted perspective that international markets always simply exist to be exploited. Our view is that international entrepreneurship scholarship offers unexploited research prospects if the view is taken that markets are made by the entrepreneurial firm and that strategies towards optimal distinctiveness can assist in a market-making activity. We accept that markets are made by entrepreneurial endeavour, and that firms exist in markets that are defined and bounded by the exchange of products and services. How these products and services are portrayed to stakeholders, and how stakeholders perceive them, determines the markets in which the firm will compete (Porac *et al.*, 1989). The firm identifies with a particular market in which it seeks a competitive advantage. Herein lies the optimal distinctiveness puzzle — the firm joins a market for legitimation but other firms will also inhabit the market should it provide an opportunity for exploitation and capture (Navis and Glynn, 2010; McKnight and Zietsma, 2018).

We also add to the discussion on optimal distinctiveness in entrepreneurship research highlighting the portrayal of both uniqueness and similarity in new ventures (Navis and Glynn, 2010; Garud *et al.* 2018; McKnight and Zietsma, 2018). Our framework corresponds with the latest turn in this discussion arguing that the formation of optimal distinctiveness is not a process oriented towards a stable threshold, but that organisations engage in threshold orchestration through compensation and integration of seemingly paradoxical forces (Zhao *et al.*, 2017; McKnight and Zietsma, 2018). In the domestic context, it might be difficult or even impossible to observe firms progressing across different stages of industry development and operating under multiple legitimacy scripts and diverse stakeholders' expectations (Zhao *et al.*, 2017). Therefore, our contribution to this domain brings in the international business context with its unique constraints — the liability of foreignness and the multiplicity of markets in which the firm can operate (Kostova *et al.*, 2008). As entrepreneurs make claims to audiences located and embedded in different contexts, the narratives around optimal distinctiveness change not only in time and but also in space (Lamb *et al.*, 2011; Haley and Boje, 2014). Therefore, we posit that legitimation of new ventures does not only depend on the age of the venture (Fisher *et al.*, 2016), role of stakeholders (Fisher *et al.*, 2017), industry incumbents (McKnight and Zietsma, 2018), homogeneity of firms within categories (Haans, 2018) or stage of industry development (Navis and Glynn, 2010) but also on geographical differences defined by national boundaries.

Limitations

We are aware that the conceptual nature of this paper has limitations, but these offer inviting opportunities for future research. First, our treatment of the industry context of entrepreneurs defined by cultural or technological innovation is not conclusive. For example, Zhao *et al.* (2017) raised the specificity of fashion industries with a more dynamic evolution. Similarly, Lounsbury and Glynn (2001) acknowledged that only a small number of technology ventures are real inventors (e.g. Apple and Google), while many others follow or enhance an existing design. Further investigation into optimal distinctiveness of various types of innovations could provide a more detailed understanding of this observation. Scholars might also explore corporate entrepreneurship in established organisations and activities of international mergers and acquisitions, and how multinational firms with established reputations identify and acquire new innovative firms that operate in nascent industries.

Second, future research could apply our framework to assess the relationship of particular strategies with the performance of the firm in foreign markets. For example, the empirical study of Martens *et al.* (2007) reported that well-crafted entrepreneurial storytelling leads to more assured resource acquisition. However, researchers should not blindly make assumptions that this would be the case across other contexts (e.g. industry or country). Similarly, scholars might address further implications of optimal distinctiveness by including extreme cases of decoupling those activities that deviate from the legitimacy scripts of given concepts through international outsourcing or incorporation (McGaughey, 2007). Third, research might also explore our typology of strategies in various geographies. While we do not emphasise any particular countries to be more suitable for our framework than others, as we expect generalisability of our findings, we also believe that as some countries are more supportive of entrepreneurial venturing, country context is likely to have an influence on firm strategies.

Conclusion

We address the puzzle of optimal distinctiveness, and we posed the following question: how does the entrepreneurial firm resolve the tension between uniqueness and similarity when innovation in the firm can be technological or cultural? To provide the theoretical and empirical links between the world of information flow and the world of material flow as articulated by (Casson, 2003), we appealed to the strategies entrepreneurs employ to make markets tangible. We present a theoretical framework for determining optimal distinctiveness for the international market-making entrepreneur, and identify and elaborate four strategies: *assembling* and *upholding* technological market referent, and *sharpening* and *delimitating* within market movement boundaries. To do so, we have adopted the context of international market-making, which is characterised by the simultaneous presence in multiple and diverse contexts, and hence, a need to meet different optimal distinctiveness demands. Our contributions highlight not only further challenges firms might experience in their endeavours to gain both legitimacy and competitive advantage but also how well-crafted and optimally balanced strategies might help them achieve these ends.

References

Aldrich, H. E. and C. M. Fiol (1994). Fools rush in? The institutional context of industry creation. *Academy of Management Review*, 19(4), 645–670.

Andersen, P. H. and M. Rask (2014). Creating legitimacy across international contexts: The role of storytelling for international new ventures. *Journal of International Entrepreneurship*, 12(4), 365–388.

Anderson, P. and M. L. Tushman (1990). Technological discontinuities and dominant designs: A cyclical model of technological change. *Administrative Science Quarterly*, 35(4), 604–633.

Barlow, M. A., J. C. Verhaal, and J. D. Hoskins (2018). Guilty by association: Product-level category stigma and audience expectations in the U.S. craft beer industry. *Journal of Management*, 44(7), 2934–2960.

Beckman, C., K. Eisenhardt, S. Kotha, A. Meyer, and N. Rajagopalan (2012). Technology entrepreneurship. *Strategic Entrepreneurship Journal*, 6(2), 89–93.

Beverland, M. B. (2005). Crafting brand authenticity: The case of luxury wines. *Journal of Management Studies*, 42(5), 1003–1029.

Bhattacharya, A. (2018). India is just not enough for some Indian startups. *Quartz India*. https://qz.com/india/1311099/from-oyo-to-ola-indian-startups-are-going-international/ (accessed on February 27, 2019).

Boulard, S. (2018). Non-tech startups: Silicons valley's most prized secrets.... *Entrepreneur Handbook*. https://entrepreneurhandbook.co.uk/non-tech-startups/ (accessed on February 25, 2019).

Brannen, M. Y. (2004). When mickey loses face: Recontextualization, semantic fit, and the semiotics of foreignness. *Academy of Management Review*, 29(4), 593–616.

Carroll, G. R. and A. Swaminathan (2000). Why the microbrewery movement?: Organizational dynamics of resource partitioning in the U.S. brewing industry. *American Journal of Sociology*, 106(3), 715–762.
Casson, M. (2003). *The Entrepreneur: An Economic Theory*. Cheltenham, UK: Edward Elgar.
Clegg, S. R., C. Rhodes, and M. Kornberger (2007). Desperately seeking legitimacy: Organizational identity and emerging industries. *Organization Studies*, 28(4), 495–513.
Delmestri, G. and F. C. Wezel (2011). Breaking the wave: The contested legitimation of an alien organizational form. *Journal of International Business Studies*, 42(6), 828–852.
DiMaggio, P. J. (1983). State expansion and organizational fields. *Organizational Theory and Public Policy*. R. H. Hall and R. E. Quinn. Beverly Hills, CA, SAGE Publications, pp. 147–161.
Dobrev, S. D., S. Z. Ozdemir, and A. C. Teo (2006). The ecological interdependence of emergent and established organizational populations: Legitimacy transfer, violation by comparison, and unstable identities. *Organization Science*, 17(5), 577–597.
Farjoun, M. (2010). Beyond dualism: Stability and change as a duality. *Academy of Management Review*, 35(2), 202–225.
Fisher, G., S. Kotha, and A. Lahiri (2016). Changing with the times: An integrated view of identity, legitimacy, and new venture life cycles. *Academy of Management Review*, 41(3), 383–409.
Fisher, G., D. F. Kuratko, J. M. Bloodgood, and J. S. Hornsby (2017). Legitimate to Whom? The challenge of audience diversity and new venture legitimacy. *Journal of Business Venturing*, 32(1), 52–71.
Fligstein, N. (1991). The structural transformation of American industry: An institutional account of the cases of diversification in the largest firms, 1919–1979. *The New Institutionalism in Organisational Analysis*. W. Powell and P. J. DiMaggio. Chicago, IL: The University of Chicago Press, pp. 311–336.
Fox, J. (2018). Why Elon Musk's brain is different to yours. *The Sydney Morning Herald*. https://www.smh.com.au/business/companies/why-elon-musk-s-brain-is-different-to-yours-20180911-p502y2.html (accessed on January 12, 2019).
Garud, R., S. Jain, and A. Kumaraswamy (2002). Institutional entrepreneurship in the sponsorship of common technological standards: The case of sun microsystems and java. *Academy of Management Journal*, 45(1), 196–214.
Garud, R., T. Lant, and K. H. A. Schildt (2018). Generative imitation, strategic distancing and optimal distinctiveness during the growth, decline and stabilization of Silicon Alley. *Innovation: Organization & Management*, 21(1), 187–213.

Grant, A. (2016). *Originals: How Non-conformists Move the World.* New York, NY: Penguin Random House.

Grodal, S., A. Gotsopoulos, and F. F. Suarez (2015). The coevolution of technologies and categories during industry emergence. *Academy of Management Review*, 40(3), 423–445.

Haans, R. F. J. (2018). What's the value of being different when everyone is? The effects of distinctiveness on performance in homogeneous versus heterogeneous categories. *Strategic Management Journal*, 40(1), 3–27.

Haley, U. C. V. and D. M. Boje (2014). Storytelling the internationalization of the multinational enterprise. *Journal of International Business Studies*, 45(9), 1115–1132.

Hannan, M. T. and J. Freeman (1977). The population ecology of organizations. *American Journal of Sociology*, 82(5), 929–964.

ITU News (2018). Four ways entrepreneurs can promote innovation in emerging markets. *ITU News*, https://news.itu.int/four-ways-entrepreneurs-can-promote-innovation-emerging-markets/ (accessed on February 26, 2019).

Jasovska, P. (2019). Tapping into foreign markets: Internationalisation of the craft beer industry from small open economic. Sydney, University of Technology Sydney. Unpublished PhD dissertation.

Johanson, J. and J.-E. Vahlne (2009). The uppsala internationalization process model revisited: From liability of foreignness to liability of outsidership. *Journal of International Business Studies*, 40(9), 1411–1431.

Kodeih, F. and R. Greenwood (2014). Responding to institutional complexity: The role of identity. *Organization Studies*, 35(1), 7–39.

Kostova, T. and S. Zaheer (1999). Organizational legitimacy under conditions of complexity: The case of the multinational enterprise. *Academy of Management Review*, 24(1), 64–81.

Kostova, T., K. Roth, and M. T. Dacin (2008). Institutional theory in the study of multinational corporations: A critique and new directions. *Academy of Management Review*, 33(4), 994–1006.

Kriz, A. and C. Welch (2018). Innovation and internationalisation processes of firms with new-to-the-world technologies. *Journal of International Business Studies*, 49(4), 496–522.

Lamb, P. W., J. Sandberg, and P. W. Liesch (2011). Small firm internationalisation unveiled through phenomenography. *Journal of International Business Studies*, 42(5), 672–693.

Leblebici, H., G. R. Salancik, A. Copay, and T. King (1991). Institutional change and the transformation of interorganizational fields: An organizational history of the U.S. radio broadcasting industry. *Administrative Science Quarterly*, 36(3), 333–363.

Lee, B. H., S. Hiatt, and M. Lounsbury (2017). Market mediators and the trade-offs of legitimacy: Seeking behaviors in a nascent category. *Organization Science*, 28(3), 447–470.

Liesch, P. W., L. S. Welch, and P. J. Buckley (2011). Risk and uncertainty in internationalisation and international entrepreneurship studies. *Management International Review*, 51(6), 851–873.
Lounsbury, M. and M. A. Glynn (2001). Cultural entrepreneurship: Stories, legitimacy, and the acquisition of resources. *Strategic Management Journal*, 22(6–7), 545–564.
Lounsbury, M., M. Ventresca and P. M. Hirsch (2003). Social movements, field frames and industry emergence: A cultural–political perspective on US recycling. *Socio-Economic Review*, 1(1), 71–104.
Lounsbury, M., J. Cornelissen, N. Granqvist, and S. Grodal (2018). Culture, innovation and entrepreneurship. *Innovation*, 1–12.
Mainela, T., V. Puhakka and P. Servais (2014). The concept of international opportunity in international entrepreneurship: A review and a research agenda. *International Journal of Management Reviews*, 16(1), 105–129.
Marinova, P. (2017). Why China is crucial for Airbnb's global ambitions. *Fortune*, http://fortune.com/2017/12/05/airbnb-china-growth/ (accessed on February 25, 2019).
Martens, M. L., J. E. Jennings, and P. D. Jennings (2007). Do the stories they tell get them the money they need? The role of entrepreneurial narratives in resource acquisition. *Academy of Management Journal*, 50(5), 1107–1132.
Mathias, B. D., A. Huyghe, C. J. Frid, and T. L. Galloway (2018). An identity perspective on coopetition in the craft beer industry. *Strategic Management Journal*, 39(12), 3086–3115.
McCarthy, J. D. and M. N. Zald (1977). Resource mobilization and social movements: A partial theory. *American Journal of Sociology*, 82(6), 1212–1241.
McGaughey, S. L. (2007). Hidden ties in international new venturing: The case of portfolio entrepreneurship. *Journal of World Business*, 42(3), 307–321.
McKnight, B. and C. Zietsma (2018). Finding the threshold: A configurational approach to optimal distinctiveness. *Journal of Business Venturing*, 33(4), 493–512.
Meyer, J. W. and B. Rowan (1977). Institutionalized organizations: Formal structure as myth and ceremony. *American Journal of Sociology*, 83(2), 340–363.
Mikkeller (2015). Brewery. *Mikkeller Website*, http://mikkeller.dk/brewery/ (accessed on November 7, 2015).
Muzychenko, O. and P. W. Liesch (2015). International opportunity identification in the internationalisation of the firm. *Journal of World Business*, 50(4), 704–717.
Navis, C. and M. A. Glynn (2010). How new market categories emerge: Temporal dynamics of legitimacy, identity, and entrepreneurship in satellite radio, 1990–2005. *Administrative Science Quarterly*, 55(3), 439–471.

Navis, C. and M. A. Glynn (2011). Legitimate distinctiveness and the entrepreneurial identity: Influence on investor judgments of new venture plausibility. *Academy of Management Review*, 36(3), 479–499.

Nummela, N., S. Saarenketo, and S. Loane (2016). The dynamics of failure in international new ventures: A case study of Finnish and Irish software companies. *International Small Business Journal*, 34(1), 51 –69.

Nussey, S. and D. Ingram (2018). In Japan, twitter sees a surge of users — and revenue. *Reuters*, https://www.reuters.com/article/us-twitter-japan/in-japan-twitter-sees-a-surge-of-users-and-revenue-idUSKCN1GC17T (accessed on February 28, 2019.

Owens, M., M. Palmer, and A. Zueva-Owens (2013). Institutional forces in adoption of international joint ventures: Empirical evidence from British retail Multinationals. *International Business Review*, 22(5), 883–893.

Pareek, S. (2013). 25 great frugal innovations from around the world. *The Alternative*, http://www.thealternative.in/lifestyle/25-great-frugal-innovations-from-around-the-world/ (accessed on February 26, 2019).

Pikeswines (2015). Some silverware for the 'Trad'. *Pikeswines Website*, http://www.pikeswines.com.au/some-silverware-for-the-trad/ (accessed on December 8, 2015).

Pontikes, E. G. and W. P. Barnett (2015). The persistence of lenient market categories. *Organization Science*, 26(5), 1415–1431.

Porac, J. F. and H. Thomas (1990). Taxonomic mental models in competitor definition. *Academy of Management Review*, 15(2), 224–240.

Porac, J. F., H. Thomas, and C. Baden-Fuller (1989). Competitive groups as cognitive communities: The case of Scottish knitwear manufacturers. *Journal of Management Studies*, 26(4), 397–416.

Psomadelis, R. (2018). Rethinking our mobile growth strategies. *Canva*, https://product.canva.com/mobile-growth-strategies/ (accessed on February 27, 2019).

Rao, H., P. Monin, and R. Durand (2003). Institutional change in Toque Ville: Nouvelle cuisine as an identity movement in French gastronomy. *American Journal of Sociology*, 108(4), 795–843.

Rao, H., C. Morrill, and M. N. Zald (2000). Power plays: How social movements and collective action create new organizational forms. *Research in Organizational Behavior*. B. M. Staw and R. I. Sutton. London: JAI Press, pp. 237–281.

Regnér, P. and J. Edman (2014). MNE institutional advantage: How subunits shape, transpose and evade host country institutions. *Journal of International Business Studies*, 45(3), 275–302.

Reuber, A. R., G. A. Knight, P. W. Liesch, and L. Zhou (2018). International entrepreneurship: The pursuit of entrepreneurial opportunities across national borders. *Journal of International Business Studies*, 49(4), 395–406.

Rindova, V. P. and C. J. Fombrun (2001). Entrepreneurial action in the creation of the speciality coffee niche. *The Entrepreneurship Dynamic: Origins of Entrepreneurship and the Evolution of Industries*. C. B. Schoonhoven and E. Romanelli. Stanford, CA: Stanford University Press, pp. 236–261.

Santos, F. M. and K. M. Eisenhardt (2009). Constructing markets and shaping boundaries: Entrepreneurial power in nascent fields. *Academy of Management Journal*, 52(4), 643–671.

Schumpeter, A. (1942/2003). *Capitalism, Socialism and Democracy*. London, Routledge.

Shashidhar, A. (2018). HUL has increased its focus on foods, will it succeed? *Business Today*, https://www.businesstoday.in/opinion/perspective/hul-has-increased-its-focus-on-foods-will-it-succeed/story/281106.html (accessed on February 25, 2019).

Srikanth, A. N. (2018). 5 remarkable tech entrepreneurs you must know of. *Shout Me Loud*, https://www.shoutmeloud.com/famous-tech-entrepreneurs.html (accessed on February 25, 2019).

Stinchcombe, A. L. (1965). Social structure and organizations. *Handbook of Organizations*. J. G. March. Chicago, IL: Rand McNally & Company, pp. 142–193.

Suarez, F. F., S. Grodal, and A. Gotsopoulos (2015). Perfect timing? Dominant category, dominant design, and the window of opportunity for firm entry. *Strategic Management Journal*, 36, 437–448.

Suárez, F. F. and J. M. Utterback (1995). Dominant designs and the survival of firms. *Strategic Management Journal*, 16(6), 415–430.

Swaminathan, A. and J. B. Wade (2001). Social movement theory and the evolution of new organisational forms. *The Entrepreneurship Dynamic: Origins of Entrepreneurship and the Evolution of Industries*. C. B. Schoonhoven and E. Romanelli. Stanford, CA: Stanford University Press, pp. 286–313.

Tracey, P., E. Dalpiaz, and N. Phillips (2018). Fish out of water: Translation, legitimation, and new venture creation. *Academy of Management Journal*, 61(5), 1627–1666.

Turcan, R. (2013). International new venture legitimation: An exploratory study. *Administrative Sciences*, 3(4), 237–265.

Tushman, M. and J. P. Murmann (2002). Dominant designs, technology cycles, and organizational outcomes. *Managing in the Modular Age: Architectures, Networks, and Organizations*. R. Garud, A. Kumaraswamy and R. Langlois. Hoboken, NJ: Blackwell Publishing, pp. 316–348.

Tushman, M. L. and P. Anderson (1986). Technological discontinuities and organizational environments. *Administrative Science Quarterly*, 31(3), 439–465.

Utterback, J. M. and W. J. Abernathy (1975). A dynamic model of process and product innovation. *Omega, The International Journal of Management Science*, 3(6), 639–656.

Vaara, E. and J. Tienari (2010). On the narrative construction of multinational corporations: An antenarrative analysis of legitimation and resistance in a cross-border merger. *Organization Science*, 22(2), 370–390.

Wade, J. (1995). Dynamics of organizational communities and technological bandwagons: An empirical investigation of community evolution in the microprocessor market. *Strategic Management Journal*, 16(Special Issue: Technological transformation and the new competitive landscape (Summer, 1995)), 111–133.

Wry, T., M. Lounsbury, and M. A. Glynn (2011). Legitimating nascent collective identities: Coordinating cultural entrepreneurship. *Organization Science*, 22(2), 449–463.

Zaheer, S. (1995). Overcoming the liability of foreignness. *Academy of Management Journal*, 38(2), 341–363.

Zhao, E. Y., G. Fisher, M. Lounsbury, and D. Miller (2017). Optimal distinctiveness: Broadening the interface between institutional theory and strategic management. *Strategic Management Journal*, 38(1), 93–113.

Zietsma, C. and B. McKnight (2009). Building the iron cage: Institutional creation work in the context of competing proto-institutions. *Institutional Work: Actors and Agency in Institutional Studies of Organizations*. T. B. Lawrence, R. Suddaby and B. Leca. Cambridge, UK: Cambridge University Press, pp. 143–177.

Zimmerman, M. A. and G. J. Zeitz (2002). Beyond survival: Achieving new venture growth by building legitimacy. *Academy of Management Review*, 27(3), 414–431.

https://doi.org/10.1142/9789811228445_0003

Chapter 3

Effect of International Entrepreneurial Orientation on the Organisational Performance of Brazilian Exporting Companies

Rodrigo Marques de Almeida Guerra[*,†] and
Roberta Gizelle Macêdo Alves Farinha[*,‡]

[*]*Federal University of Pará, Belém, Brazil*

[†]*rmaguerra1@gmail.com*

[‡]*gizelle.farinha@gmail.com*

Abstract

Although international entrepreneurial orientation (IEO) is a topic widely discussed in national and international journals, little is known about its relationship with organisational performance (OP), particularly of exporting companies located in emerging economies. Research involving the theory of Resource-based Vision (RBV) may depend on the context in which companies operate. We measure the strength of the dimensions of innovativeness, proactivity and risk-taking in relation to the variables' growth in sales and profitability of companies located in the states of the North and Northeast regions of Brazil, which is an emerging economy. The data were collected through a questionnaire completed by 121 companies registered in the database of the MDIC (Ministry of Economy, Development, Industry and Commerce) related to three sectors of the National Classification of Economic Activity (CNAE) The five-point Likert scale involved the dimensions of IEO and organisational performance. The data were analysed using descriptive statistics, correlation, confirmatory factor analysis and modelling of structural equations. The results of this study have generated several practical implications for managerial decision-making due to the fact that the regions covered have strategic resources, export potential and diversity of human resources. This research contributed to fill the literature gap in the relationship between the dimensions of IEO and the OP of exporting companies located in an emerging-economy country. The results revealed a positive and significant effect for seven of the nine hypotheses. Only the links between innovativeness and profitability, and risk-taking and profitability have not been confirmed. The other hypotheses about innovativeness, proactivity, sales growth, profitability and stakeholders were statistically supported. Empirical evidence of the effect of the dimensions of IEO on OP reinforces the results of previous research, in addition to expanding the scope of investigation for future research.

Keywords: International entrepreneurial orientation; Innovativeness; Proactivity; Risk-taking; Organisational performance.

Introduction

Entrepreneurial orientation (EO) is considered part of a company's strategic resources and can be used to identify innovation opportunities in international markets (Lumpkin and Dess, 1996; Tang *et al.*, 2012). Organisations based on OE are more effective because they have the capacity to expand a new resource base, mainly if directed to the international market. However, it is necessary to develop new skills for decision-making in order to achieve superior performance in a complex international environment (Reuber *et al.*, 2017; Bauweraerts, 2018; Saeed and Ziaulhaq, 2018).

Recent research (Jones *et al.*, 2011; McDougall *et al.*, 2014; Reuber *et al.*, 2018) has stimulated theoretical and empirical investigations involving new international ventures (INVs), or related themes, due to the rapid conceptual growth. However, not everything is clear, since the term international entrepreneurship (IE) still influences other areas of knowledge in a transversal way (McDougall *et al.*, 2014): organisational structure, intangible resources and organisational performance, among others.

Due to the complexity of variables that can interfere in IE, this chapter will emphasise the organisational aspect, according to the assumption of Zahra (1993, 2005). Understanding the context of IE and corporate strategy can assist several companies in managing and expanding their business, both in relation to INVs and organisations with traditional management. Therefore, it is necessary to understand the concept of IE and its consequences.

The academic literature disregards the conceptual difference between IE, EO and International Entrepreneurial Orientation (IEO). Miller (2011) suggests that EO should be applied when seeking to understand the company as "being entrepreneur". In turn, Freeman and Cavusgil (2007) state that IEO is a behaviour of EO within a global context involving the three main elements of EO, postulated by Miller (1983) and expanded by Lumpkin and Dess (1996). To generate a better understanding of this theoretical gap, it is necessary to analyse the conceptual origin and the application environment of IE, EO and IEO, aiming at appropriate use.

Academic debates about entrepreneurial organisational strategy were disseminated from Mintzberg (1973). Ten years later, Miller (1983) suggests three key concepts for an entrepreneurial company: innovation, pioneering spirit (proactivity) and risk-taking. Covin and Slevin (1989) corroborate the initial idea of Miller (1983) when they consider the three elements of EO as being from a composite perspective, that is from the common behaviour of the three dimensions.

Only in the 1990s, Lumpkin and Dess (1996) expanded Miller's initial view (1983) from the recommendation of two new dimensions for EO (autonomy and competitive aggressiveness), which were added to the initial proposal of Miller (1983). Almost thirty years after the initial publication, Miller (2011) confirms the contributions of Lumpkin and Dess (1996) regarding the components of autonomy and competitive aggressiveness necessary for an entrepreneurial organisation.

The dimensions of EO suggest unique characteristics about innovativeness, proactivity, risk-taking, autonomy and competitive aggressiveness. These attributes are a consequence of a natural evolution; however, they do not prove to be equally valid for all organisations. In other words, some companies can develop certain dimensions and others cannot. Thus, in order to achieve internationalisation, the organisation needs to develop a set of skills and competences that facilitate operations in new markets.

Knight and Cavusgil (2004) indicate that companies that are pioneers in internationalising have characteristics aimed at innovative culture, knowledge, reduction of transaction costs in the foreign market and development of different capacities. In addition, the internationalisation of new ventures requires a distinct combination of guidelines and strategies for organisational success in international markets.

The concept of IEO has suffered conceptual influence both from IE and from organisational strategy, which in turn complement the RBV Theory. Barney (1991, 2001) states that organisations that seek sustainable competitive advantage should emphasise the use of idiosyncratic and heterogeneous resources, aiming to enhance their value through VRIO (valuable, rare, difficult to imitate and irreplaceable resources).

However, not all organisations own VRIO resources (valuable, rare, difficult to imitate and irreplaceable) and, even so, they operate competitively in the market. Knight and Cavusgil (2004) reopen this discussion by stating that, regardless of age, experience and obtaining tangible resources, reopen this discussion and state that any company is capable of competing in the international market by using knowledge, innovation, capabilities and appropriation of organisational culture.

McDougall (1989) states that the concept of IE is related to the development of new ventures with international operations, mainly of start-ups or born globals (BGs). For that, it is necessary that the organisation has mastery of international operations from the beginning. Since then, the concept of IE has been evolving. McDougall *et al.* (1994) claim that IE makes it possible to create hybrid structures to preserve scarce resources. This idea refers to the concept of RBV, defined by Barney (1991).

Companies located in emerging markets are characterised by having scarce resources, low (or none) experience related to internationalisation and limited access to relevant information, decisive for the development of strategies aimed at the foreign market (Samiee and Chirapanda, 2019). In this context, and based on the theory of RBV and IE, this chapter aims to measure the strength of the dimensions of innovativeness, proactivity and risk-taking in relation to the variables' growth in sales and profitability of Brazilian exporting companies located in the states of the North and Northeast regions of Brazil, a market for an emerging economy.

Theoretical Background

Resource-based View (RBV)

The seminal article "Firm Resources and Competitive Advantage", written by Jay Barney in 1991, suggests that organisations gain competitive advantage through resources that are valuable, rare, difficult to imitate and replace, denoted by the acronym VRIO. From this conception, the concept of RBV is born, which emphasises the need for the use of idiosyncratic and heterogeneous resources on the part of the company in order to enhance its value (Barney, 1991, 2001).

RBV presupposes that organisations improve existing capacities and develop new capacities, in order to obtain a competitive advantage in the long term (Barney, 1991, 2001). Due to its conceptual breadth, RBV influences the conception of several theories, such as strategic assets (Amit and Schoemaker, 1993), core competencies (Prahalad and Hamel, 1990), knowledge-based vision (Grant, 1996), EO (Grande *et al.*, 2011; Adomako *et al.*, 2016) and IE (McDougall *et al.*, 1994). This conceptual link can enhance the firm's competitive advantage.

The achievement of competitive advantage through the use of strategically valuable resources occurs when the organisation operates in the international market and is guided based on deliberate strategies. Thus, companies with IE are more likely to have a positive relationship about organisational performance, especially when they invest in resources based on VRIO (Adomako *et al.*, 2016). For Grande *et al.* (2011), entrepreneurial activities and attitudes are considered relevant and encourage organisations to create, reconsider and apply their resources more efficiently.

The evolution of the RBV Theory gave rise to the concept of Dynamic Capabilities (Teece *et al.*, 1997). Dynamic Capabilities are recognised as key factors for adapting the firm to the changing environment, and are clearly necessary for organisational sustainability (Teece *et al.*, 1997; Teece, 2007). Dynamic capabilities can be more valuable when the external environment presents itself in an unpredictable way (Zahra and George, 2002).

International Entrepreneurship

The concept of internationalisation emerged in the 1970s from macroeconomic concepts from the United States, Germany and Singapore (Knight and Liesch, 2016). Only around the 1980s did the concept of IE arouse the interest of researchers in understanding the mechanisms for generating new international ventures (INVs), start-ups or born globals (BGs) (McDougall *et al.*, 2014). These companies are being created and managed very quickly. The early rise indicates the use of different drives compared to traditional companies. The predominance of intensive use of technology may be the main characteristic for the emergence of these new international ventures; however, there are other attributes.

In the case of developed countries, the 1980s were marked by global factors that made international trade more dynamic, with lower transaction costs, reduced trade barriers and industry deregulation. In addition, the speed in sending products to their final destination contributed to the internationalisation of these companies (McDougall *et al.*, 2014)

For McDougall (1989), IE must encompass a broad market coverage strategy, diversity and control of distribution channels, and expansion of customers in various segments based on a high visibility of the market or product. For this, it is necessary to develop a more aggressive strategy, taking advantage of external financial and production resources to expand operations in geographic markets.

Knight and Cavusgil (2004) warn that the precocity in the internationalisation of companies is due to the development of knowledge, innovation and capacity, associated with the appropriation of the organisational culture. McDougall *et al.* (2014) state that IE must involve alternative theoretical perspectives, new problems and comparisons between countries, covering a significant number of related areas. However, one should avoid the lack of authenticity in relation to the theme, increase the methodological rigour and the scientific contribution to the literature (Coviello *et al.*, 2011; McDougall *et al.*, 2014).

Contrary to what may be thought initially, the absence of tangible and intangible resources is not the central problem for the internationalisation of companies. Over time, organisations have come to realise the importance of forming a set of strategic capabilities, the need for innovation and mastery of organisational culture, aiming at access to internationalisation, sometimes developed in an accelerated way (Knight and Cavusgil, 2004).

International Entrepreneurial Orientation

The concept of IEO is still neglected in international publications. For decades, researchers have sought to broaden the concepts of EO and IEO. Throughout this evolution, several publications contributed significantly to theoretical advances (Miller, 1983, 2011; George and Marino, 2011; Anderson *et al.*, 2015). Within this context, it can be said that much needs to be done to improve these definitions. An example of this is the discussion of the use of terminology in research developed within the context of IE.

Table 1: Conceptual Evolution of IE

Authors	IE Concept
McDougall (1989)	IE is considered as the development of new ventures or international start-ups that, since the beginning, have been involved in international business.
McDougall *et al.* (1994)	New international ventures are individuals who see opportunities to establish ventures that operate across national borders. They are "alert" to the possibilities of combining resources from different national markets due to the skills (networks, knowledge and background) that they have developed from their previous activities.
Oviatt and McDougall (1994)	IE is defined as a commercial organisation that, from the beginning, seeks to obtain a significant competitive advantage from the use of resources and the sale of products in several countries.
Oviatt and McDougall (1994)	New international ventures are characterised by multinational companies, with their own structure, integrated with business with other countries, entrepreneurship and related to the theory of strategic management.
Knight and Cavusgil (2004)	Any company, regardless of age, experience and tangible resources, can be an active participant in international business.
Jones *et al.* (2011)	Instead of defining IE, the authors reviewed several scientific articles in order to integrate the current concepts from the application of a rigid methodology, making it possible to replicate them. Theoretical scarcity suggests conceptual evolution, identification of border areas and comparison between countries, in order to improve management practices. Due to the theoretical scarcity, it was necessary to build a conceptual map through the ontological domain of transversal themes.
McDougall, Jones and Serapio (2014)	The concept of IE is related to unusual internationalisation patterns involving frontier areas of science, identification and exploitation of new business opportunities, cognitive and behavioural characteristics of individuals and their work teams. Despite this, the concept still needs to be refined.
Cavusgil and Knight (2015)	IE advances due to innovation in the company's value chain. This perspective creates an opportunity to explore and expand the advantage over the competition.
Knight and Liesch (2016)	The concept of IE is evolving and can be applied to organisations of any size, age, experience and use of resources. Future research should identify the reasons for the precocity and rapid internationalisation of organisations worldwide. It is important to encourage the publication of robust theoretical papers on the subject.
Reuber, Dimitratos and Kuivalainen (2017)	Early companies operating in international markets have identified a business opportunity. For that, it is necessary to develop new management methods and tools that reinforce this opportunity.
Pruthi, Mitra and Mitra (2020)	Researching different bases of the phenomenon, such as ethnicity, tensions between the concepts of migrant, returnee, diasporan and transnational entrepreneurship and their association with IE, can be an opportunity for future studies.

Source: Elaborated by the authors (2020).

Recent research should be cautious with the use of the terms EO and IEO, since internationalisation can expand the context of the company's performance (Covin and Miller, 2014).

Table 1 shows the conceptual evolution of the term EO.

The conceptual discussion between the use of EO or IEO can be extensive, and it can be justified by the high dynamism, turbulence and complexity in the corporate environment, particularly of organisations with international scope. The organisational logic is not as simple as it seems, especially when the company exports products and services to demanding markets.

International business theory suggests that internationalisation is a phenomenon subsequent to organisational origin (McDougall, 1989). Acting globally can leverage sales growth and accelerate the emergence of international ventures (McDougall and Oviatt, 2000), since the logic of the international market is different from the domestic market (McDougall, 1989; Covin and Miller, 2014).

Thus, it is clear that the conceptual difference between EO and IEO can be tenuous. An example of this is the measurement instruments used in past research. Often, the dimensions applied to measure OE are the same as those of IEO, although the context of application is different (Miller, 1983, 2011; Lumpkin and Dess, 1996; Covin and Miller, 2014). IE should be applied to INVs operating outside the home country's domestic borders (McDougall, 1989), so that it is possible to measure IEO.

In this sense, what can still be done to improve the use of terms? Can the concept of IEO be improved? If so, in what way (Covin and Miller, 2014; Anderson *et al.*, 2015)? One possible answer may be the contextual difference, new inputs and the use of a wide resource base (Covin and Miller, 2014; Anderson and Eshima, 2013; Eshima and Anderson, 2017), since the constructs have multiple attributes (Lumpkin and Dess, 1996; Miller, 2011).

The bases and exploitation of resources can restrict or expand the organisational capacity to operate in domestic or international markets (McDougall, 1989; McDougall and Oviatt, 2000). Thus, export performance, organisational culture, consumer preference and beliefs can be favourable (or not) indicators for targeting the domestic market, international market or both (Knight and Cavusgil, 2004; Kreiser *et al.*, 2010; Wales *et al.*, 2019). In addition, the performance of INVs in the

Table 2: Conceptual Evolution of Entrepreneurial Orientation

Authors	**EO Concept**
Miller (1983)	EO refers to the application of its operations in product or service innovation, which occurs, basically, through risk-taking and proactivity.
Covin and Slevin (1989)	EO involves organisational business practices, which determine which strategies will be applied to face difficulties due to hostile environments.
Covin and Slevin (1991)	By presenting strong interference on organisational performance, EO can be characterised as one of the origins of competitive advantage.
Lumpkin and Dess (1996)	EO is related to the use of methods, practices and decision-making style employed in an entrepreneurial way, resulting in the emergence of new business opportunities.
Covin *et al.* (2006)	An EO is based on a strategy in which the understanding of the structure encompasses results at the level of the organisation, these belonging to the managerial preferences, beliefs and behaviours manifested among the managers of the organisation.
Lumpkin *et al.* (2009)	Decision-making and autonomy are essential elements of an EO, resources capable of providing a direction to achieve strategic advantages and business results in the organisation.
Miller (2011)	EO is broadly related to theories in strategy, organisational theory and economics.
Wales *et al.* (2013)	EO can be defined as an organisational phenomenon, which changes over time, due to the way in which EO is applied in organisations.
Lechner and Gudmundsson (2014)	EO influences the relationship between competitive strategy and organisational performance.
Anderson *et al.* (2015)	EO represents the study of the company's strategic behaviour in reference to entrepreneurship.
Eshima and Anderson (2017)	By increasing adaptive capacity, organisations are able to expand their business activities in the same proportion as they increase their EO.

Source: Elaborated by the authors (2020).

international environment can further expand the organisation's performance in the business environment (McDougall *et al.*, 2003).

Dimensions of International Entrepreneurial Orientation (IEO)

Innovativeness

Innovativeness is based on the stimulus generated to companies with decisions that involve possibilities, determined by the creation and development of new ideas, new products and services (Lumpkin and Dess, 1996). Through innovation, organisations can have resources and actions (Miller and Friense, 1982) capable of developing and/or making new products available on the market, facilitating their access to new domestic and/or international markets (Kreiser *et al.*, 2013; Dai *et al.*, 2014). Innovativeness can help companies to associate strategic capacity aimed at new businesses (Avlonitis and Salavou, 2007).

Innovativeness can be the basis of strategic conduct for an organisation. Thus, companies with a greater emphasis on innovation will be able to obtain better results with the insertion of new technologies in innovative products and services (Lee and Peterson, 2000), which may contribute to the economic growth of developed or developing countries (Martinez and Santiso, 2003; Radas and Božić, 2009). The innovation process can be different even in developing countries. Chile is driven by technological innovation (products and processes); on the contrary, in Peru, the most evident innovation was non-technological (organisational and marketing). Consequently, the dissimilarity of innovation influences organisational performance (OP) in different ways (Pérez *et al.*, 2019). For these reasons, innovativeness must be investigated with greater attention, especially in relation to the dimensions of organisational performance: sales growth, stakeholders and profitability.

Hypothesis H1a: There is a positive relationship between innovativeness and sales growth.

Hypothesis H1b: There is a positive relationship between innovativeness and stakeholders.

Hypothesis H1c: There is a positive relationship between innovativeness and profitability.

Risk-taking

Risk-taking is related to the way in which the organisation works. Investment in new international ventures (INVs) requires financial resources, which have no guarantee of return (Lumpkin *et al.*, 2013; Pukall and Calabrò, 2014). Risk-taking becomes a peculiarity of IE, since it maintains a certain degree of indeterminacy, regarding expectations in obtaining positive results and profit generation, enhancing the risk–return link (Lumpkin and Dess, 1996; Brulhart *et al.*, 2019). Despite the limited availability of financial resources, some new international ventures seek to develop skills and abilities to achieve success in the foreign market (Kinghit and Cavusgil, 2004). Thus, risk-taking can significantly decrease organisational performance, since high risk can be counterproductive for the company (Kollmann and Stöckmann, 2014). Therefore, this investigation needs to be deepened.

Hypothesis H2a: There is a positive relationship between risk-taking and sales growth.

Hypothesis H2b: There is a positive relationship between risk-taking and stakeholders.

Hypothesis H2c: There is a positive relationship between risk-taking and profitability.

Proactivity

The proactivity dimension introduces the perspective of creating new opportunities, anticipating changes, awakening new capacities with a tendency to generate competitive behaviours (Kreiser *et al.*, 2013). Proactivity is an anticipation of actions in the face of changes or problems that may arise, through entrepreneurial behaviour (Lumpkin and Dess, 2005). For Kreiser *et al.* (2013), proactivity strengthens the performance of small and medium-sized companies, favouring their positioning in the market, when they act in advance in the face of future situations that demand the search for better results, regulating and interacting with the external environment. EO may be able to expand the international performance of small- and medium-sized companies (Brouthers *et al.*, 2014).

Different levels of proactivity and innovativeness (low or high) can help advance the company's internationalisation. In turn, moderate levels decrease the demand for new markets (Dai *et al.*, 2014). Similarly, it is important to analyse how much proactivity can influence the dimensions of OP (e.g. sales growth, stakeholders and profitability) and, consequently, contribute to the internationalisation of companies already operating in foreign markets.

Hypothesis H3a: There is a positive relationship between proactivity and sales growth.

Hypothesis H3b: There is a positive relationship between proactivity and stakeholders.

Hypothesis H3c: There is a positive relationship between proactivity and profitability.

Organisational Performance (OP)

OP can be measured in several ways, being considered an important multidimensional construct and difficult to measure (Behrman and Perreault, 1982; Richard *et al.*, 2009). The most traditional way of measuring an indicator is quantitatively, such as profitability (Narver and Slater, 2006), sales growth, operational efficiency and value generation, among others (Sharma, 2005).

OP is a construct that is difficult to measure on the part of organisational management (Dess and Robinson, 1984; Hubbard, 2009). Thus, it is recommended that the business environment has efficient management (Venkatraman and Ramanujam, 1986), aiming to manage resources in a sustainable way (Dess and Robinson, 1984; Narver and Slater, 2006). However, in order to obtain superior performance in relation to the main rivals (Venkatraman and Ramanujam, 1986), it is necessary that organisations make use of different measurement indicators, such as profitability and sales growth (Dess and Robinson, 1984).

The use of non-financial indicators can be useful to expand the company's operations, going beyond economic dimensions. An organisation can use both objective measures (financial indicators) and subjective measures (non-financial indicators) to measure OP (Dess and Robinson, 1984). Some examples of subjective measures can be quality of service, levels of productivity, rate of innovation, customer satisfaction, brand

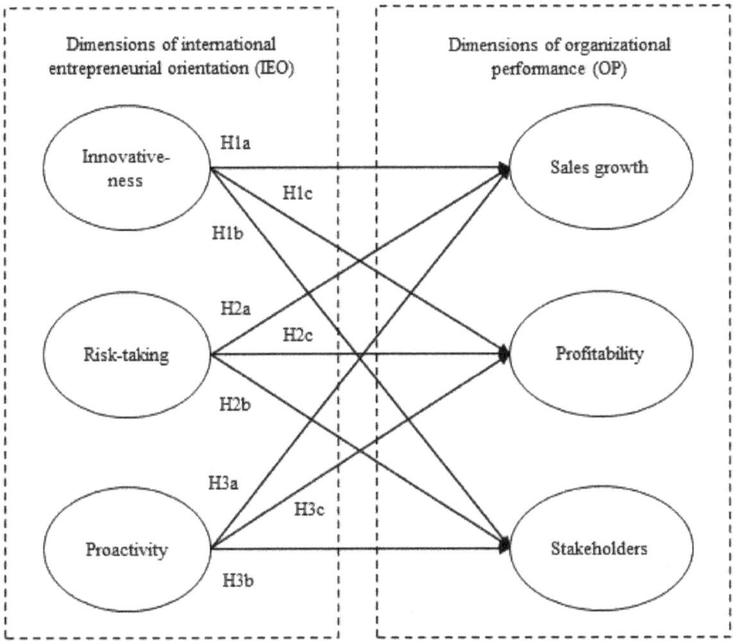

Figure 1: Framework of the Proposed Empirical Model

Source: Research data (2020).

value and stakeholders, among others (Richard *et al.*, 2009; Mazur and Pisarski, 2015; Singh *et al.*, 2016).

Figure 1 presents the hypotheses of the empirical model through the connection between the dimensions of IEO and OP.

Methodological Procedures

Data were collected through a questionnaire completed by 121 companies registered in the CNAE (National Classification of Economic Activity) in three sectors of activity. The five-point Likert scale involved the dimensions of IEO and organisational performance. The data were analysed using descriptive statistics, Pearson's correlation, confirmatory factor analysis and modelling of structural equations.

Data Collection and Sample

The research involved companies registered in the MDIC database (Ministry of Economy, Development, Industry and Commerce). This study took into account the exporting companies that commercialised their products in the last five years. The universe of identified companies brought together 2,255 organisations based in the North and Northeast regions of different sectors of activity in four states in the Brazilian territory. To classify companies, the CNAE (National Classification of Economic Activity) criterion was adopted, resulting in three participation groups, namely agriculture, livestock, forest production, research and aquaculture; extractive industries; and manufacturing industry.

Data collection was carried out between September and November 2019, through an electronic link made available to all companies listed in the MDIC database, in order to test the proposed hypotheses. In order to avoid any doubts regarding the two waves of responses, it was decided to compare them, and it was not possible to identify significant differences between the two groups. The initial valid sample obtained was 134 companies. After the exclusion of 13 severe outliers, through the calculation of the Mahalanobis distance (D^2), the final valid sample was 121 cases. Thus, the rate of return was 90.30% of the final sample obtained; however, if we consider the total number of companies in the database (2,255 companies), the rate of return was 5.36% of the cases. In addition, to ensure the number of responses obtained, telephone calls were made to verify the companies' intention to participate in the survey. The questionnaire was completed by only one respondent from each participating company.

The questionnaire was adapted from Hughes and Morgan (2007), Covin and Slevin (1989), Naman and Slevin (1993) and Guerra (2017), comprising 27 specific questions distributed in the three dimensions of IEO: innovativeness (INN), proactivity (PRO) and risk-taking (RT). The dimensions of OP were divided as follows: growth in sales (SALES) and profitability (PROFIT). The applied questionnaire is available in Appendix A. The target audience of the research involved employees at the tactical or strategic levels, which is important for organisational decision-making.

Research Environment

Agriculture in Brazil is one of the main elements of the country's economy. Given the degree of importance, it is essential that research in this sector can collaborate for better economic performance, contributing to the expansion of production, as well as identifying limitations and opportunities for growth.

Initially, an analysis of the industrial production of the states involved (Amazonas/AM, Bahia/BA, Pará/PA and Pernambuco/PE) was carried out in order to verify the contribution to the investigated region. Companies in the North and Northeast have a prominent role in the regional economy due to their strategic resources, export potential and diversity of human resources. The production of the northern region is related to the primary sector, with emphasis on extraction (vegetable, animal and mineral) and agriculture.

Data Analysis

The cross-sectional survey was applied to a sample of 121 small, medium and large companies based in states in the North and Northeast regions of Brazil. For that, it was necessary to analyse the data obtained using the statistical software IBM SPSS® (Statistical Package for the Social Sciences) and Amos® (Analysis of Moment Structures). The applied multivariate statistics involved the statistical procedures: Pearson's correlation, confirmatory factor analysis (CFA) and structural equation modelling (SEM).

Results

Descriptive Statistics

The results of descriptive statistics showed that the percentage of male respondents (51.2%) was higher than that of women (48.8%). Regarding the area of work, the commercial/sales sector has a number of respondents amounting to 27.3%. As for the position of the company, the highest percentage of respondents involved the position of manager (31%). In relation to the states, Pará/PA obtained 38.8% of valid responses, followed by the state of Pernambuco/PE with 25.6%.

The survey involved large (44.6%), medium (38.0%) and small (17.4%) companies. Regarding the economic activities of these companies, the manufacturing industry obtained the highest response rate (77.0%). This percentage can be considered high in relation to agriculture, livestock, forest production, research and aquaculture (19.0%). As for the time of existence of the companies, the number of companies with a lifespan of over 51 years reached a percentage of 18.2%, and 11.6% for companies between 31 and 40 years of existence.

The respondents' area of activity was distributed as follows: industrial (n = 13; 10.7%), human resources (n = 24; 19.8%), commercial/sales (n = 33; 27.3%), logistics (n = 14; 9.1%), marketing (n = 4; 3.3%), financial/accounting (n = 12; 9.9%) and import/export (n = 10; 8.3%). Despite this, it is important to state that all the companies investigated have been active in foreign trade in the last five years. The functions of the participants in the companies were as follows: partner/owner (n = 10; 8.3%), manager (n = 38; 31.4%), analyst (n = 9; 7.4%), coordinator of area (n = 0; 41.3%) and technician/supervisor (n = 14; 11.6%).

Correlation and Discriminant Analysis

Table 3 indicates a strong correlation between the observable variables (range from 0.72 to 0.82), which suggests a result that is higher than that indicated by the academic literature (0.7), according to the assumptions of Hair *et al.* (2009) and Fávero *et al.* (2009). In addition, the mean, standard deviation and Cronbach's alpha values were analysed. The latter must be

Table 3: Mean, Standard Deviation, Cronbach's Alpha (α), CR, AVE and Pearson's Correlation

							Pearson's Correlation					
Variables	**Items**	**M**	**SD**	α	**AVE**	**CR**	**1**	**2**	**3**	**4**	**5**	**6**
1. INN	5	18.00	4.55	0.87	0.61	0.88	**0.78**	—	—	—	—	—
2. PRO	5	19.14	4.13	0.84	0.52	0.85	.459**	**0.72**	—	—	—	—
3. RT	5	19.15	4.30	0.89	0.64	0.90	.464**	.431**	**0.80**	—	—	—
4. SALES	4	12.56	3.99	0.89	0.63	0.87	.507**	.503**	.482**	**0.79**	—	—
5. PROFIT	4	12.82	3.82	0.76	0.49	0.83	.098†	.388**	.150†	.305**	**0.70**	—
6. SKH	4	11.74	4.72	0.90	0.66	0.89	.489**	.420**	.465**	.683**	.291**	**0.82**
	—	—	**M**	**0.86**	**0.59**	**0.87**	—	—	—	—	—	—

Notes: M = Mean; SD = Standard Deviation; α = Cronbach's Alpha; CR = Composite Reliability; AVE = Average Variance Extracted; INN = Innovativeness; PRO = Proactivity; RT = Risk-taking; SALES = Sales growth; PROFIT = Profitability; and SKH = Stakeholders.

†$p \geq 0.1$ *$p < 0.05$; **$p < 0.01$.

Source: Research data (2020).

greater than 0.8, as indicated by Hair *et al.* (2009) and Fávero *et al.* (2009).

Table 3 also demonstrates the convergent validity and internal consistency from the results of the AVE (Average Variance Extracted) (>0.5) and CR (Composite Reliability) (>0.8) (Fornell and Larcker, 1981). Regarding the discriminant analysis, the bold values of the correlation diagonal indicate the result of the square root of the stroke. Values above those indicated by the line and column of the correlation matrix suggest suitability for the discriminant analysis.

Structural Equation Modelling (SEM)

The values of modelling structural equations should be analysed with caution (Hair *et al.*, 2009). Thus, the researcher must be careful to evaluate a set of indicators, never a single index in isolation (Marôco, 2010). With regard to the present study, the MEE adjustment indices were as follows: the CFI (Comparative Fit Index), GFI (Goodness of Fit Index) and IFI (Incremental Fit Index) indices must present values equal to or greater than 0.9 (Hair *et al.*, 2009; Vieira and Ribas, 2011).

In turn, the RMSEA (Root of Approximate Mean Square Error) should vary between 0.05 and 0.08 (Hair *et al.*, 2009; Vieira and Ribas, 2011). The chi-square test (χ^2) suggests the adjustment of the model, and should present the lowest possible value (Hair *et al.*, 2009); the only exception is when the model demonstrates complexity of the constructs. The result of the x^2/df ratio must be between >1.0 and < 3.0 (Marôco, 2010).

After defining the reference indices, the CFA indicated a good level of adjustment for the structural model: $x^2 = 531.249$; $df = 314$; $p = 0.000$; $x^2/df = 1.692$; CFI = 0.884; GFI = 0.766; IFI = 0.887; RMSEA = 0.076; P(rmsea) <0.001. The result of the structural model meets the theoretical assumptions (Hair *et al.*, 2009; Vieira and Ribas, 2011; Marôco, 2010).

Table 4 shows that Model 3 presents the best fit for MEE. A possible justification for this may have happened due to the sample having surpassed 100 cases, a fact that proves the adequacy of the results of the complete model.

Discussion

The results indicate a positive and significant effect of seven of the nine hypotheses (Table 5). Only the links between innovativeness and

Table 4: Result of MEE Adjustment by Surveyed Region

Model	*N*	χ^2	gl	χ^2/gl	*P*	GFI	CFI	IFI	RMSEA
Model 1 - North	65	473.972	314	1.509	0.000	0.848	0.672	0.853	0.089
Model 2 - Northeast	56	598.381	314	1.906	0.000	0.739	0.619	0.747	0.128
Model 3 - Complete	121	531.249	314	1.692	0.000	0.884	0.766	0.887	0.076
Model adjustment indexes	Bigger, better	Smaller, better	—	< 3.0	< 0.001	≥ 0.9	≥ 0.9	≥ 0.9	≥ 0.05 a ≤ 0.08

Notes: *N* = Sample; x^2 = Chi-square; gl = Degrees of freedom; χ^2/gl = Chi-square by degrees of freedom; *p* = Significance level; GFI = *Goodness of Fit Index*; CFI = *Comparative Fit Index*; IFI = *Incremental Fit Index*; and RMSEA = *Root Mean Square Error of Approximation.*
Source: Research data (2020).

Table 5: Result of the Hypothesis Test

Hypotheses	Relations	Loading	S.E.	CR	*p*-value	Supported?
H1a	INN→SALES	0.398	0.105	3.778	***	Yes
H1b	INN→SKH	0.399	0.116	3.429	***	Yes
H1c	INN→PROFIT	−0.112	0.110	−1.021	0.307	No
H2a	RT→SALES	0.309	0.099	3.115	0.002	Yes
H2b	RT→SKH	0.321	0.109	2.934	0.003	Yes
H2c	RT→PROFIT	−0.007	0.104	−0.071	0.943	No
H3a	PRO→SALES	0.408	0.101	4.051	***	Yes
H3b	PRO→SKH	0.277	0.105	2.637	0.008	Yes
H3c	PRO→PROFIT	0.586	0.127	4.621	***	Yes

Note: *** < 0.001.
Source: Research data (2020).

profitability (H1c), and risk-taking and profitability (H2c) have not been confirmed. The other hypotheses that involved the variables innovativeness, proactivity, sales growth, profitability and stakeholders were statistically supported.

The results of the hypothesis test reveal support for seven of the nine hypotheses proposed (Table 5). The **H1a hypothesis was supported**

(INN→SALES) ($\beta = 0.398$; S.E. = 0.105; CR = 3.778; p-value < 0.001). Previous studies involving the innovativeness dimension demonstrated a predominantly positive relationship with the growth in sales and the offer of new products enhancing the current and emerging needs of the market (Kuratko *et al.*, 2009; Wiklund *et al.*, 2009). The **H1b hypothesis was accepted** (INN→SKH) ($\beta = 0.399$; S.E. = 0.116; CR = 3.429; p-value < 0.001). Recent research has found that the proactivity dimension has significant value when it comes to efforts to satisfy multiple stakeholders and reach solutions in new markets (Lumpkin *et al.*, 2013). The **H1c hypothesis was rejected** (INN→PROFIT) ($\beta = -0.112$; S.E. = 0.110; CR = −1.021; p-value<0.307). Although previous research relates innovation positively to OP (Kollmann and Stöckmann, 2014), it must be considered that innovation costs can be high, requiring resources and infrastructure from the organisation, which can impact the company's profitability (Kreiser *et al.*, 2012).

The **H2a hypothesis was accepted** (RT→SALES) ($\beta = 0.309$; S.E. = 0.099; CR = 3.155; p-value <0.005). Preliminary research has shown that risk-taking has a positive impact on sales growth, when companies expand their exploration possibilities, take advantage of market opportunities (Dess and Lumpink, 2005). Lumpkin and Dess (1996) claim that EO is related to obtaining new business opportunities. Risk-taking is related to the opportunity cost (Reuber *et al.*, 2018), which can be exploited by market dysfunctions, that is gaps that cause the organisation to take a risk in relation to the gain with the increase in sales. Thus, the greater the risk, the greater the chance of obtaining sales growth. Similarly, the entrepreneurial opportunity is related to how much the company is willing to take risks and take advantage (increase sales) in relation to its rivals (Shane and Venkataraman, 2000), e.g. a new international market (Chandra *et al.*, 2012).

The **H2b hypothesis was supported** (RT→SKH) ($\beta = 0.309$; S.E. = 0.099; CR = 3.155; p-value<0.005). Stakeholders have a high potential when they involve the risk-taking dimension, increasing expectations of gain in organisations (Lumpkin *et al.*, 2013; John *et al.*, 2008). Internationalisation is associated with the risk, level of knowledge and breadth of the company's network of contacts (Pukall and Calabrò, 2014). International ventures are related to the opportunity to generate new business beyond national borders (McDougall *et al.*, 1994; Lumpkin and Dess, 1996). To this end, it is important that international ventures take risks, seek out stakeholders and develop a network of contacts, aiming to cross the domestic market. Pukall and Calabrò (2014) state that risk-taking is related to access to interested parties, resources and financing.

The **H2c hypothesis was rejected** (RT→PROFIT) (β = −0.007; S.E. = 0.104; CR = −0.071; *p*-value <0.943). Risk-taking and profitability diverge when the probability of failure in the strategy is enhanced (Miller, 2011); greater profitability requires greater investment in differentiation (Lechner and Gudmundsso, 2012). Risk entrepreneurship is related to how much the organisation is willing to generate radical innovation (Lassen *et al.*, 2006). Radical innovation foresees discontinued innovation in the offer/production of products, services, technology and/or current markets in exchange for inserting a different paradigm from the usual (Christensen, 1997; Hamel and Prahalad, 2000). Because of this, the respondents of this research probably associated the risk of (radical) innovation with the possibility of obtaining greater profits.

The **H3a hypothesis was supported** (PRO→SALES) (β = 0.408; S.E. = 0.101; CR = 4.051; *p*-value <0.001). This hypothesis is consistent with previous research that suggests that proactivity at higher levels is capable of leveraging growth in sales (Lumpink and Dess, 2001; Venkatraman, 1989). Proactivity is positively related to sales growth. For Zahra (1996), dynamic environments contribute to the emergence of new ventures, particularly with pioneering characteristics. Lumpkin and Dess (2001) state that proactivity significantly interferes with sales growth. Kreiser and Davis (2010) suggest that dynamic and magnificent environments present high innovativeness, proactivity and risk-taking, in addition to contributing to organisational performance.

The **H3b hypothesis was accepted** (PRO→SKH). The hypothesis test revealed a positive and significant relationship (β = 0.277; S.E. = 0.105; CR = 2.637; *p*-value<0.01). Stakeholder participation has the potential to strongly influence the level of proactivity within an organisation, raising the prospect of new opportunities, awakening competitive behaviours (Kreiser *et al.*, 2012; Lumpkin *et al.*, 2013; Brulhart *et al.*, 2019). The **H3c hypothesis was accepted** (PRO→PROFIT) (β = 0.561; S.E. = 0.077; CR = 7.262; *p*-value <0.001). According to previous studies, proactivity is a dimension capable of exploiting opportunities that already exist in the market, thus reinforcing the company's profitability (Lumpink and Dess, 2001). Brulhart, Gherra and Quelin (2019) suggest, based on stakeholder theory and RBV, that there is a link between stakeholders, proactivity and profitability.

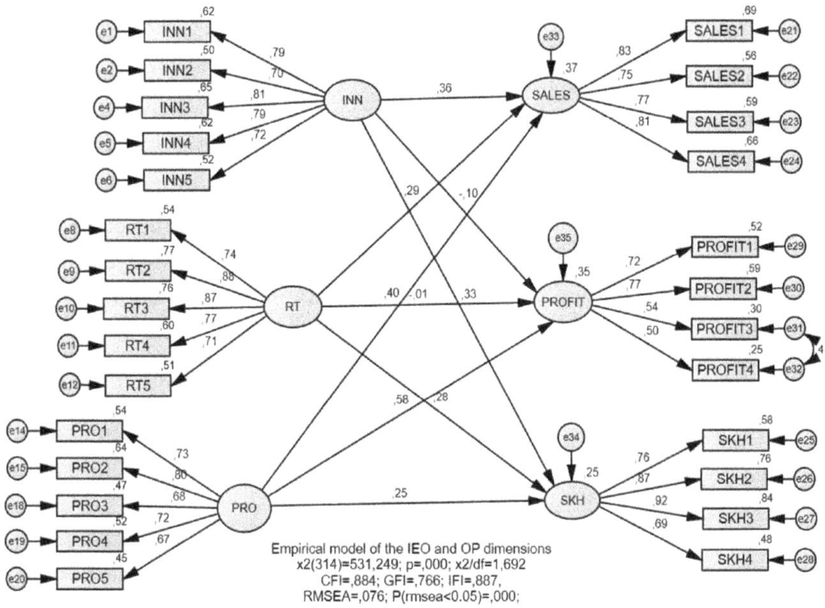

Figure 2: Result of Hypothesised Relationships

Source: Research data (2020).

Figure 2 suggests the empirical model of the relationship between the dimensions of IEO and OP.

Theoretical Contributions

The research contributes to the academic literature by testing three models of IEO in relation to the dimensions of OP (sales growth, profitability and stakeholders). The analysis was carried out within the context of Brazilian exporting companies, parents of the emerging economy. Studies involving this configuration and research environment should be further explored in the international literature due to the importance for the local and regional economy. The study offers theoretical and practical implications to three dimensions of IEO: innovativeness, risk-taking and proactivity.

The main contribution of this chapter is in the statistical confirmation of six of the nine hypotheses tested. In other words, it can be inferred that innovation and risk-taking influence, positively and significantly, the variables' sales growth and stakeholders. The second contribution suggests that innovativeness and risk-taking do not positively and statistically influence the profitability dimension. This finding may be important, since the research was applied during the Brazilian electoral period, considered to be of economic and political instability due to the uncertainty regarding the direction of the country. Martínez and Santiso (2003) suggest that electoral results influence countries in emerging economies to a greater extent compared to industrialised or developed countries. This fact may be related to possible market turbulence, economic instability and uncertainty regarding the future of foreign investment generated in developing countries. Hoskisson *et al.* (2000) postulate that countries in emerging economies (e.g. countries in Latin America) need to develop strategies, such as the RBV, to deal with rapid political and economic changes due to the different stages of economic liberalisation that they have.

The third contribution refers to the business tradition of the companies surveyed. Previous studies (McDougall *et al.*, 2014; Knight and Liesch, 2016) reinforce the need to investigate new international ventures (INVs, start-ups or BGs), which did not happen in this research. However, this study proved a large part of the tested hypotheses, reinforcing its empirical contribution to the theory of internationalisation and IE.

The fourth contribution suggests that the group of companies investigated is considered relevant, since it covers a sample of organisations located in regions with the presence of strategic resources, potential for export and diversity of human resources. In addition, the fact that the research was developed in a country with an emerging economy was decisive in identifying characteristics related to the RBV theory.

The fifth contribution refers to the concept of IEO. This theoretical gap makes it possible to advance theoretical discussions, since the theory of IE is limited to the context of IE. Clarifying the need of having a guiding vision (international entrepreneurial orientation) for the organisation is vital. This finding may be important for proposing a specific concept, as well as possible drives that differentiate IE, EO and IEO. This comparison can be made based on the theory of RBV or dynamic capabilities. One needs to be aware that developments that contribute to the theory of IE may be important for advances within the science of management.

Practical Implications

The results of this study generated several practical implications for managerial decision-making due to the fact that the surveyed regions have strategic resources, export potential and diversity of human resources. The investigated environment seems to be favourable to the generation of incremental innovation, the development of new capacities and the acquisition of knowledge. Internationalisation has generated a closer relationship with the organisation culture of the destination countries. These findings confirm previous results (Knight and Cavusgil, 2004; Cavusgil and Knight, 2015).

Innovativeness is important for the creation and development of new products. This characteristic is particularly identified in entrepreneurial companies, regardless of their level of maturity, since they need innovative resources aimed at differentiation. Proactivity awakens the organisation's ability to change the current situation by encouraging the competitive and proactive behaviour of its employees.

The search for the anticipation of the competitor's actions is a decisive factor for the generation of new products, processes and specific technology for the company to take advantage of the pioneering spirit. For that, it is necessary that organisations take a certain degree of risk, aiming at obtaining favourable results, greater profitability and reduced competition. The risk environment is natural in international markets, since the scenario is unpredictable.

Search Limitations

As for research limitations, there is a lack of exploration of the dimensions: autonomy and competitive aggressiveness, as well as the dimension called networks. This dimension proposes that organisations need to build relationship networks, aiming to direct the entry into new markets. The research was restricted to a sample of Brazilian international companies located in the North and Northeast regions, a country with an emerging economy. These two regions are vulnerable in terms of industrialisation and participation in the Brazilian territory. Despite the asymmetry, in relation to other regions of the country, the surveyed places are important due to cultural diversity, obtaining strategic resources and potential for export. There may have been some response bias, because data collection was carried out during the electoral period. Uncertainties caused in periods of turbulence (e.g. financial, economic, market or political) are typical of developing countries or those with industrial backwardness, due to making the organisational environment even more unstable and uncertain.

Future Studies

It is hoped that future research will be able to offer a deeper analysis of how the dimensions of IEO can impact the performance of new international ventures in emerging countries. New empirical research can conceptualise and reveal the functioning of the mechanisms of IEO. This point is fundamental for the consolidation of the term. Countries operating in the context of the domestic economy may reveal different findings in developed and developing economies. This seems to be key to the composition of the definition of IEO.

Studying elements that reinforce emerging concepts related to the theory of IE seems to be key to the consolidation of the area. What corroborates this is the expansion of terminologies involving the theory of IE, such as multidisciplinary, multi-method and cross-border business activities. Expanding the dimensions of IE seems to be reasonable, since the theory is still under construction. Perhaps the multicriteria of these dimensions of IE can influence the evidence in different international markets.

Conclusion

Although the field of research related to IE and organisational strategy is more explored in developed countries, analysing the context of emerging countries seems to be useful to stimulate the vocation of this group of companies, particularly in regions with growth potential. The academic literature lacks empirical research involving the relationship between the constructs of IEO and organisational performance. The findings of this research further reinforce the results of previous research, in addition to expanding the scope for further investigations.

This article aimed to measure the strength of the dimensions of innovativeness, proactivity and risk-taking in relation to the variables' growth in sales and profitability of Brazilian exporting companies located in the states of the North and Northeast regions of Brazil, parents of the emerging economy. The survey results confirmed seven of the nine hypotheses tested.

Thus, this chapter contributes to IE and organisational strategy, from the perspective of the RBV theory. IE is associated with new theories, complex concepts and a breakdown of the *status quo*, due to its multidisciplinary characteristics (McDougall *et al.*, 2014). RBV can be important for managers' decision-making, since VRIO-based resources can differentiate companies from rivals and facilitate resource management, particularly in emerging economies, where the economic and political scenario is more unpredictable for resource-dependent organisations.

The North region of Brazil stands out for its vocation for entrepreneurship in activities related to agriculture, livestock, forestry production, research and aquaculture, in addition to acting differently in the extractive industry. The Northeast region is driven by the manufacturing industry, mainly related to the manufacture of rubber and plastic products, beverages, computer equipment, electronic and optical products, and cellulose, paper and paper products. Despite the difference between the two regions, both have similar characteristics, which may have contributed to the regional economy, more precisely to strategic resources, export potential and diversity of human resources. These capacities need to be stimulated, aiming at differentiating the analysed business sectors.

Finally, research on quantitative approaches is relevant to analyse the impact of constructs from a sample of companies. Thus, the results obtained must be analysed with caution, being restricted to the cases studied.

Appendix A: Research Questionnaire

IEO dimensions	**I totally disagree** **I totally agree**
RT1. The term "risk taker" is considered a positive attribute for people in our business.	1. ☐ 2. ☐ 3. ☐ 4. ☐ 5. ☐
RT2. Your company people are encouraged to take calculated risks with new ideas.	1. ☐ 2. ☐ 3. ☐ 4. ☐ 5. ☐
RT3. The company emphasizes exploring and experimenting with opportunities.	1. ☐ 2. ☐ 3. ☐ 4. ☐ 5. ☐
RT4. The company has a strong tendency towards the high risk/high return project.	1. ☐ 2. ☐ 3. ☐ 4. ☐ 5. ☐
RT5. The company has bold and comprehensive actions to achieve our goals.	1. ☐ 2. ☐ 3. ☐ 4. ☐ 5. ☐

(*Continued*)

(*Continued*)

IEO dimensions	**I totally disagree**	**I totally agree**
INN1. The company frequently introduces improvements and innovations in the business.	1. ☐ 2. ☐ 3. ☐ 4. ☐ 5. ☐	
INN2. The company is creative in its methods of operation.	1. ☐ 2. ☐ 3. ☐ 4. ☐ 5. ☐	
INN3. The company is looking for new ways of doing things.	1. ☐ 2. ☐ 3. ☐ 4. ☐ 5. ☐	
INN4. The company has a strong emphasis on R&D, technological leadership and innovation.	1. ☐ 2. ☐ 3. ☐ 4. ☐ 5. ☐	
INN5. The company has had many new product lines in the past five years (or since its inception).	1. ☐ 2. ☐ 3. ☐ 4. ☐ 5. ☐	
PRO1: The company initiates actions in the market to which competitors respond.	1. ☐ 2. ☐ 3. ☐ 4. ☐ 5. ☐	
PRO2: The company is the first to introduce new products/services on the market, new administrative techniques, new operational technologies, etc.	1. ☐ 2. ☐ 3. ☐ 4. ☐ 5. ☐	
PRO3: Monitoring the environment is a constant practice in the company (customers, competitors, search for opportunities, etc.).	1. ☐ 2. ☐ 3. ☐ 4. ☐ 5. ☐	
PRO4: Top management tends to be ahead of other competitors in introducing new ideas and products.	1. ☐ 2. ☐ 3. ☐ 4. ☐ 5. ☐	
PRO5: The company has the capacity to anticipate future problems and/or the need for changes in order to enter new markets.	1. ☐ 2. ☐ 3. ☐ 4. ☐ 5. ☐	

Organisational performance dimensions	**I totally disagree**	**I totally agree**
SALES1. The company is able to sell products with higher profit margins.	1. ☐ 2. ☐ 3. ☐ 4. ☐ 5. ☐	
SALES2. The company is able to quickly generate sales of new products.	1. ☐ 2. ☐ 3. ☐ 4. ☐ 5. ☐	
SALES3. The company is capable of producing a high market share in relation to the territory in which it operates.	1. ☐ 2. ☐ 3. ☐ 4. ☐ 5. ☐	
SALES4. The company is able to exceed our sales goals and objectives.	1. ☐ 2. ☐ 3. ☐ 4. ☐ 5. ☐	

(*Continued*)

IEO dimensions	I totally disagree — I totally agree
PROFIT1. The company has the capacity to generate profitable sales.	1. ☐ 2. ☐ 3. ☐ 4. ☐ 5. ☐
PROFIT2. The greater the market orientation, the greater the company's profitability.	1. ☐ 2. ☐ 3. ☐ 4. ☐ 5. ☐
PROFIT3. Sales training increases the commercialization of products, consequently the company's profit.	1. ☐ 2. ☐ 3. ☐ 4. ☐ 5. ☐
PROFIT4. Exporting products increases the company's profit.	1. ☐ 2. ☐ 3. ☐ 4. ☐ 5. ☐
SKH1. The company is competent and fully capable of establishing a relationship with one of the interested parties.	1. ☐ 2. ☐ 3. ☐ 4. ☐ 5. ☐
SKH2. The company realizes that the attributes are suitable for establishing relationships with stakeholders.	1. ☐ 2. ☐ 3. ☐ 4. ☐ 5. ☐
SKH3. The company finds it easy to maintain a relationship with one of the interested parties.	1. ☐ 2. ☐ 3. ☐ 4. ☐ 5. ☐
SKH4. The company is competent and fully capable of maintaining a relationship with one of the interested parties.	1. ☐ 2. ☐ 3. ☐ 4. ☐ 5. ☐

Source: Adapted from Guerra (2017).

References

Adomako, S., S. H. Quartey, and B. Narteh (2016). Entrepreneurial orientation, passion for work, perceived environmental dynamism and firm performance in an emerging economy. *Journal of Small Business and Enterprise Development*, 23(3), 728–752.

Amit, R. and P. J. Schoemaker (1993). Strategic assets and organizational rent. *Strategic Management Journal*, 14(1), 33–46.

Anderson, B. S. and Y. Eshima (2013). The influence of firm age and intangible resources on the relationship between entrepreneurial orientation and firm growth among Japanese SMEs. *Journal of Business Venturing*, 28(3), 413–429.

Anderson, B. S., P. M. Kreiser, D. F. Kuratko, J. S. Hornsby, and Y. Eshima (2015). Reconceptualizing entrepreneurial orientation. *Strategic Management Journal*, 36(10), 1579–1596.

Avlonitis, G. J. and H. E. Salavou (2007). Entrepreneurial orientation of SMEs, product innovativeness, and performance. *Journal of Business Research*, 60(5), 566–575.

Barney, J. B. (1991). Firm resources and sustained competitive advantage. *Journal of Management*, 17(1), 99–120.

Barney, J. B. (2001). Resource-based theories of competitive advantage: A ten-year retrospective on the resource-based view. *Journal of Management*, 27(6), 643–650.

Bauweraerts, J. (2019). Entrepreneurial orientation and performance in private family firms: A configurational model. *Canadian Journal of Administrative Sciences/Revue Canadienne des Sciences de l'Administration*, 36(3), 418–431.

Behrman, D. N. and W. D. Perreault, Jr. (1982). Measuring the performance of industrial salespersons. *Journal of Business Research*, 10(3), 355–370.

Brouthers, K. D., G. Nakos, and P. Dimitratos (2015). SME entrepreneurial orientation, international performance, and the moderating role of strategic alliances. *Entrepreneurship Theory and Practice*, 39(5), 1161–1187.

Brulhart, F., S. Gherra, and B. V. Quelin (2019). Do stakeholder orientation and environmental proactivity impact firm profitability? *Journal of Business Ethics*, 158(1), 25–46.

Cavusgil, S. T. and G. A. Knight (2015). The born-global firm: An entrepreneurial and capabilities perspective on early and rapid internationalization. *Journal of International Business Studies*, 46(1), 3–16.

Chandra, Y., C. Styles, and I. F. Wilkinson (2012). An opportunity based view of rapid internationalization. *Journal of International Marketing*, 20(1), 74–102.

Christensen, C. M. (1997). *The Innovators Dilemma: When New Technologies Cause Great Firms to Fail*. Harvard Business School Press: Boston, MA.

Coviello, N. E., P. P. McDougall, and B. M. Oviatt (2011). The emergence, advance and future of international entrepreneurship research: An introduction to the special forum. *Journal of Business Venturing*, 26(6), 625–631.

Covin, J. G. and D. Miller (2014). International entrepreneurial orientation: Conceptual considerations, research themes, measurement issues, and future research directions. *Entrepreneurship Theory and Practice*, 38(1), 11–44.

Covin, J. G. and D. P. Slevin (1989). Strategic management of small firms in hostile and benign environments. *Strategic Management Journal*, 10(1), 75–87.

Covin, J. G. and D. P. Slevin (1991). A conceptual model of entrepreneurship as firm behavior. *Entrepreneurship Theory and Practice*, 16(1), 7–26.

Covin, J. G., K. M. Green, and D. P. Slevin (2006). Strategic process effects on the entrepreneurial orientation–sales growth rate relationship. *Entrepreneurship Theory and Practice*, 30(1), 57–81.

Dai, L., V. Maksimov, B. A. Gilbert, and S. A. Fernhaber (2014). Entrepreneurial orientation and international scope: The differential roles of innovativeness, proactiveness, and risk-taking. *Journal of Business Venturing*, 29(4), 511–524.

Dess, G. G. and G. T. Lumpkin (2005). The role of entrepreneurial orientation in stimulating effective corporate entrepreneurship. *Academy of Management Perspectives*, 19(1), 147–156.

Dess, G. G. and R. B. Robinson, Jr. (1984). Measuring organizational performance in the absence of objective measures: The case of the privately-held firm and conglomerate business unit. *Strategic Management Journal*, 5(3), 265–273.

Eshima, Y. and B. S. Anderson (2017). Firm growth, adaptive capability, and entrepreneurial orientation. *Strategic Management Journal*, 38(3), 770–779.

Fávero, L. P. L., P. P. Belfiore, F. L. D. Silva, and B. L. Chan (2009). *Análise de dados*: modelagem multivariada para tomada de decisões. Rio de Janeiro: Elsevier, 646.

Fornell, C. and D. F. Larcker (1981). Structural equation models with unobservable variables and measurement error. *Journal of Marketing Research*, 18(3), 382–388.

Freeman, S. and S. T. Cavusgil (2007). Toward a typology of commitment states among managers of born-global firms: A study of accelerated internationalization. *Journal of International Marketing*, 15(4), 1–40.

George, B. A. and L. Marino (2011). The epistemology of entrepreneurial orientation: Conceptual formation, modeling, and operationalization. *Entrepreneurship Theory and Practice*, 35(5), 989–1024.

Grande, J., E. L. Madsen, and O. J. Borch (2011). The relationship between resources, entrepreneurial orientation and performance in farm-based ventures. *Entrepreneurship and Regional Development*, 23(3–4), 89–111.

Guerra, R. M. A. (2017). Capacidades dinâmicas e ambidestria organizacional como variáveis mediadoras da relação entre orientação empreendedora e performance organizacional. *Tese de Doutorado*, Universidade de Caxias do Sul, Caxias do Sul, RS, Brasil.

Hair, J. F., W. C. Black, B. J. Babin, R. E. Anderson, and R. L. Tatham (2009). *Análise multivariada de dados*. 6 ed. Porto Alegre: Bookman.

Hamel, G. and C. K. Prahalad (2000). *Leading the Revolution*. Boston, MA, USA: Harvard Business School Press, pp. 343–354.

Hoskisson, R. E., L. Eden, C. M. Lau, and M. Wright (2000). Strategy in emerging economies. *Academy of Management Journal*, 43(3), 249–267.

Hubbard, G. (2009). Measuring organizational performance: Beyond the triple bottom line. *Business Strategy and the Environment*, 18(3), 177–191.

Hughes, M. and R. E. Morgan (2007). Deconstructing the relationship between entrepreneurial orientation and business performance at the embryonic stage of firm growth. *Industrial Marketing Management*, 36(5), 651–661.

John, K., L. Litov, and B. Yeung (2008). Corporate governance and risk-taking. *The Journal of Finance*, 63(4), 1679–1728.

Jones, M. V., N. Coviello, and Y. K. Tang (2011). International entrepreneurship research (1989–2009): A domain ontology and thematic analysis. *Journal of Business Venturing*, 26(6), 632–659.

Knight, G. A. and S. T. Cavusgil (2004). Innovation, organizational capabilities, and the born-global firm. *Journal of International Business Studies*, 35(2), 124–141.

Knight, G. A. and P. W. Liesch (2016). Internationalization: From incremental to born global. *Journal of World Business*, 51(1), 93–102.

Kollmann, T. and C. Stöckmann (2014). Filling the entrepreneurial orientation–performance gap: The mediating effects of exploratory and exploitative innovations. *Entrepreneurship Theory and Practice*, 38(5), 1001–1026.

Kreiser, P. M. and J. Davis (2010). Entrepreneurial orientation and firm performance: The unique impact of innovativeness, proactiveness, and risk-taking. *Journal of Small Business & Entrepreneurship*, 23(1), 39–51.

Kreiser, P. M., L. D. Marino, D. F. Kuratko, and K. M. Weaver (2013). Disaggregating entrepreneurial orientation: The non-linear impact of innovativeness, proactiveness and risk-taking on SME performance. *Small Business Economics*, 40(2), 273–291.

Kuratko, D. F. and D. B. Audretsch (2009). Strategic entrepreneurship: Exploring different perspectives of an emerging concept. *Entrepreneurship Theory and Practice*, 33(1), 1–17.

Lassen, A. H., F. Gertsen, and J. O. Riis (2006). The nexus of corporate entrepreneurship and radical innovation. *Creativity and Innovation Management*, 15(4), 359–372.

Lechner, C. and S. V. Gudmundsson (2014). Entrepreneurial orientation, firm strategy and small firm performance. *International Small Business Journal*, 32(1), 36–60.

Lee, S. M. and S. J. Peterson (2000). Culture, entrepreneurial orientation, and global competitiveness. *Journal of World Business*, 35(4), 401–416.

Lumpkin, G. T. and G. G. Dess (1996). Clarifying the entrepreneurial orientation construct and linking it to performance. *Academy of Management Review*, 21(1), 135–172.

Lumpkin, G. T. and G. G. Dess (2001). Linking two dimensions of entrepreneurial orientation to firm performance: The moderating role of environment and industry life cycle. *Journal of Business Venturing*, 16(5), 429–451.

Lumpkin, G. T., C. C. Cogliser, and D. R. Schneider (2009). Understanding and measuring autonomy: An entrepreneurial orientation perspective. *Entrepreneurship Theory and Practice*, 33(1), 47–69.

Lumpkin, G. T., T. W. Moss, D. M. Gras, S. Kato, and A. S. Amezcua (2013). Entrepreneurial processes in social contexts: How are they different, if at all? *Small Business Economics*, 40(3), 761–783.

Marôco, J. (2010). *Análise de Equações Estruturais: Fundamentos Teóricos, Software & Aplicações*. Report Number.

Martinez, J. and J. Santiso (2003). Financial markets and politics: The confidence game in Latin American emerging economies. *International Political Science Review*, 24(3), 363–395.

Mazur, A. K. and A. Pisarski (2015). Major project managers' internal and external stakeholder relationships: The development and validation of measurement scales. *International Journal of Project Management*, 33(8), 1680–1691.

McDougall, P. P. (1989). International versus domestic entrepreneurship: new venture strategic behavior and industry structure. *Journal of Business Venturing*, 4(6), 387–400.

McDougall, P. P. and B. M. Oviatt (2000). International entrepreneurship: The intersection of two research paths. *Academy of Management Journal*, 43(5), 902–906.

McDougall, P. P., M. V. Jones and M. G. Serapio (2014). High–potential concepts, phenomena, and theories for the advancement of international entrepreneurship research. *Entrepreneurship Theory and Practice*, 38(1), 1–10.

McDougall, P. P., B. M. Oviatt, and R. C. Shrader (2003). A comparison of international and domestic new ventures. *Journal of International Entrepreneurship*, 1(1), 59–82.

McDougall, P. P., S. Shane and B. M. Oviatt (1994). Explaining the formation of international new ventures: The limits of theories from international business research. *Journal of Business Venturing*, 9(6), 469–487.

Miller, D. (1983). The correlates of entrepreneurship in three types of firms. *Management Science*, 29(7), 770–791.

Miller, D. (2011). Miller (1983) revisited: A reflection on EO research and some suggestions for the future. *Entrepreneurship Theory and Practice*, 35(5), 873–894.

Miller, D. and P. H. Friesen (1982). Innovation in conservative and entrepreneurial firms: Two models of strategic momentum. *Strategic Management Journal*, 3(1), 1–25.

Mintzberg, H. (1973). *The Nature of Managerial Work*. New York: Harper & Row.

Naman, J. L. and D. P. Slevin (1993). Entrepreneurship and the concept of fit: A model and empirical tests. *Strategic Management Journal*, 14(2), 137–153.

Narver, J. C. and S. F. Slater (2006). Efeito da orientação para o mercado sobre a lucratividade da empresa. *RAE — Revista de Administração de Empresas*, 46(2), 61–81.

Oviatt, B. M. and P. P. McDougall (1994). Toward a theory of international new ventures. *Journal of International Business Studies*, 25(1), 45–64.

Pérez, J. A. H., C. Geldes, M. H. Kunc, and A. Flores (2019). New approach to the innovation process in emerging economies: The manufacturing sector case in Chile and Peru. *Technovation*, 79, 35–55.

Pestana, M. H. and J. N. Gageiro (2005). *Descobrindo a regressão*: com a complementaridade do SPSS. 4 ed. Edições Sílabo: Lisboa.

Prahalad, C. K. and G. Hamel (1990). The core competence of the corporation. *Harvard Business Review*, 68(3), 79–91.

Pruthi, S., J. Mitra, and J. Mitra (2020). Special Issue on Migrant and Transnational Entrepreneurs: International Entrepreneurship and Emerging Economies. *Journal of Entrepreneurship and Innovation in Emerging Economies*, 6(1), 7–11.

Pukall, T. J. and A. Calabrò (2014). The internationalization of family firms: A critical review and integrative model. *Family Business Review*, 27(2), 103–125.

Radas, S. and L. Božić (2009). The antecedents of SME innovativeness in an emerging transition economy. *Technovation*, 29(6–7), 438–450.

Ribas, Jr. and P. D. C. Vieira (2011). *Análise Multivariada com o Uso do SPSS.* Rio de Janeiro: Ciência Moderna.

Richard, P. J., T. M. Devinney, G. S. Yip, and G. Johnson (2009). Measuring organizational performance: Towards methodological best practice. *Journal of Management*, 35(3), 718–804.

Reuber, A. R., P. Dimitratos, and O. Kuivalainen (2017). Beyond categorization: New directions for theory development about entrepreneurial internationalization. *Journal of International Business Studies*, 48, 411–422.

Saeed, A.. and H. M. Ziaulhaq (2018). The Impact of CEO Characteristics on the Internationalization of SMEs: Evidence from the UK. *Canadian Journal of Administrative Sciences/Revue Canadienne des Sciences de l'Administration*, 36(3), 322–335.

Samiee, S. and S. Chirapanda (2019). International marketing strategy in emerging-market exporting firms. *Journal of International Marketing*, 27(1), 20–37.

Shane, S. and S. Venkataraman (2000). The promise of entrepreneurship as a field of research. *Academy of Management Review*, 25(1), 217–226.

Sharma, D. S. (2005). The association between ISO 9000 certification and financial performance. *The International Journal of Accounting*, 40(2), 151–172.

Singh, S., T. K. Darwish, and K. Potočnik (2016). Measuring organizational performance: A case for subjective measures. *British Journal of Management*, 27(1), 214–224.

Tang, Z. and C. Hull (2012). An investigation of entrepreneurial orientation, perceived environmental hostility, and strategy application among Chinese SMEs. *Journal of Small Business Management*, 50(1), 132–158.

Teece, D. J. (2007). Explicating dynamic capabilities: The nature and microfoundations of (sustainable) enterprise performance. *Strategic Management Journal*, 28(13), 1319–1350.

Teece, D. J., G. Pisano, and A. Shuen (1997). Dynamic capabilities and strategic management. *Strategic Management Journal*, 18(7), 509–533.

Venkatraman, N. (1989). The concept of fit in strategy research: Toward verbal and statistical correspondence. *Academy of Management Review*, 14(3), 423–444.

Venkatraman, N. and V. Ramanujam (1986). Measurement of business performance in strategy research: A comparison of approaches. *Academy of Management Review*, 11(4), 801–814.

Wales, W. J., V. K. Gupta, and F. T. Mousa (2013). Empirical research on entrepreneurial orientation: An assessment and suggestions for future research. *International Small Business Journal*, 31(4), 357–383.

Wiklund, J., H. Patzelt, and D. A. Shepherd (2009). Building an integrative model of small business growth. *Small Business Economics*, 32(4), 351–374.

Zahra, S. A. (1993). A conceptual model of entrepreneurship as firm-level behaviour: A critique and extension. *Entrepreneurship Theory and Practice*, 17(4), 5–21.

Zahra, S. A. (1996). Technology strategy and financial performance: Examining the moderating role of the firm's competitive environment. *Journal of Business Venturing*, 11(3), 189–219.

Zahra, S. A. (2005). The theory of international new ventures: A decade of research. *Journal of International Business Studies*, 36(1), 20–29.

Zahra, S. A. and G. George (2002). The net-enabled business innovation cycle and the evolution of dynamic capabilities. *Information Systems Research*, 13(2), 147–150.

https://doi.org/10.1142/9789811228445_0004

Chapter 4

Piecing Together a Jigsaw Puzzle on Intermittent Internationalisation

Zubair Ali Shahid*,‡ and Leonie Hallo†,§

Mesal Global Consulting, Pakistan

†*The University of Adelaide, Adelaide, South Australia, Australia*

‡*shahid.zubairali@gmail.com*

§*leonie.hallo@adelaide.edu.au*

Abstract

Global disruption has forced all types of international firms to take tough decisions to move in and out of international markets. Internationalisation of firms is a complex phenomenon. International businesses are not only dealing with product-market complexities but are also required to develop new ways of understanding the business world by applying principles of knowledge, networks and psychology. Drawing on internationalisation models (intermittent internationalisation theory), network theory, knowledge-based view and entrepreneurial psychology, this chapter reviews the existing literature on international exit and re-entry and explores how the phenomenon of intermittent internationalisation should be explored from multi-theoretical perspectives. The chapter offers a way to move forward by better comprehending the intermittent internationalisation process.

A Commentary on the Current State of Intermittent Internationalisation Literature

Intermittent internationalisation is characterised by substantial increases and decreases in sales and or profits and commitment to international partners and operations. While these phenomena create great challenges for international firms from both developed and emerging economies, the current literature has neglected nonlinear internationalisation, considering it as an outlier in the experience of international firms. We contribute to the existing internationalisation literature by refining the dynamic internationalisation process model to highlight the importance of entrepreneurial psychology, network relationships, individual behaviour and knowledge across different levels of commitment, i.e. de- and re-internationalisation (intermittent internationalisation) to underpin the multi-layered complexities experienced by international entrepreneurial firms. Criticism of internationalisation models (for example, by Vissak and Francioni, 2013) suggests a new way forward in exploring alternative models such as adding de-internationalisation and re-internationalisation activities as part of the overall internationalisation process. However, there remains a paucity of research on international withdrawals from and re-engagement in international markets (Shahid and Hallo, 2019; Lafuente *et al*., 2019; Choquette, 2019; Surdu *et al*., 2019).

Recent studies on internationalisation suggest an alternative view of venturing in overseas markets (Bernini *et al*., 2016). For example, (1) the international activity of firms is seen as a result of active adjustment to their external environments, and (2) this requires them to continuously configure both internal and external activities of the firm. As firms proactively adjust to their international markets, some markets are likely to become more important than others. For instance, lower sales in some markets will allow firms to diversify their existing international portfolios and look for opportunities in other markets. Firms are likely to demonstrate both passive and active adjustments to international markets. Welch and Welch (2009) and Javalgi *et al.* (2011) commented that withdrawals from international markets could be associated with a lack of the firm's internal capabilities, such as their inability to conduct proper marketing campaigns in foreign markets. Additionally, Crick *et al.* (2020) argue that international marketing activities play a key role for start-ups. New firms are required to be cautious when dealing with overseas customers to avoid hazardous consequences and a forced exit. Thus, timely understanding of consumer insights, expectations and needs will reduce performance barriers. Similarly, a market orientation and identifying consumer needs and satisfaction levels allow international firms to be flexible with their overseas clients, and understanding the timings of consumer demands allows firms to create customer value and mitigate damage to any future relationships. Table 1 provides a summary of findings of recent studies published on de-internationalisation and re-internationalisation within the fields of international business and international entrepreneurship. Additionally, Figure 1 demonstrates conceptual framework of the intermittent internationalisation process.

Intermittent Internationalisation in Export Markets

International firms engaged in exporting and importing activities continuously demonstrate intermittent behaviours. Exporters and importers contract and expand their international activities based on accumulated learnings from international markets (Choquette, 2019). For some firms, exporting into international markets may be just a one-time activity (Crick, 2004), and could be viewed as an experimental stage of internationalisation (preferably starting initial international activity with a low-commitment mode in exporting instead of a high-commitment mode such as foreign direct investment). Experimentation in the long run allows firms to accumulate additional knowledge about export markets which could lead to additional advancements (via re-entries) into those markets. Past international experiences create what can be called an "international heritage" (Welch and Welch 2009) or "stock of knowledge" (Javalgi *et al.*, 2011) for firms. These "...experience[s] may help or hinder future attempts to re-enter international markets" (Choquette, 2019, p. 1073). However, switching behaviour between export and import markets (for example, leaving export markets to focus on import markets) remains an under-explored area of research, as is the area of withdrawals from international export markets. Choquette (2019) suggested that "import-based market experience ought to reduce export market exit, whereas, from a sunk cost logic, it ought to increase export market exit". Consequently, firms may perceive international withdrawals as potentially positive outcomes.

Vissak and Francioni (2013) moved internationalisation research in a new direction by identifying the concept of "serial nonlinear", defined as "... it encompasses several de- and re-internationalization and the time perspective is longer". More recently, Vaillant and Lafuente (2019) observed greater international propensity in serial export entrepreneurs in

Table 1: Studies Published on De-internationalisation and Re-internationalisation (Summary of Relevant Studies) Within the Fields of International Business and International Entrepreneurship

S. No.	Study	Summary of Findings
1	Lafuente *et al.* (2019)	• Results from the sequential deductive triangulation analysis reveal that practical experience is an essential prerequisite for entrepreneurial learning, and that the resilience of those with negative entrepreneurial experience induces the generative entrepreneurial learning especially suitable for subsequent internationally oriented ventures.
2	Welch and Welch (2009)	• The limited, sketchy evidence is considered and it is argued that some re-internationalisers will go into the re-entry process with a significant international heritage from previous activities, including relevant knowledge and networks, enabling faster re-entry and take-off. However, other firms will have exited in such negative circumstances that international re-entry initially is rejected as an option, and may be slow to respond to new international opportunities. Much depends on what happens during the international time-out period, particularly in terms of changes in management and/or ownership; the nature and strength of new re-entry influences; and how the re-entry process unfolds.
3	Javalgi *et al.* (2011)	• The authors present a knowledge utilisation framework for international market re-entry, along with an international market re-entry matrix that encompasses host country attractiveness, risk and firm resources and capabilities. The article qualitatively evaluates a sample of firms for their return to previously exited international markets and discusses the lessons learned from their experience.
4	Benito and Welch (1997)	• While there are numerous reasons for various types of de-internationalisation, it is indicated that, as might be expected, companies do not readily entertain withdrawal, particularly as they become more committed to, and dependent on, international operations.
5	Choquette (2019)	• The study found that the sunk cost logic primarily explains the relationship between import-based market experience and a firm's probability to exit an export market, and that the effect is strongest for exports to similar destinations. Further analysis shows that this result is partly driven by experimentation-like export behaviour by firms with import-based market experience.
6	Surdu *et al.* (2019)	• Contrary to the predictions of learning theory, the authors did not find support for the effect of experience accumulated during the initial market endeavour on the re-entry commitment strategies of MNEs. In turn, exit motives significantly impact the re-entrant's decision to re-enter via a different mode of operation, by either increasing or decreasing their commitment to the market. The study shows that re-entrants do not replicate unsuccessful operation mode strategies if they had previously underperformed in the market. When favourable host institutional changes occur during the time-out period, re-entrants tend to increase commitment in the host market irrespective of the degree of prior experience accumulated in the market.
7	Vissak and Francioni (2013)	• A single case study concludes that despite having had a year or more without export activities in 29 countries (in eight of them twice or more) and activities only in seven countries in 2011, this firm has been relatively successful. Thus, de-internationalisation is not automatically a sign of failure. Moreover, subsequent de- and re-internationalisations are normal for other firms besides project businesses, especially if their markets are small and exit/re-entry costs low.

8	Dominguez and Mayrhofer (2017)	• The findings indicate that the internationalisation process of SMEs continues to follow several stages, but that their commitment to foreign markets may increase, decrease and re-increase. The identified stages, which can be triggered by internal and external factors, reflect characteristics of different internationalisation models proposed in the literature.
9	Bernini *et al.* (2016)	• Smaller and less productive firms are more likely to exit exporting, and react more strongly to changes in both domestic and foreign markets than larger firms. Exit and re-entry are closely linked. Firms with a low exit probability also have a high likelihood of re-entry, and vice versa. However, the way in which firms react to market conditions at the time of exit matters greatly in determining the likelihood of re-entry: thus, re-entry depends crucially on the strategic rationale for exit.
10	Ciravegna *et al.* (2019)	• Strategic internationalisers choose markets and entry modes using an economic rationale, often becoming multinational enterprises. Entrepreneurial internationalisers expand in ways that mirror entrepreneurial features, which may lead them to become multinationals, change business models or continue expanding within their region. Serendipitous internationalisers may not be ready for international expansion, and may de-internationalise after an initial spurt, or continue a learning process and grow as exporters.
11	Vaillant and Lafuente (2019)	• Consistent with the theoretical arguments on the relevance of generative-based cognitive agility, the results of this paper reveal that serial entrepreneurs demonstrate a greater export propensity. Additionally, the authors found that serial entrepreneurs who also demonstrate process agility show superior export propensity levels, compared to the group of business owners outside this ambidextrous group (first-time business owners without process agility).
12	Tan and Sousa (2019)	• The findings indicate that innovation capability moderates the relationship between performance and exit decision. However, and contrary to expectations, the study suggests that incremental and radical innovations have an opposite contingent effect on the performance–exit relationship. In addition, the moderating effect of innovation capability on the performance–exit relationship was further moderated by international experience.
13	Chen *et al.* (2019)	• The results indicate the importance of the exit stage in shaping re-entry decisions, price/quality ratio and export performance, where the time-out period plays a significant role in varying these effects.
14	Surdu *et al.* (2018)	• The study finds that the length of experience accumulated between initial entry and exit does not lead to earlier re-entries. In turn, the depth of experience accumulated through operating via joint ventures and the nature of the experience determined by the exit process have a significant impact for early re-entrants. Host country institutional quality leads to early re-entry and, under certain circumstances, moderates the relationship between learning from past experiences and re-entry speed. The findings reveal experience-based learning to be a complex and dynamic process, one highly dependent on the quality of the institutional setting of the firm.

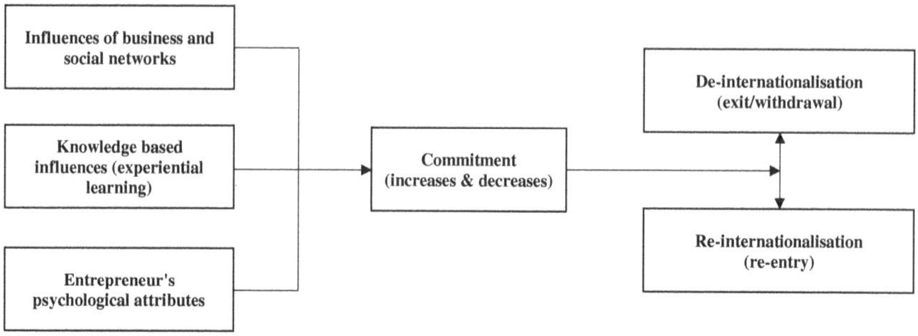

Figure 1: Conceptual Framework of Intermittent Internationalisation Process

terms of increased process agility. Larger firms approach foreign market commitments differently than smaller firms. Multinational enterprises (MNEs) are likely to make bold decisions post-exit. These types of enterprises are known to be larger in size and capital intensive. Also, MNEs do not replicate prior unsuccessful operation mode strategies (Surdu *et al.*, 2018). However, small entrepreneurial firms' commitment decisions in foreign markets have been viewed as occurring in five stages: (1) starting international expansion, (2) increasing internationalisation, (3) changing or decreasing internationalisation, (4) re-internationalisation and (5) increasing internationalisation (Dominguez and Mayrhofer, 2017). Small to medium-sized enterprises (SMEs) are likely to make smaller commitments to international markets post-exit. Additionally, SMEs are engaged as international suppliers for MNEs producing value-added products. Hence, being engaged in the upstream (supply side) and downstream (distribution side) is a common activity for these types of firms (Dominguez and Mayrhofer, 2017). International supply chains are highly network dependent, composed of channel members, buyers, suppliers, distributors and other network relationships. Therefore, withdrawal from these networks could be costly for smaller firms. However, the international business literature remains silent on how smaller firms navigate such tightly knit network relationships and move through international market exit or re-entry. In order to deepen our understanding of intermittent internationalisation outcomes, it is important to explore the role of network relationships. The next section discusses how network relationships facilitate through the processes of international withdrawal. Later sections discuss entrepreneurial knowledge and entrepreneurs' psychological attributes.

Network Relationships and Intermittent Internationalisation

The international business literature has recognised the importance of the use of network relationships for entrepreneurial ventures to accelerate penetration in foreign markets through the ability to gain knowledge, identify market opportunities and gather information about new customers (for example, see Chetty and Holm, 2000). The literature has continued to highlight the importance of different types of network relationships involved in facilitating firms' re-entries into foreign market activities (Halinen *et al.*, 2013; Ellis, 2011). These types of network relationships could be based on business and/or social contacts. Business network relationships are defined as "a set of connected actors that perform different types of business activities in interaction with each other" (Holmlund and Törnroos, 1997, p. 304). On the contrary, social network relationships would include an entrepreneur's friends, family, relatives and contacts with informal communication, which could provide information on potential business opportunities in foreign markets (Ellis, 2011). However, the precise role of network relationships, both business and social, in the international context remains ambiguous (Ciravegna *et al.*, 2014). In order to develop a holistic understanding of entrepreneurial firm globalisation outcomes, and specifically internationalisation-related outcomes, a better approach to integrating these types of network relationships in all phases of the internationalisation processes is needed and these should include foreign market withdrawals.

Role of Network Relationships During International Withdrawals

Recent literature on internationalisation and network relationships has focused mainly on successful attempts in developing and nurturing business and social network relationships in foreign markets (for example, see Dabić *et al.*, 2019). However, the literature has ignored the damaging effects or the dark side of these types of relationships, for example how international entrepreneurial firms navigate the contractual agreements with their foreign partners during the withdrawal (Shahid and Hallo, 2019; Welch and Welch, 2009). Researchers within the field of industrial marketing have labelled the process of disconnecting from network relationships as "*relationship dissolution*" (Payan *et al.*, 2010). Alajoutsijärvi *et al.* (2000) recommended that managers operating in business-to-business markets execute dissolution through the process of a "beautiful exit". For less capital-intensive and network-dependent SMEs, managing business relationships requires a careful approach (Habib *et al.*, 2020). Conversely, poor management of foreign market network relationships when leaving international markets is likely to become a liability (Javalgi *et al.*, 2011).

Business partners may avoid ending a relationship because of switching cost, lost market opportunity and a potential negative impact on reputation (Tähtinen and Vaaland, 2006). Further, some SME entrepreneurs, particularly born global entrepreneurs, may have a long-term relationship orientation and consciously avoid "competitiveness" and "self-interest" (Freeman and Cavusgil, 2007). Therefore, significant scholarly attention is needed to develop frameworks and explanations to better understand how international entrepreneurial ventures deal with a relational crisis in foreign markets. Both proactive and reactive strategies for relationship dissolutions leading to de-internationalisation include managing the dark sides of relationships (Abosag *et al.*, 2016; Johnsen and Lacoste, 2016), for example managing international partners' betrayal (Leonidou *et al.*, 2017), opportunism (Yang *et al.*, 2018) and other negative activities.

Configuring Network Relationships to Revive Internationalisation Activities

Commercialisation in internationally oriented firms is an outcome of networking efforts generated by proactive entrepreneurs. Nurturing these relationships allows firms to further develop product and marketing competencies. As an internationally oriented venture moves through the different stages of its firm life cycles, the demand for rapid innovation and finding a new niche in markets increases. Firms that are unable to meet these demands in existing markets may converge current international operations and focus on domestic markets, or they may enter new markets with existing or new products. International entrepreneurial firms that leave markets may have intentions to re-enter later on. Hence, network linkages in previous markets represent opportunities. As demand pressures reduce in previous markets, international ventures may contemplate re-entries into previously exited markets. To re-enter, they need to proactively rekindle relationships with previous network partners. International ventures operate in narrow niche markets and are forced to search constantly for new opportunities in existing or previous markets. The quest for a better opportunity in international markets allows this type of firm to demonstrate proactiveness, innovativeness and risk-taking behaviours as they switch between opportunities and markets.

Javalgi *et al.* (2011) suggest that positive and strong relationships in a previously exited market may entice a firm to attempt re-entry into that market more quickly. However, Welch and Welch (2009) suggest that higher levels of differences in re-entry situations in terms of country, culture, line of business and network relationships may make the previous international experience less useful. Thus, experience in one market does not necessarily mean success in another market. A study conducted on UK-based exporters found that after leaving certain foreign markets, these entrepreneurs did have intentions to restart international activities and to re-enter those previously exited markets. Therefore, entrepreneurs and managers of these SMEs are motivated to collect information from network partners about foreign market opportunities (Crick, 2004).

International ventures that move through the process of exit(s) and re-entry(ies) may undergo a time-out stage (Welch and Welch, 2009). During this time-out stage, they may or may not be actively looking for international opportunities. Both business relationships and previous market experience play an important role for internationalising firms moving on from the time-out stage. With regard to the importance of reconnecting relationships, Welch and Welch (2009) acknowledge the significance of networks in the firm's re-internationalisation process. However, the intermittent internationalising literature remains silent on the "process" through which firms move in and out of a market, specifically for those firms applying networking strategies to re-enter both new and old markets.

Shahid and Hallo (2019) call for attention on how entrepreneurial ventures can repair foreign market trust and commitments after a negative experience. As suggested by Hurmelinna (2018, p.113), "...less is known about the phases following termination of relationships in networks". For network-dependent international entrepreneurial firms, "good reputations" among their networking partners, both social and business, could be a significant source of advantage. For example, reputation in delivering commitments and fulfilling business promises will help firms to remain competitive among international competitors. On the contrary, entrepreneurial firms with repeated mistakes and failure to sustain commitments are likely to experience early exits from foreign markets, potentially leading to stigmatised situations and bad reputations. In summary, the international business literature suggests that in order to remain competitive, networks, both business and social, are important sources of knowledge for opportunity development in foreign markets and should be nurtured.

Entrepreneurial Knowledge and Intermittent Internationalisation

The international entrepreneurship and international business literatures widely acknowledge the role entrepreneurial knowledge plays in foreign market developments (Martin and Javalgi, 2019; Nordman and Melen, 2008). Various types of knowledge have been discussed including product, market, institutional and network. There is a focus in the international business literature on the importance of entrepreneurs' "international experiential knowledge" (Chetty *et al.*, 2006). Experiential knowledge is referred to thus: "when firms enter foreign markets, we assume that they exploit previous experiences and gain new experiences". "We refer to this experience as internationalization knowledge" (Hilmersson and Jansson, 2012, p. 99). Internationalisation knowledge is a unique experience that comes from ongoing international business activities, leading to it being specific to the person (Chetty *et al.*, 2006). It is "tacit" and can only be acquired through an entrepreneur's personal experience. This is knowledge which is generally not shared with others.

Knowledge Development in Foreign Markets

Nordman and Melen (2008) studied knowledge-based internationalisation to capture the phenomena of "opportunity discovery" and "exploitation" in evaluating opportunities for SMEs. They suggested that entrepreneurs with higher levels of international knowledge and technological knowledge are able to make sound decisions that have a positive impact on the early internationalisation of SMEs. Freeman, Hutchings, Lazaris and Zyngier (2010) developed a model of SME rapid knowledge development integrating both the knowledge-based and the network-based views, arguing that SMEs proactively utilise both existing and newly developed networks in their internationalisation. They emphasised that future empirical research should explore how knowledge develops in SMEs and the implications for their performance outcomes.

Martin and Javalgi (2019) investigated the performance outcomes of international new ventures while applying the *knowledge-based view* (*KBV*). Their study concludes that international entrepreneurs who possess information and knowledge about competitors, doing business in export markets, sales promotion and distribution, are likely to increase the performance prospects of their organisation. In particular, marketing capabilities in foreign markets are considered to be a knowledge-based resource. Tan and Sousa (2019) observed innovation capability and international experience as moderators to foreign market exit decisions and firm performance. International managers may advise making a cautious decision before contemplating exit strategies, for instance proceeding through the process of knowledge acquisition (acquiring proper knowledge about markets, products, and networks) before leaving or re-entering international markets (Javalgi *et al.*, 2011). Failing to do so may result in repeated failure or permanent exit from foreign markets. The re-entry process may also require knowledge utilisation. Acquiring and utilising knowledge about past decisions could help support international managers in organising what resources and capabilities are required to contemplate successful re-entries into particular foreign markets.

Underpinning Entrepreneurial Knowledge through De- and Re-internationalisation

Unlearning previous ways of doing business in foreign markets may be important (Casillas *et al.*, 2010; Javalgi *et al.*, 2011). International entrepreneurs should be aware of any changes, both societal and institutional, occurring in previous foreign markets. Acting on previously acquired market knowledge could be associated with competitive disadvantage under some circumstances. Unlearning requires both individuals and organisations to demonstrate their intention to unlearn and search for new and more relevant knowledge (Casillas *et al.*, 2010). However, this may be a time-consuming process. The current international business literature ignores what happens to the stock of knowledge when firms leave foreign markets. How do international managers use these knowledge sources, for example previously learnt country-specific marketing, innovation and production capabilities? Do they reapply these capabilities or do they learn new ways of doing business in foreign markets?

Crick *et al.* (2020) provide early insights into the phenomenon of de-internationalisation and entrepreneurial marketing capabilities of start-up firms. Within the framework of effectuation theory; international ventures that demonstrate a potential to re-internationalise previously held foreign market knowledge; for instance after de-internationalisation, may use the "lemonade principle" ("make the best of unexpected situations" Duening *et al.*, 2012, p. 208) to re-evaluate foreign market strategies. In using the effectual approach/lens, "*the environment is endogenous to the actions of effectuators* [entrepreneurs], *who therefore attempt to cocreate it through commitments with a network of partner, investor, and customer stakeholders*" (Read *et al.*, 2009, p. 2). Therefore, entrepreneurs at the early stages of start-ups are likely to be means oriented instead of goal oriented.

Knowledge about foreign market operations possessed by international managers is largely "tacit" and gained through personal experiences. International managers leaving firms post-exit could leave with these assets of knowledge (Welch and Welch, 2009). Hence, retaining these employees could become a priority for international firms. If entrepreneurs are serious about international re-entry decisions, this knowledge could be embedded into the individual (entrepreneur's) experience, networks, culture, products and markets specific to regions, countries and industries. While it is important to unlearn previous international market experiences, it is also important for firms to nurture previously held information and knowledge, or firm heritage, to make future decisions (Welch and Welch, 2009). Experiential internationalisation knowledge held by individuals could be used and articulated in a number of ways, as knowledge is acquired to reduce foreign market uncertainty (Hilmersson and Jansson, 2012). How individuals interpret and use these sources of knowledge could influence future decision-making. One important factor that could be associated with perceiving and interpreting internationalisation knowledge could be the individual entrepreneur's psychological attributes. The next section highlights how entrepreneurial psychological factors may influence intermittent internationalising decisions

Entrepreneurial Psychological Factors Associated with Intermittent Internationalisation

Internationalisation, like any other activity, involves risk and stress. Various psychological factors are relevant when considering individual responses to the highs and lows of this type of endeavour. This section will consider individual personality strengths as these relate to intermittent internationalisation endeavours.

Resilience/Growth Mindset

Much recent work has emerged from the positive psychology movement, which considers character strengths leading to individual well-being, happiness and flourishing (Seligman and Csikszentmihalyi, 2014). This movement explores ways in which positive attitudes can influence outcomes. Two important features here are psychological resilience and growth mindset. Resilience is the ability to cope with stress and quickly return to a state of stasis and stability. Remaining calm during a crisis is a powerful personal weapon against the inevitable negative features of life, both business and personal. Positive affect is associated with good health and it is useful in buffering harmful effects of stress. The relationship between positive emotions and reactions to stress has been explored in many ways, including through the "broaden and build" theory of Fredrickson (Fredrickson, 2004), in which positive emotions can form important personal resources against future stress. Growth mindset (Dweck, 2008; Dweck, 2016) is another popular current approach to strengthening the individual against the negative effects of challenge and failure. People with a growth mindset interpret failure as an invitation to develop further through effort and persistence. People with a fixed mindset interpret failure as a personal lack of the necessary abilities. Encouraging people to take on a growth mindset has been shown to be powerful in terms of pressing on under adversity, especially in the context of education and learning new skills (Claro *et al.*, 2016).

Self-determination and Self-efficacy

Self-determination theory (SDT) is a theory of motivation. People inherently want to grow and achieve, to learn and explore and to develop new skills. Human beings do have an inherent motivation to grow and to achieve. They have a natural tendency towards wanting to learn, explore and develop new skills. People want to be competent, they like autonomy and the ability to choose how to do their work or live their life, and they like to relate to others; we are on the whole social animals. Motivation can be either intrinsic or extrinsic. Intrinsic motivation arises due to enjoyment from an activity itself, something you enjoy doing. Extrinsic reinforcement is a reward which is externally provided, such as money or approval. Self-determination is strongly related to a sense of autonomy. A person who is self-determining can choose what they decide to do (Deci *et al.*, 1989; Heywood *et al.*, 2017). People experience a sense of self-determination when they can voluntarily get involved in a task rather than being forced to do it. People who are empowered do have a sense of responsibility in terms of their work (Staples, 1990). The self-determined person views themselves as a proactive person, a self-starter. They take initiative and try out new ideas (Conger and Kanungo, 1988). They have internal locus of control; that is, they feel that they control what happens to them (Heywood *et al.*, 2017). Self-determination is associated with higher work satisfaction and work performance. People who are highly self-determined are more likely to be entrepreneurial and innovative (Hsiao *et al.*, 2016).

Self-efficacy theory was originally proposed by the psychologist Albert Bandura (Bandura *et al.*, 1999) who defined it as your own judgement and belief about how well you can succeed in certain situations or accomplish certain tasks. This plays a major role in how a person approaches challenges. Valuing our own abilities is obviously very empowering. In developing self-efficacy, we are highly influenced by what we observe in other people. People with high self-efficacy who believe that they can do well are much more likely to see a challenging task as something to be mastered and not something to be avoided. A person who believes they have low self-efficacy is likely to avoid that kind of work. This avoidance may not be based upon fact. People with high self-efficacy will try harder to complete a task and will persist longer. People with low self-efficacy are more likely to experience a state called learned helplessness or a feeling of lack of control. There are obvious linkages here between SDT, self-efficacy and entrepreneurial intermittent internationalisation behaviour.

Tolerance of Ambiguity and Reactions to Entrepreneurial Failure

Some people perceive ambiguous situations as sources of threat, whereas others do not. This characteristic is associated with the propensity for risk and has been associated with entrepreneurship (Chaudhary, 2017; Nasip *et al.*, 2017). People with low tolerance of ambiguity prefer certainty and the familiar. This is a black-and-white view of life. Such people often conclude their decision-making too early because of this tendency to reject the unfamiliar, and to respond differently to experiences of failure. Learned optimism theory (the ability to remain optimistic even in the face of difficulty) has been employed to explain why some people may be able to come back from failure more readily than others. Confidence has also been suggested as a trait which could facilitate entrepreneurial resilience and mitigate the emotional cost of failure (Hayward *et al.*, 2010). Finally, emotional intelligence may help people to be able to better understand information about their loss. Quintillán and Peña-Legazkue (2019) noted a positive relationship between emotional intelligence and early internationalisation in a group of entrepreneurs.

Shepherd (2003, 2009) has drawn on the wider grief and loss literature to come up with suggestions as to how entrepreneurs may better be able to recover from a business loss. In grief recovery, one must confront the loss, accept the loss, work through the events surrounding the loss and eventually recover. This may involve seeking out people to talk to about one's experiences. The recovery process will be different for everyone and will depend on external factors such as support of various sorts, and an ability to face the loss rather than using strategies such as avoidance, denial and distraction. Entrepreneurs who experience failure may benefit from speaking to others about their feelings of loss.

Cognitive Style

Much literature suggests that there are two main approaches to decision-making or cognitive style, analysis and intuition, and that managers can use both styles, although they most likely tend towards one or the other (Evans, 2011); (Hodgkinson and Sadler-Smith, 2018). Intuition is variously viewed as a shortcut or alternatively as a highly efficient method of decision-making, especially when a person has a great deal of experience in the area (Kahneman, 2011). Thus, experienced managers can create a detailed cognitive understanding of the situation and a more accurate mental model (Maitland and Sammartino, 2015). This enables rapid and effective decision-making under complex conditions. The strategic choices made by individual upper echelon managers are critical in decisions about internationalising. The systematic review by Niittymies and Pajunen (2019) examined management rationality in decision-making in the very uncertain and ambiguous case of decisions to internationalise. The authors comment that how managers learn from experience and transfer this knowledge during internationalisation needs further research in terms of the relationship between cognitive decision-making style and outcomes.

Conclusion and Recommendations

This chapter has examined various approaches to the understanding of intermittent internationalisation and moving in and out of international markets. This complex activity will be influenced by many factors including the precise nature of the venturing, the size of the firm and the quality of the network relationships both business and social between the firm and the target of entry or re-entry. In addition, the knowledge contained within the firm including the tacit knowledge of individual managers and their psychological attributes will be important factors to consider. The process of intermittent internationalisation is dynamic and complex. Clearly, this chapter has just skimmed the surface of the contribution of these factors and in-depth research is needed to come up with definitive statements about their role and impact.

References

Abosag, I., D. A. Yen, and B. R. Barnes (2016). What is dark about the dark-side of business relationships? *Industrial Marketing Management*, 55, 5–9.

Alajoutsijärvi, K., K. Möller, and J. Tähtinen (2000). Beautiful exit: How to leave your business partner. *European Journal of Marketing*, 34(11–12), 1270–1290.

Benito, G. R. and L. S. Welch (1997). De-internationalization. *MIR: Management International Review*, 37, 7–25.

Bandura, A., W. H. Freeman, and R. Lightsey (1999). *Self-efficacy: The Exercise of Control*, Springer.

Bernini, M., J. Du, and J. H. Love (2016). Explaining intermittent exporting: Exit and conditional re-entry in export markets. *Journal of International Business Studies*, 47(9), 1058–1076.

Chen, J., C. M. Sousa, and X. He (2019). Export market re-entry: Time-out period and price/quality dynamisms. *Journal of World Business*, 54(2), 154–168.

Chaudhary, R. (2017). Demographic factors, personality and entrepreneurial inclination. *Education+ Training*, 59(2), 171–187.

Casillas, J. C., F. J. Acedo, and J. L. Barbero (2010). Learning, unlearning and internationalization: Evidence from the pre-export phase. *International Journal of Information Management*, 30(2), 162–173.

Conger, J. A. and R. N. Kanungo (1988). The empowerment process: Integrating theory and practice. *Academy of Management Review*, 13(3), 471–482.

Choquette, E. (2019). Import-based market experience and firms' exit from export markets. *Journal of International Business Studies*, 50(3), 423–449.

Crick, J. M., D. Crick, and S. Chaudhry (2020). Entrepreneurial marketing decision-making in rapidly internationalising and de-internationalising start-up firms. *Journal of Business Research*, 113, 158–167.

Ciravegna, L., S. K. Kundu, O. Kuivalainen, and L. E. Lopez (2019). The timing of internationalization–Drivers and outcomes. *Journal of Business Research*, 105, 322–332.

Chetty, S. and D. B. Holm (2000). Internationalization of small to medium-sized manufacturing firms: A network approach. *International Business Review*, 9(1), 77–93.

Chetty, S., K. Eriksson, and Lindbergh, J. (2006). The effect of specificity of experience on a firm's perceived importance of institutional knowledge in an ongoing business. *Journal of International Business Studies*, 37(5), 699–712.

Ciravegna, L., S. B. Majano, and G. Zhan (2014). The inception of internationalization of small and medium enterprises: The role of activeness and networks. *Journal of Business Research*, 67(6), 1081–1089.

Claro, S., D. Paunesku and, and C. S. Dweck (2016). Growth mindset tempers the effects of poverty on academic achievement. *Proceedings of the National Academy of Sciences*, 113(31), 8664–8668.

Crick, D. (2004). UK SMEs' decision to discontinue exporting: An exploratory investigation into practices within the clothing industry. *Journal of Business Venturing*, 19(4), pp. 561–587.

Dominguez, N. and U. Mayrhofer (2017). Internationalization stages of traditional SMEs: Increasing, decreasing and re-increasing commitment to foreign markets. *International Business Review*, 26(6), 1051–1063.

Dweck, C. S. (2008). *Mindset: The New Psychology of Success*. Random House Digital, Inc.

Dweck, C. S. (2016). What having a "growth mindset" actually means. *Harvard Business Review*, *13*, 213–226.

Deci, E. L., J. P. Connell, and R. M. Ryan (1989). Self-determination in a work organization. *Journal of Applied Psychology*, 74(4), 580.

Duening, T., M. Shepherd, and A. Czaplewski (2012). How entrepreneurs think: Why effectuation and effectual logic may be the key to successful enterprise entrepreneurship. *International Journal of Innovation Science*, 4(4), 205–216.

Dabić, M., J. Maley, L. P. Dana, I. Novak, M. M. Pellegrini, and A. Caputo (2019). Pathways of SME internationalization: A bibliometric and systematic review. *Small Business Economics*, 1–21.

Ellis, P. D. (2011). Social ties and international entrepreneurship: Opportunities and constraints affecting firm internationalization. *Journal of International Business Studies*, 42(1), 99–127.

Evans, J. S. B. (2011). Dual-process theories of reasoning: Contemporary issues and developmental applications. *Developmental Review*, 31(2–3), 86–102.

Freeman, S. and S. T. Cavusgil (2007). Toward a typology of commitment states among managers of born-global firms: A study of accelerated internationalization. *Journal of International Marketing*, 15(4), 1–40.

Freeman, S., K. Hutchings, M. Lazaris, and S. Zyngier (2010). A model of rapid knowledge development: The smaller born-global firm. *International Business Review*, 19(1), 70–84.

Fredrickson, B. L. (2004). The broaden–and–build theory of positive emotions. *Philosophical Transactions of the Royal Society of London. Series B: Biological Sciences*, 359(1449), 1367–1377.

Heywood, J. S., U. Jirjahn, and C. Struewing (2017). Locus of control and performance appraisal. *Journal of Economic Behavior & Organization*, 142, 205–225.

Holmlund-Rytkönen, M. and J.-Å. Törnroos (1997). What are relationships in business networks? *Management Decision*, 5(4), 304–309.

Hilmersson, M. and H. Jansson (2012). Reducing uncertainty in the emerging market entry process: On the relationship among international experiential knowledge, institutional distance, and uncertainty. *Journal of International Marketing*, 20(4), 96–110.

Hurmelinna, P. (2018). Exiting and entering relationships: A framework for re-encounters in business networks. *Industrial Marketing Management*, 70, 113–127.

Habib, F., M. Bastl, A. Karatzas, and C. Mena (2020). Treat me well and I may leave you kindly: A configurational approach to a buyer's relationship exit strategy. *Industrial Marketing Management*, 84, 237–250.

Halinen, A., J. Å. Törnroos, and M. Elo (2013). Network process analysis: An event-based approach to study business network dynamics. *Industrial Marketing Management*, 42(8), 1213–1222.

Hayward, M. L., W. R. Forster, S. D. Sarasvathy, and B. L. Fredrickson (2010). Beyond hubris: How highly confident entrepreneurs rebound to venture again. *Journal of Business Venturing*, 25(6), 569–578.

Hodgkinson, G. P. and E. Sadler-Smith (2018). The dynamics of intuition and analysis in managerial and organizational decision making. *Academy of Management Perspectives*, 32(4), 473–492.

Hsiao, C., Y. H. Lee, and H. H. Chen (2016). The effects of internal locus of control on entrepreneurship: The mediating mechanisms of social capital and human capital. *The International Journal of Human Resource Management*, 27(11), 1158–1172.

Javalgi, R. R. G, S. Deligonul, A. Dixit, and S. T. Cavusgil (2011). International market reentry: A review and research framework. *International Business Review*, 20(4), 377–393.

Johnsen, R. E. and S. Lacoste (2016). An exploration of the 'dark side 'associations of conflict, power and dependence in customer–supplier relationships. *Industrial Marketing Management*, 59, 76–95.

Kahneman, D. (2011). *Thinking, Fast and Slow*. Macmillan.

Leonidou, L. C., B. Aykol, T. A. Fotiadis, P. Christodoulides, and A. Zeriti (2017). Betrayal in international buyer-seller relationships: Its drivers and performance implications. *Journal of World Business*, 52(1), 28–44.

Lafuente, E., Y. Vaillant, F. Vendrell-Herrero, and E. Gomes (2019). Bouncing back from failure: Entrepreneurial resilience and the internationalization of subsequent ventures created by serial entrepreneurs. *Applied Psychology*, 68(4), 658–694.

Martin, S. L. and R. R. G. Javalgi (2019). Explaining performance determinants: A knowledge based view of international new ventures. *Journal of Business Research*, 101, 615–626.

Maitland, E. and A. Sammartino (2015). Managerial cognition and internationalization. *Journal of International Business Studies*, 46(7), 733–760.

Niittymies, A. and K. Pajunen (2020). Cognitive foundations of firm internationalization: A systematic review and agenda for future research. *International Business Review*, 29(4), 101654.

Nordman, E. R. and S. Melén (2008). The impact of different kinds of knowledge for the internationalization process of born globals in the biotech business. *Journal of World Business*, *43*(2), 171–185.

Nasip, S., S. R. Amirul, S. L. Sondoh Jr., and G. H. Tanakinjal (2017). Psychological characteristics and entrepreneurial intention: A study among university students in North Borneo, Malaysia. *Education+ Training*, 59(7/8), 825–840.

Payan, J. M., C. Obadia, J. Reardon, and I. Vida (2010). Survival and dissolution of exporter relationships with importers: A longitudinal analysis. *Industrial Marketing Management*, 39(7), 1198–1206.

Quintillán, I. and I. Peña-Legazkue (2019). Emotional intelligence and venture internationalization during economic recession. *International Journal of Entrepreneurial Behavior & Research*, 26(2), 246–265.

Read, S., N. Dew, S. D. Sarasvathy, M. Song, and R. Wiltbank (2009). Marketing under uncertainty: The logic of an effectual approach. *Journal of Marketing*, 73(3), 1–18.

Seligman, M. E. and M. Csikszentmihalyi (2014). Positive psychology: An introduction. In *Flow and the Foundations of Positive Psychology*, pp. 279–298. Springer, Dordrecht.

Staples, L. H. (1990). Powerful ideas about empowerment. *Administration in Social Work*, 14(2), 29–42.

Surdu, I., K. Mellahi, and K. W. Glaister (2019). Once bitten, not necessarily shy? Determinants of foreign market re-entry commitment strategies. *Journal of International Business Studies*, 50(3), 393–422.

Surdu, I., K. Mellahi, K. W. Glaister, and G. Nardella (2018). Why wait? Organizational learning, institutional quality and the speed of foreign market re-entry after initial entry and exit. *Journal of World Business*, 53(6), 911–929.

Shepherd, D. A. (2003). Learning from business failure: Propositions of grief recovery for the self-employed. *Academy of Management Review*, 28(2), 318–328.

Shepherd, D. A. (2009). Grief recovery from the loss of a family business: A multi-and meso-level theory. *Journal of Business Venturing*, 24(1), 81–97.

Shahid, Z. A. and L. Hallo (2019). A network perspective on the intermittent internationalising experiences of emerging economy entrepreneurial SMEs. In *International Entrepreneurship in Emerging Markets: Nature, Drivers, Barriers and Determinants*. Emerald Publishing Limited.

Tan, Q. and C. M. Sousa (2019). Why poor performance is not enough for a foreign exit: The importance of innovation capability and international experience. *Management International Review*, 59(3), 465–498.

Tähtinen, J. and T. I. Vaaland (2006). Business relationships facing the end: Why restore them? *Journal of Business & Industrial Marketing*.

Vaillant, Y. and E. Lafuente (2019). The increased international propensity of serial entrepreneurs demonstrating ambidextrous strategic agility. *International Marketing Review*, 36(2), 239–259.

Vissak, T. and B. Francioni (2013). Serial nonlinear internationalization in practice: A case study. *International Business Review*, 22(6), 951–962.

Welch, C. L. and L. S. Welch (2009). Re-internationalization: Exploration and conceptualisation. *International Business Review*, 18(6), 567–577.

Yang, D., S. Sheng, S. Wu, and K. Z. Zhou (2018). Suppressing partner opportunism in emerging markets: Contextualizing institutional forces in supply chain management. *Journal of Business Research*, 90, 1–13.

Part 2

International Entrepreneurship in Action

https://doi.org/10.1142/9789811228445_0005

Chapter 5

Entrepreneurship in Cross-border Investments: Cases of Emerging Multinationals' Strategic Asset-seeking Internationalisation

Ayşe Kayacı

Dicle University, Department of Management, Diyarbakır, Turkey

ayse.kayaci@dicle.edu.tr

Abstract

Drawing from the literature about international entrepreneurship and emerging multinationals, this chapter undertakes a comparative analysis of three cases of Turkish infant multinationals to understand how entrepreneurial internationalisation works in emerging market contexts. The accelerated internationalisation process of these multinationals is analysed under the light of their historical progress. The findings of the study suggest that the increased presence of emerging multinationals in global foreign direct investment is primarily based on the success of these firms' founding entrepreneur's vision and ability to manage the underdeveloped institutional context. Another finding highlights the changing entrepreneurial process and behaviour of these firms as new generations started to control these firms. Finally, the impact of the entrepreneurial background on corporate entrepreneurship has been identified as the determinant factor of internationalisation for these cases. The differences and similarities between emerging multinationals and "born global" firms are also mentioned to link the international business and international entrepreneurship sides of the literature.

Keywords: International entrepreneurship; Emerging multinationals; Corporate entrepreneurship; Business groups; Turkey.

Introduction

Over the last two decades, Emerging Multinational Corporations (EMNCs) have succeeded in achieving a remarkable growth in outward foreign direct investment (OFDI), thanks in part to emerging markets following neo-liberal economic policies in the 1990s (Child and Rodrigues, 2005). OFDI by emerging markets (EMs) accounted for $417 billion in 2018, despite decreasing global FDI (UNCTAD, 2019). Cross-border merger and acquisitions (CBMAs) have been a significant part of this accelerated internationalisation of EMNCs to access strategic capabilities, which are generally available in developed markets and to advanced-country MNCs (Meyer *et al.*, 2018). Similar to other emerging markets, Turkey has amplified its OFDI via CBMAs of Turkish firms with $1856 million net sales value in 2016 (UNCTAD, 2017). Despite the increased attention by scholars regarding the rapid internationalisation process, and the paths and scope of EMNCs, the entrepreneurial processes and motivations of EMNCs still need to be investigated by international business (IB) scholars (Cuervo-Cazurra and Genc, 2008; Ramamurti, 2009b; Madhok and Keyhani, 2012). Understanding EMNCs' rapid internationalisation via entrepreneurial motivations is a flourishing area for international entrepreneurship research, since this stream has been highly dominated by the "born global" phenomenon and small and medium-sized enterprises' (SMEs) internationalisation (Jones *et al.*, 2011).

EMs are known for their underdeveloped institutional environments and factor markets, which result in high transaction costs for entrepreneurial activity of both individuals and ongoing corporations (Khanna and Palepu, 1997). Additionally, firms from EMs are not endowed with proprietary advantages like advanced technology and reputable brands, especially when venturing in foreign markets and competing with advanced-country MNCs (Madhok and Keyhani, 2012; Ramamurti, 2012). As a mid-range emerging market, Turkey has acceptable infrastructural development but insufficient institutional development among other emerging markets. This may lead firms to choose OFDI as an exit option from limited factor markets at home and use their capabilities in foreign markets. Besides, outward internationalisation can be used as a corporate entrepreneurial activity via searching and exploiting valuable resources in foreign markets by EMNCs (Hoskisson *et al.*, 2013). On the contrary, firms in EMs have developed distinct entrepreneurial responses to overcome institutional voids and imperfect market conditions for effective resource acquisition and allocation of their operations (Guillen, 2000). As a response to underdeveloped markets, business groups (BGs) have been national pioneers for many years, forming economic and entrepreneurial activity in many EMs (Khanna and Yafeh, 2010) and are defined as "a set of firms which, though legally independent, are bound together by a constellation of formal and informal ties and are accustomed to taking coordinated action" (Khanna and Rivkin, 2001, p. 47). In spite of the common argument that BGs would disappear after the development of free markets in emerging economies, they still play a significant role in EMs and the global economy via outward internationalisation activities (Carney *et al.*, 2018). In the case of BGs from Turkey, this argument weakens more than other EMs' cases since most of the FDI and CBMA activities have been employed by BGs or their affiliates (Deloitte, 2016). The success of BGs in Turkey (for instance, Koç Holding) is primarily due to the founding entrepreneur's ability to create financial resources in underdeveloped financial markets and to identify new opportunities after World War II in Turkey's statist economic policies (Colpan and Jones, 2016).

While BGs are known for their resilience in operating in both imperfect and liberalised markets, internationalisation of EMNCs has been explained by resource (strategic asset)-seeking motivation in recent approaches (Mathews, 2006; Luo and Tung, 2007) rather than the OLI paradigm's asset exploitation view (Dunning, 1988). Considering internationalisation studies of EMNCs and BGs' entrepreneurial success in EMs, it would be beneficial for IB studies to examine how BGs exploit entrepreneurial opportunities in foreign markets and expand their ownership advantages by CBMAs. As a result of this, investigating different cases of EMNCs like Arçelik, Kordsa and Ülker, which are some of the leading BGs of Turkey, may amplify our understanding of entrepreneurial processes and strategic entrepreneurship in EMs. This chapter also provides insights about how entrepreneurship works at the corporate level during the establishment of an international strategy for BG affiliates in Turkey. Moreover, studying EMNCs' internationalisation with the lens of the international entrepreneurship domain would expand and enrich the IB-based research domain. In this manner, the role of entrepreneurship in

EM contexts could also be extended to the IB literature. This chapter is also one of the unique examples that consider the entrepreneurial side of Turkish MNCs in recent years.

International Entrepreneurship

For more than two decades, the international entrepreneurship research domain has been shaped by the intersection of innovation, economic change, internationalisation, networks and cross-cultural studies (McDougall and Oviatt, 2000; Jones *et al.*, 2011). This eclectic nature of the research domain has made it difficult to develop theory building in this area since the two intersected research domains (international business and entrepreneurship) have different focus points. While international business (IB) scholars have focused on multinational corporations (MNCs), the entrepreneurship domain has studied the creation of new ventures and small and medium-sized enterprises (SMEs) generally in domestic markets (McDougall and Oviatt, 2000). However, increased attention and economic activity in global markets has led the scholars to propose different definitions of international entrepreneurial activity or international new ventures during this time. The foremost and comprehensive definition of international entrepreneurship is "a combination of innovative, proactive, and risk-seeking behaviour that crosses national borders and intended to create value in organizations" (McDougall and Oviatt, 2000, p. 903). This definition shows that international entrepreneurship is different from entrepreneurial research by considering entrepreneurial behaviour at individual, group and organisational levels.

Furthermore, international entrepreneurship involves a cyclical process of entrepreneurial and firm behaviours that are shaped by environmental changes and produces value creation across borders. In this manner, internationalisation of a firm occurs as a firm-level entrepreneurial behaviour (Jones and Coviello, 2005). However, initial studies of international entrepreneurship research have proposed diverse concepts and terms which seem to contradict IB theories. For instance, "born global" and "international new venture" concepts have defined early internationalising firms which have a non-gradual internationalisation process (Oviatt and McDougall, 1994; Knight and Cavusgil, 2004). Changing market conditions in diverse economic activities for SMEs, increased technology in production, transportation and communication, the significance of availability of global networks and alliances, and entrepreneurs of early internationalising firms with extensive competences initiated the rise of these concepts in both the practical and scholarly fields (Rialp *et al.*, 2005). On the contrary, every international expansion attempt can involve some kind of entrepreneurial activity like managerial experience (Verbeke and Ciravegna, 2018). Thus, it is important to understand the entrepreneurial side of the internationalisation of firms even if they are of a certain age or size. This can lead scholars to evaluate the effect of individual behaviour on the internationalisation process of firms that have established both domestic and international operations for a long time. MNCs can be an important example for understanding the international entrepreneurship phenomenon since they redistribute certain goods and services through global supply chains and bring incentives, opportunities and resources for local firms across national borders (Hill and Mudambi, 2010, p. 322). Even if MNCs' increased existence in the global economy has been studied comprehensively by IB scholars for years (Buckley and Casson, 1976; Rugman and Verbeke, 2003; Ramamurti, 2009b), international entrepreneurship research has mainly focused on rapidly internationalising firms and skipped the significance of opportunity seeking of these firms in different regions (Reuber *et al.*, 2018). Furthermore, seeking opportunities across the globe can not only be considered for "born global" firms but also for MNCs since their basic motivations are getting opportunities of valuable natural resources, strategic assets, efficiencies and markets in different parts of the world (Dunning, 1998). Consequently, any kind of internationalisation activity by MNCs could not be disregarded as "non-entrepreneurial" and out of the international entrepreneurship domain.

Business Groups and Multinational Corporations from Emerging Markets

Different formations of capitalism in distinct national business systems have not only affected the relationships between economic actors but also the development of big businesses in these economies (Whitley, 1998). EMs are composed of underdeveloped institutions and product markets that have awoken scholarly interest about organisations and business systems in recent years (Khanna and Palepu, 2006; Hoskisson *et al.*, 2013). BGs are prominent organisational forms in these markets with operations in multiple diversified industries and a high level of control by a well-known family in general (Leff, 1978). Moreover, the relationships between state and economic actors in EMs have been close and sophisticated, which provides grounds for the formation of BG-type organisations (Khanna and Yafeh, 2010; Schneider, 2010). South Korea, Taiwan, Brazil, Chile, Indonesia, India and Turkey are well-known examples of EMs with BGs as pioneer economic actors in their national business systems even if they have different names, like "chaebol", "guanxi qiye", "business houses" or "family holdings", and definitions (Yiu *et al.*, 2007). BGs are formed as a collection of legally independent firms that have connections with each other through cross-shareholdings, diversified in multiple unrelated industries and controlled by an umbrella company whose shares are owned by a sole family or ethnic group (Granovetter, 2005; Colpan and Hikino, 2010). BGs allow their affiliates to share a common resource base via an established network among firms from diversified industries to escape from risk and uncertainty of underdeveloped market conditions (Leff, 1978; Guillen, 2000). Moreover, BGs have attracted scholars' attention due to governance problems like tunnelling wealth and profit of affiliates to the controlling shareholders since these shareholders generally involve family or kinship networks (Morck and Yeung, 2003; Granovetter, 2005). The reason for the pivotal role of BGs in EMs is the underdeveloped legal and economic institutions and the rent-seeking ability of the founding entrepreneur or her/his offspring. Also, governments' privatisation policies to establish a free market economy in EMs after the 1990s have strengthened BGs' positions as rivals for foreign MNCs in EMs (Khanna and Palepu, 2006; Yiu *et al.*, 2007). For instance, Chari and Dixit (2015) have found that the ability of BGs is greater than independent firms to start new businesses in privatised industries as an evidence of how BGs use their entrepreneurial assets effectively in EMs like India. This may be a confirmation of resistance and ongoing accomplishment of BGs in EMs despite attempts to establish a free market economy and MNCs' increasing presence.

Besides, MNCs and their increasing FDI operations from these markets (called as EMNCs) have also attracted the interest of researchers and practitioners in recent years (Child and Rodrigues, 2005; Ramamurti, 2009b; Peng, 2012; Meyer *et al.*, 2018). EMNCs have followed unconventional internationalisation strategies like searching for valuable assets in developed markets via high levels of involvement in entry modes rather than an incremental route (Mathews, 2006; Luo and Tung, 2007). This kind of opportunity-seeking behaviour is similar to the patterns observed in the internationalisation of "born global" firms who prioritise international operations from their inception (Knight and Cavusgil, 2004). However, EMNCs and BGs from EMs do not share the same characteristics as developed market "born global" firms, especially in relation to the internationalisation process. For example, EMNCs generally do not have firm-specific advantages (FSAs) such as globally known brands, technological assets and managerial ability of international operations (Rugman and Verbeke, 2003; Ramamurti, 2009a). On the contrary, EMNCs have country-specific advantages (CSAs) which are lower labour costs, easy access to natural and financial resources, arm's length relations with the state and policymakers, and the ability to operate in uncertain environments (Hennart, 2012; Peng, 2012; Ramamurti, 2012). Furthermore, most EMNCs and BGs commence their internationalisation activities when a considerable amount of time passes after their inception. For instance, it was not until the 1990s' neo-liberal economy policies in EMs that prompted EMNCs, who were known giants in their home markets, to expand their investments across borders (Child and Rodrigues, 2005; Khanna and Palepu, 2006). Moreover, most of the EMNCs and BGs like Haier, Tata Group, Koç Holding and Cemex belong to mature manufacturing and service industries. Despite the presence of EMNCs, "born global" firms and international new ventures have generally operated in technology-intensive sectors and started to internationalise a short time after their founding (Khanna and Palepu, 2006; Jones *et al.*, 2011). Besides, the theoretical foundations of studying EMNCs and BGs, which are mainly based on resource-based, institution-based and transaction-based views, have been differentiated from the international entrepreneurship research domain (Hoskisson *et al.*, 2000; Yamakawa *et al.*, 2008). On the contrary, entrepreneurial and network-based approaches have shaped international entrepreneurship literature so far (Rialp *et al.*, 2005; Jones *et al.*, 2011; Verbeke and Ciravegna, 2018).

Ultimately, EMNCs and BGs have been generally explained through different theoretical and practical implications than the "born global" and "international new venture" phenomena in IB studies, and the international entrepreneurship literature has been neglected so far. The role of the entrepreneurial intentions of these firms should be considered through a different perspective to bring together IB and international entrepreneurship studies. In this way, both internationalisation studies of EM firms and international entrepreneurship research can give insights to scholars and practitioners for expanding the literature.

The Turkish Context

Turkey has shown mid-range emerging economy qualifications through lower development in institutional environment and a moderate level of infrastructural development. This leads firms to internationalise out of national markets as a corporate entrepreneurial activity (Hoskisson *et al.*, 2013). Moreover, institutional voids in EMs have caused BGs to escape uncertainty in factor and product markets (Khanna and Yafeh, 2010). Like other EMs, BGs continue to be dominant economic actors in Turkey's economy despite the liberalisation policies of the 1980s that attempted to develop the country's institutional environment and factor markets (Buğra, 1995; Colpan, 2010). BGs in Turkey have shown similar qualities, like unrelated diversification strategies, a high level of family control and tunnelling problems, as other EM BGs (Yurtoglu, 2000; Yaprak *et al.*, 2006; Colpan, 2010). Besides, most of the EMNCs from Turkey are affiliate companies of these BGs and have gathered international experience through exporting and JVs in the home market with advanced MNCs (Yaprak and Karademir, 2011). Knowledge transfer through these alliances has played an important role for Turkish BGs and MNCs while expanding abroad as other EM firms (Xia *et al.*, 2014). This shows that the internationalisation pattern of EMNCs can be differentiated for each EM context despite the relevant literature of asset exploration motivation of EM firms.

For example, the internationalisation of EMNCs from Turkey has shown how firm- and country-specific advantages play a significant and interactive role in strategy formation for inward and outward internationalisation of these firms (Yaprak *et al.*, 2018). Moreover, previous studies about Turkish MNCs have generally relied on frequently used IB theories (institution based, transaction cost based, resource based, eclectic paradigm, linkage-leverage-learning paradigm) to investigate their internationalisation behaviour and motivations (Demirbag *et al.*, 2010; Yaprak and Karademir, 2010, 2011; Anil *et al.*, 2014). These studies have focused on diverse or single industries; the main findings are clustered around the characteristics of home country context, market-seeking motivations, significant effect of inward internationalisation, and exploring and exploiting assets through outward internationalisation in general (Erdilek, 2008; Eren-Erdogmus *et al.*, 2010; Yaprak and Karademir, 2011). While these studies have explained the entry mode decisions and motivations of Turkish MNCs, entrepreneurial motivations, or behaviour, seem to be understudied by researchers. As mentioned earlier, international entrepreneurial behaviour can occur at individual, group and organisational levels, which would make understanding EMNCs' motivations valuable within this research domain. If the context of EMNCs shapes strategic decisions of the firms, it can also form their entrepreneurial behaviour at all levels. As a result, exploring the internationalisation strategies of significant EMNCs from Turkey as a mid-range EM can highlight how corporate entrepreneurial behaviour is important for international entrepreneurship literature. For this reason, this study tries to answer the following specific research questions:

How can EMNCs and BGs exploit entrepreneurial opportunities during outward internationalisation?

How do EMNCs as BGs affiliates use international entrepreneurship at the corporate level for the establishment of an international strategy?

Methodology

The case study methodology has been selected to understand how entrepreneurial processes and behaviour could form and explain the internationalisation of EMNCs. The case study methodology has been widely used in international entrepreneurship and international business research domains in recent years to explain the motivations and reasons for outward internationalisation of EM firms (Child and Rodrigues, 2005; Bonaglia *et al.*, 2007; Eren-Erdogmus *et al.*, 2010; Vissak and Zhang, 2014; Yaprak *et al.*, 2018). Besides, the case study method gives the opportunity to ask "how" and "why" questions while focusing extensively on a research question that deals with processes and extending previous theories or building new theories (Eisenhardt, 1989; Yin, 2018, pp. 35–39). The case study methodology can help researchers form new knowledge about corporate processes like outward internationalisation and consider context-specific issues for constructing new theories (Guercini, 2004).

Three cases from Turkey were selected with purposeful sampling to understand the role of international entrepreneurship in the internationalisation of EMNCs. Even if the sample of the research is quite small and generalisation of the results would be difficult (Vissak and Zhang, 2014), the sample of the study has the power to represent EMNCs in the Turkish context and the ability to investigate the research questions in depth. Moreover, the cases in the sample were selected through their corporate performance in the domestic market, media coverage of their latest internationalisation attempts (Bloomberg, 2001; Daneshkhu, 2016; Bigan *et al.*, 2017;

Boorer, 2018) and scholarly interest in these firms in previous studies (Bonaglia *et al.*, 2007; Erdilek, 2008; Colpan and Hikino, 2010; Yaprak and Karademir, 2010).

The data were collected through annual reports, corporate websites, news in the media about FDI announcements of the firms and previous scholarly work. Due to time-based constraints and hardship to access key managers in the selected firms for a short period of time, the data coverage was limited. However, the current data sources of the related firms can give rich information about the historical and current processes of these EMNCs, which would eliminate the shortcomings of not having semi-structured interviews with decision-makers in these firms.

Cases

Arçelik

Arçelik was founded in 1955 by Vehbi Koç who was also the founder of Koç Holding in Turkey. Since that year, Arçelik has played a significant role in both Turkey's growing manufacturing industry and Koç Holding's growth via exporting, licensing agreements with western firms and cross-border acquisitions in different parts of the world. Arçelik produced Turkey's first washing machine in 1959 and the first refrigerator (Bonaglia *et al.*, 2007). Arçelik has reached a net sales value of 4,75 billion US dollars by offering products and services in 146 different countries (Arçelik, 2018). The success of Arçelik can be attributed to the ambition of Vehbi Koç (founding entrepreneur) who also established a giant company (Koç Holding) in Turkey during statist economy conditions. The growth agenda of Arçelik was defined by Vehbi Koç at the beginning with his entrepreneurial vision, and expanded through his offspring in the following years. By means of this vision and by transferring individual entrepreneurial vision into the corporate level, Arçelik generated approximately 60% of its revenues from international operations (Colpan and Jones, 2016; Bigan *et al.*, 2017). Vehbi Koç's entrepreneurial vision also helped build Turkey's first private sector Research and Development (R&D) Center in 1973, which helped Koç Holding adopt foreign technology into local needs in its affiliates, like Arçelik (Colpan and Jones, 2016). The first internationalisation attempt of Arçelik started in the 1980s with exporting of its products to neighbouring countries, and increased through an original equipment manufacturing (OEM) contract with Sears

Rebuck in 1988 to produce refrigerators under the Kenmore brand. This initial step for internationalisation has also been considered as an entrepreneurial response to increased incentives for exporting activities that was encouraged by the 1980s' neo-liberal economy policy by the state (Önis, 1992). BGs and their affiliates have generally been the first movers to exploit state incentives in the domestic market of Turkey, and this situation has continued to expand internationally.

Arçelik invested in research and development to build its own technology and global brand, and followed these attempts with acquisitions of foreign brands like Arctic in Romania and Defy in South Africa (Bonaglia *et al.*, 2007; Arçelik, 2018). The main reason for the cross-border investments of Koç Holding's Arçelik was the saturation of the home market (Verma *et al.*, 2011). Arçelik's outward internationalisation accelerated through the 2000s as Turkey's economy became more stable, and demonstrated significant growth. This can be a sign of how the controlling family still has an influence on entrepreneurial decisions of BG affiliates by following opportunities in different markets. As can be seen in Table 1, Arçelik's accelerated acquisitions have helped it build its brand and technology base with risk-taking, proactive and innovative behaviours (McDougall and Oviatt, 2000).

Moreover, Arçelik has continued to form JVs both in domestic (Beko-LG) and foreign (Voltas-Beko) markets to seek opportunities in innovative technologies. In conclusion, Arçelik's growth journey has been shaped by not only the institutional conditions of Turkey's economy but also the opportunity-seeking behaviour of its founders and owners throughout the years.

Kordsa

Kordsa was established in 1973 as the Kordsa Tire Cord Fabric Plant in İzmit as an affiliate of Sabancı Holding. Sabancı Holding controlled

Table 1: Cross-border Acquisitions of Arçelik through the 2000s

2002	Acquisitions in Europe (Elektra Bregenz, Blomberg, Leisure, Flavel, Arctic)
2006	Acquisition of Grundig
2011	Acquisition of Defy Appliances Limited
2015	Acquisition of Dawlance (Pakistan)

71.11% of Kordsa's shares as of 2018. Kordsa's first internationalisation attempt was exporting to Yugoslavia in 1976, a few years after its founding. Kordsa reached a gross profit of 794 million TL for the year 2018. It operates in 13 countries across Europe, the Middle East, Asia, North Africa and America. Kordsa gained 820 million USD revenue in 2018 (Kordsa, 2018). Like Arçelik, Kordsa was also an OEM supplier of industry leaders and has built on its technology through these partnerships. It is also successful in cost efficient nylon manufacturing via its Turkey facility, and produces composite and construction reinforcement materials (Yaprak *et al.*, 2018, p. 203). Kordsa started to expand its international production facilities by forming an alliance with DuPont under the DUSA International name (50/50 JV agreement) at the end of 2000 (Bloomberg, 2001). Kordsa still continues to acquire DUSA's shares to operate its foreign operations as the ultimate owner.

As can be seen in Table 2, most of the foreign subsidiaries of Kordsa were established through this JV agreement and helped Kordsa increase its geographic expansion. Moreover, the JV agreement with DuPont has

Table 2: Kordsa's Foreign Subsidiaries (Kordsa, 2018)

Subsidiaries	Country	Activity Subject	Share (%)
Kordsa Inc.	USA	Industrial Fibre and Cord Fabric Production and Trade	100
Fabric Development, Inc.	USA	Advanced Composite Material Production for Civil Aviation Industry	100
Textile Products, Inc.	USA	Advanced Composite Material Production for Civil Aviation Industry	100
Advanced Honeycomb Technologies Corporation	USA	Advanced Composite Material Production for Civil Aviation Industry	100
Kordsa Brasil S.A.	Brazil	Industrial Fibre and Cord Fabric Production and Trade	97.31
PT Indo Kordsa Tbk	Indonesia	Industrial Fibre and Cord Fabric Production and Trade	61.58
PT Indo Kordsa Polyester	Indonesia	Cord Fabric Production and Trade	99.97
Thai Indo Kordsa Co. Ltd.	Thailand	Cord Fabric Production and Trade	64.19
Nile Kordsa Company SAE	Egypt	Cord Fabric Production and Trade	51

given Kordsa the chance of becoming the sole licensee of DuPont technologies across international markets. By this alliance, Kordsa got access to new technologies and used them for further FDI activities (Erdilek, 2008). This strategy has been a signature of Sabancı Holding for its affiliates for many years. Forming alliances with Western companies to develop production technologies and a brand image has been an entrepreneurial choice of Turkish BGs. Similar to Koç Holding, Sabancı Holding also manifests the strategic vision and international strategic behaviour of its affiliates. This indicates that Turkish BGs can control their affiliates by not only family member shareholders but also establishing an entrepreneurial orientation among their member firms. Rather than applying the risk and opportunity-seeking style of Arçelik (Koç Holding), Kordsa (Sabancı Holding) has preferred to choose an incremental internationalisation approach (Erdilek, 2003). At this point, Kordsa follows the routes of traditional MNCs for globalisation. Although it seems to adopt a more traditional approach than that proposed by international entrepreneurship literature, Kordsa still shows the effort to be a part of international networks like "born global" firms by JVs. Besides, it started exporting activities a short time after its founding, which is similar to the "born global" phenomenon. Kordsa's foreign subsidiaries also gave it the chance of evolving both its foreign and local operations and catching up to its foreign partners and rivals. This subsidiary evolution has been considered a type of corporate entrepreneurship since it has acquired the shares of its advanced JV partner in the following years (Hill and Mudambi, 2010). To sum up, entrepreneurial internationalisation can be a context-dependent concept especially for EM firms. Examining each firm within its context and founding entrepreneur's vision can magnify our understanding of the international entrepreneurship domain to fill research gaps.

Ülker

Ülker was established as a small biscuit factory in 1944 in İstanbul by Sabri Ülker and his brothers. As a branch and flagship of Yıldız Holding, Ülker has been the national giant in producing chocolates, chocolate-coated biscuits, biscuits and cakes for over 70 years. Ülker started its internationalisation through targeted exporting into the Middle East in 1974 and established its R&D department in the same year. In 2008, Ülker acquired 25, 23% of Godiva, which is a premium chocolate brand in the world, as a strategic asset-seeking internationalisation attempt with a value of 850 million USD. Ülker made an alliance with Kellog's to sell its products in Turkey with its own brand and Kellog's in 2005. Ülker also established international alliances as a JV with the Eckes-Granini Group and McCormick in 2010 and with Japan Nissin Foods in 2012. Ülker made another important global acquisition by buying UK's United Biscuits in 2014. After these significant acquisitions and alliances with global firms, Yıldız Holding established Pladis to merge its global brands Godiva, United Biscuits and Ülker in 2016 (Ülker, 2018b). By establishing Pladis, Yıldız Holding got the company to be quoted on the New York Stock Exchange (Carney *et al.*, 2018). Ülker reached 5.95 billion TL net sales in 2018 and achieved a 12% increase in net profit relevant to the previous year, with foreign sales breaking a record by counting 37.7% (1.30 billion TL) of total sales in the same year. Ülker employed 9029 people for the year 2018. Pladis has 51% and Yıldız Holding and family members control 7.48% of Ülker's shares as of 2018. Ülker has 6 production facilities in Turkey, 2 in Saudi Arabia and 1 each in Egypt and Kazakhstan (Ülker, 2018a).

The foreign subsidiaries of Ülker have been listed in Table 3. As shown, Ülker's production facilities have been generally located in nearby regions, which were also its first exporting destinations. Ülker's entrepreneurial internationalisation has shown a more focused approach than most BGs from Turkey. Networks and the founding entrepreneur's vision seemed to shape the first internationalisation destinations of Ülker since the Ülker family has a more Islamic point of view than other BGs and known families in Turkey. Furthermore, Ülker's close relations with state actors were amplified in the AK Party era due to a similar Islamic background of the owner family. On the contrary, Ülker's recent acquisitions

Table 3: Foreign Subsidiaries of Ülker (Ülker, 2018a)

Subsidiaries	Country	Activity Subject	Share (%)
Godiva	Belgium	Production (Turkey)-Sales	19.2
Hi-Food for Advanced Food Industries	Egypt	Production	51.4
Food Manufacturers Company	Saudi Arabia	Production-Sales	55
Hamle Company Ltd. LLP	Kazakhstan	Production-Sales	100
UI MENA-Amir Global	Saudi Arabia	Investment-Sales	100
International Biscuits Company	Saudi Arabia	Production-Sales	100

in Western countries may have been affected by the government's European Union integration at the beginning of the 2000s and the changing roles of the AK Party government in recent years (Carney *et al.*, 2018). Besides, the Godiva and United Biscuits acquisitions can be considered risky decisions for an EM firm with their high return and opportunities. Ülker's experience in the domestic market and the new generation's (Murat Ülker) asset-exploring attitude have widened the international presence of the company. Despite Sabri Ülker's religious worldview and east-oriented expansion strategy, his son Murat Ülker has made Ülker an emerging giant that can compete with Western MNCs (Turgut, 2008). This can be an indicator of Turkish BGs' evolving strategic and entrepreneurial vision across different generations. New generations in BGs seem to have more outward internationalisation-oriented entrepreneurship ideas than their ancestors. As a result, Ülker (Yıldız Holding) has been a distinct example, even for Turkish BGs with founders who have a different worldview and lifestyle and transformation, of its entrepreneurial vision according to changing conditions in the domestic market.

Findings and Discussion

According to insights from previous research and historical information about selected cases, the findings seem to be formed by both the institutional context of Turkey and the entrepreneurial behaviour of founders and their offspring. The main finding of the selected cases is the role of the controlling family and the entrepreneur in the strategy-making processes in both the domestic and international markets. Seeking opportunities and rent by BGs and EMNCs as their affiliates is not dependent on only the EM contexts and is sustained during outward internationalisation attempts by these firms. Turkey's infant MNCs like Arçelik, Kordsa and Ülker have offered new insights about entrepreneurial processes of EM firms at both the national and international levels. The founding entrepreneur's vision and resilience to expand BG affiliates' operations in Turkey's underdeveloped institutional and moderately developed infrastructural environments are also reflected in the first internationalisation attempts of these cases. Vehbi Koç and Sabri Ülker could be good examples how different worldviews shape entrepreneurs' strategic visions. While Vehbi Koç's close relations with the founding ideology and the state of the Republic of Turkey made Koç Holding and Arçelik closer to

Western allies in both the domestic and international markets (Colpan and Jones, 2016), Sabri Ülker's pious lifestyle drove Ülker into more conservative choices in the domestic markets and eastern (more Islamic-oriented) countries for internationalisation investments at the beginning (Turgut, 2008; Ülker, 2018b). Moreover, the religious worldview of the Ülker family helped the firm expand its foreign presence during first few years of the AK Party era, which occurred as the acquisition of globally known brands. However, this close relationship was also affected by the change in Turkey's institutional context in the last few years of the AK Party government. Ülker had to share a similar position with other secular BGs, which has caused the firm's controlling head company to move abroad in recent years (Carney *et al.*, 2018).

The second finding of the selected cases is the change in strategic asset-seeking and risk-taking attitude of the controlling owners through the generations. Arçelik, Kordsa and Ülker have succeeded in their accelerated internationalisation via cross-border acquisitions generally in advanced markets under the control of the second generation of the Koç, Sabancı and Ülker families. This shows how entrepreneurial vision towards internationalisation may change across generations in family-controlled firms and may also affect corporate-level entrepreneurship activities in EM contexts. The second and third generations of the controlling families have a more Western-based education and vision, which can be the reason for this changing path in international strategy (Yamak and Üsdiken, 2006). This finding is consistent with international entrepreneurship research since it considers entrepreneurship at individual, group and organisational levels. The accelerated internationalisation of these cases seems to be affected by the strategy maker's individual background and vision since the executive boards of these firms are still highly controlled by the owner families.

Another insight may be about the importance of networks for outward internationalisation of the cases. EMNCs have used international alliances like contract agreements and JVs to get involved in international networks in domestic or international markets. All three cases of EMNCs from Turkey got benefits of alliance networks as a means of entrepreneurial act at the corporate level. These networks have caused spillover effects for the EMNCs mentioned in this chapter such as developing their supply chains and distribution channels (Hill and Mudambi, 2010). Besides, these firms, by developing their FSAs through network relations, have used them in later internationalisation attempts (Yaprak *et al.*, 2018).

Conclusion

This chapter makes two main contributions to the international entrepreneurship literature. First, the study attempts to expand the knowledge about entrepreneurial internationalisation in EM contexts. This can create an opening for entrepreneurial internationalisation research since EM contexts have been shaped by prohibitive factors for entrepreneurial acts for many years. Institutional voids in factor and product markets have forced private companies to develop their own financial and human resource pools with unrelated diversification strategies and a high level of control by families in companies by cross-shareholdings (Morck and Yeung, 2003; Khanna and Palepu, 2006). These contextual factors bring out the second point of the chapter, which is discovering the outward expansion of specific organisational forms (like BGs and their affiliates as EMNCs) in EMs to understand whether the entrepreneurial success of these firms in domestic environments can be transferred into more sophisticated markets by acquiring advanced MNCs or alliance partners.

The findings can have some implications for future research on the international entrepreneurship domain in EM contexts. Most of the previous IB studies have generally underestimated the role of the controlling owners of EMNCs. This study can be a good starting point to merge EMNCs' international strategy and the hidden forces behind it. As Buckley *et al.* (2018) have mentioned, the individual-level risk propensity and the manager's attitude towards FDI risk in different locations could also explain internationalisation of EMNCs. Due to institutional voids in EMs which cause high levels of family or state control in EMNCs, these firms still have different paths in strategy formation as compared to advanced MNCs. For this reason, the international entrepreneurship domain would expand our understanding of the internationalisation of these firms and complete the shortcomings of agency theory and the institution-based view which are commonly used by scholars in IB studies. Another implication can be to discuss the relationship between SMEs in EMs and EMNCs through IB and international entrepreneurship literature. The network relationships of EMNCs could not be bounded with only foreign partners. Network relations with domestic firms as buyers and suppliers could have significant effects on both SMEs' internationalisation and EMNCs, which can use international entrepreneurship approaches for future studies. Finally, examining EM firms and EM contexts could expand our understanding of entrepreneurial processes for new venture creation in global markets for future research. BGs would be a fruitful area not only for IB studies but also for international entrepreneurship literature.

As the selected cases have indicated, the controlling entrepreneurs of Arçelik, Kordsa and Ülker have exploited current policies for their firms' first internationalisation steps in foreign markets. Policymakers should develop projects by considering all economic actors in economic environments of EMs to distribute incentives fairly among all firms of different sizes. While BGs and their affiliates are in a better position to collect firsthand benefits of international trade policies and incentives, small or medium-sized firms cannot evaluate internationalisation chances as fast as these big players. Accordingly, policies should encourage more network relations among domestic firms with relative sizes to increase both country-level and firm-level FDI and trade. Lastly, policymakers in EM firms at all levels should blend individual-level entrepreneurial behaviour with corporate-level entrepreneurship more effectively to expand their presence in global markets.

References

Anil, I., E. Tatoglu, and G. Ozkasap (2014). Ownership and market entry mode choices of emerging country multinationals in a transition country: Evidence from Turkish multinationals in Romania. *Journal for East European Management Studies*, 19(4), 413–452, doi: 10.1688/JEEMS-2014-04-Anil.

Arçelik (2018). *Annual Report*. Available at: https://www.arcelikglobal.com/media/4276/arc-elik-annual-report-18-eng.pdf (accessed on January 31, 2020).

Bigan, I., S. Decan, and B. Korkmaz (2017). *How Turkish Companies Can Become Global Successes*. Available at: https://www.mckinsey.com/industries/retail/our-insights/how-turkish-companies-can-become-global-successes# (accessed on July 31, 2019).

Bloomberg (2001). *DuPont and Sabanci Holding Finalize Expanded Industrial Nylon*. Available at: https://www.bloomberg.com/press-releases/2001-01-08/dupont-and-sabanci-holding-finalize-expanded-industrial-nylon (accessed on January 15, 2020).

Bonaglia, F., A. Goldstein, and J. A. Mathews (2007). Accelerated internationalization by emerging markets' multinationals: The case of the white goods sector. *Journal of World Business*, 42(4), 369–383, doi: 10.1016/j.jwb.2007.06.001.

Boorer, B. (2018). *Turkey's Yildiz Holding restructures $ 1bn loan, Global Capital.* Available at: https://www.globalcapital.com/article/b16x0h7dk6skfn/yildiz-holding-restructures-$1bn-loan (Accessed: October 24, 2020).

Buckley, P. J. and M. Casson (1976). *The Future of the Multinational Enterprise.* 1st ed. London: Palgrave Macmillan.

Buckley, P. J., L. Chen, L. J. Clegg, and H. Voss (2018). Risk propensity in the foreign direct investment location decision of emerging multinationals. *Journal of International Business Studies*, 49(2), 153–171, doi: 10.1057/s41267-017-0126-4.

Buğra, A (1995). *Devlet ve Işadamları: State and Business in Modern Turkey; A Comparative Study*. İletişim Yayınları.

Carney, M., M. V. Essen, S. Estrin, and D. Shapiro (2018). Business groups reconsidered: Beyond paragons and parasites. *Academy of Management Perspectives*, 32(4), 493–516, doi: 10.5465/amp.2016.0058.

Chari, M. D. R. and J. Dixit (2015). Business groups and entrepreneurship in developing countries after reforms. *Journal of Business Research*, 68(6), 1359–1366, doi: 10.1016/j.jbusres.2014.12.006.

Child, J., and S. B. Rodrigues (2005). The internationalization of Chinese firms: A case for theoretical extension? *Management and Organization Review*, 1(3), 381–410, doi: 10.1111/j.1740-8784.2005.0020a.x.

Colpan, A. M. (2010). Business groups in Turkey. In Colpan, A. M., T. Hikino, and J. R. Lincoln (eds.) *The Oxford Handbook of Business Groups*. Oxford University Press, 486–525.

Colpan, A. M. and T. Hikino (2010). Foundations of business groups: Towards an integrated framework. In Colpan, A. M., Hikino, T., and J. R. Lincoln (eds.) *The Oxford Handbook of Business Groups*. New York: Oxford University Press, 15–66.

Colpan, A. M. and G. Jones (2016). Business groups, entrepreneurship and the growth of the Koç Group in Turkey. *Business History*, 58(1), 69–88, doi: 10.1080/00076791.2015.1044521.

Cuervo-Cazurra, A. and M. Genc (2008). Transforming disadvantages into advantages: Developing-country MNEs in the least developed countries. *Journal of International Business Studies*, 39(6), 957–979, doi: 10.1057/palgrave.jibs.8400390.

Daneshkhu, S. (2016). Yildiz seeks to expand biscuit empire from London hub, *Financial Times*. Available at: https://www.ft.com/content/aa1a4d56-2cc9-11e6-a18d-a96ab29e3c95.

Deloitte (2016). *Turkish Outbound M&A Review 2014–2015.*

Demirbag, M., E. Tatoglu, and K. W. Glaister (2010). Institutional and transaction cost determinants of Turkish MNEs' location choice. *International Marketing Review*, 27(3), 272–294, doi: 10.1108/02651331011047989.

Dunning, J. H. (1988). The Eclectic paradigm of international production: A restatement and some possible extensions. *Journal of International Business Studies*, 19(1), 1–31.

Dunning, J. H. (1998). Location and the multinational enterprise: A neglected factor? *Journal of International Business Studies*, 29(1), 45–66, doi: 10.1057/palgrave.jibs.8490024.

Eisenhardt, K. M. (1989). Building theories from case study research. *The Academy of Management Review*, 14(4), 532–550.

Erdilek, A. (2003). A comparative analysis of inward and outward FDI in Turkey. *Transnational Corporations*, 12(3), 79–105, doi: 10.1007/978-3-642-22938-1.

Erdilek, A. (2008). Internationalization of Turkish MNEs. *Journal of Management Development*, 27(7), 744–760, doi: 10.1108/02621710810883634.

Eren-Erdogmus, I., E. Cobanoglu, M. Yalcin and P. N. Ghauri (2010). Internationalization of emerging market firms: The case of Turkish retailers. *International Marketing Review*, 27(3), 316–337, doi: 10.1108/02651331011048014.

Granovetter, M. (2005). Business groups and social organization. In Smelser, N. J. and R. Swedberg (eds.) *The Handbook of Economic Sociology*. Second. New Jersey, USA: Princeton University Press, 429–450, doi: 10.1515/9781400835584.429.

Guercini, S. (2004). Developing the researcher-manager interface in the case analysis process. *Management Decision*, 42, 464–472, doi: 10.1108/00251740410518921.

Guillen, M. F. (2000). Business groups in emerging economies: A resource-based view. *Academy of Management Journal*, 43(3), 362–380, doi: 10.2307/1556400.

Hennart, J.-F. (2012). Emerging market multinationals and the theory of the multinational enterprise. *Global Strategy Journal*, 2(3), 168–187, doi: 10.1111/j.2042-5805.2012.01038.x.

Hill, T. L. and R. Mudambi (2010). Far from Silicon Valley: How emerging economies are re-shaping our understanding of global entrepreneurship. *Journal of International Management*, 16(4), 321–327, doi: 10.1016/j.intman.2010.9.003.

Hoskisson, R. E., L. Eden, C. M. Lau, and M. Wright (2000). Strategy in emerging economies. *The Academy of Management Journal*, 43(3), 249–267, doi: 10.2307/1556394.

Hoskisson, R. E., M. Wright, I. Filatotchev and M. W. Peng (2013). Emerging multinationals from mid-range economies: The influence of institutions and factor markets. *Journal of Management Studies*, 50(7), 1295–1321, doi: 10.1111/j.1467-6486.2012.01085.x.

Jones, M. V. and N. E. Coviello (2005). Internationalisation: Conceptualising an entrepreneurial process of behaviour in time. *Journal of International Business Studies*, 36, 284–303, doi: 10.1057/palgrave.jibs.8400138.

Jones, M.V., N. Coviello, and Y. K. Tang (2011). International Entrepreneurship research (1989-2009): A domain ontology and thematic analysis. *Journal of Business Venturing*, 26(6), 632–659, doi: 10.1016/j.jbusvent.2011.04.001.

Khanna, T. and K. G. Palepu (1997). Why focused strategies may be wrong for emerging markets. *Harvard Business Review*, (July-August).

Khanna, T. and K. G. Palepu (2006). Emerging giants: Building world-class companies in developing countries. *Harvard Business Review*, 84(10), 1–20.

Khanna, T. and J. W. Rivkin (2001). Estimating the performance effects of business groups in emerging markets. *Strategic Management Journal*, 22(1), 45–74, doi: 10.1002/1097-0266.

Khanna, T. and Y. Yafeh (2010). Business groups in emerging markets: Paragons or parasites? *The Oxford Handbook of Business Groups*, 45(2), 331–372, doi: 10.1093/oxfordhb/9780199552863.003.0020.

Knight, G. A. and S. T. Cavusgil (2004). Innovation, organizational capabilities, and the born-global firm. *Journal of International Business Studies*, 35(2), 124–141, doi: 10.1057/palgrave.jibs.8400071.

Kordsa (2018). *Annual Report*. Available at: https://www.kordsa.com/en/images/pdf/annualreport2018.pdf.

Leff, N. H. (1978). Industrial organization and entrepreneurship in the developing countries: The economic groups. *Economic Development and Cultural Change*, 26(4), 661–675, doi: 10.1086/451052.

Luo, Y. and R. L. Tung (2007). International expansion of emerging market enterprises: A springboard perspective. *Journal of International Business Studies*, 38(4), 481–498, doi: 10.1057/palgrave.jibs.8400275.

Madhok, A. and M. Keyhani (2012). Acquisitions as entrepreneurship: Asymmetries, opportunities, and the internationalization of multinationals from emerging economies. *Global Strategy Journal*, 2(1), 26–40, doi: 10.1111/j.2042-5805.2011.01023.x.

Mathews, J. A. (2006). Dragon multinationals: New players in 21st century globalization. *Asia Pacific Journal of Management*, 23(1), 5–27, doi: 10.1007/s10490-006-6113-0.

McDougall, P. P. and B. M. Oviatt (2000). International entrepreneurship: The intersection of two research paths. *The Academy of Management Journal*, 43(5), 902–906, doi: 10.2307/1556418.

Meyer, M., N. Lang, N. Baise, K. Maggard, G. Hill, J. Wong, H. Maher, S. Verma, E. Leon, and B. Tansan (2018). *Global Challengers 2018: Digital Leapfrogs*. Boston, MA. Available at: www.digitalbcg.com (accessed on July 12, 2019).

Morck, R. and B. Yeung (2003). Agency problems in large family business groups, *Entrepreneurship Theory and Practice*, 27(4), 367–382.

Önis, Z. (1992). Redemocratization and economic liberalization in Turkey: The limits of state autonomy. *Studies in Comparative International Development*, 27(2), 3–23, doi: 10.1007/BF02687108.

Oviatt, B. M. and P. P. McDougall (1994). Toward a theory of international new ventures. *Journal of International Business Studies*, 25, 45–64, doi: 10.1057/palgrave.jibs.8400128.

Peng, M. W. (2012). The global strategy of emerging multinationals from China. *Global Strategy Journal*, 107, 97–107, doi: 10.1111/j.2042-5805.2012.01030.x.

Ramamurti, R. (2009a). What have we learned about emerging-market MNEs?. In Ramamurti, R. and J. V. Singh (eds.) *Emerging Multinationals in Emerging Markets*. Cambridge UK: Cambridge University Press, 399–426.

Ramamurti, R. (2009b). Why study emerging-market multinationals?. In Ramamurti, R. and J. V. Singh (eds.) *Emerging Multinationals in Emerging Markets*. New York: Cambridge University Press, 3–22, doi: 10.1017/CBO9780511576485.001.

Ramamurti, R. (2012). Commentaries: What is really different about emerging market multinationals? *Global Strategy Journal*, 2(1), 41–47, doi: 10.1111/j.2042-5805.2011.01025.x.

Reuber, A. R., G. A. Knight, and P. W. Liesch (2018). International entrepreneurship: The pursuit of entrepreneurial opportunities across national borders. *Journal of International Business Studies*. Palgrave Macmillan UK, 49(4), 395–406, doi: 10.1057/s41267-018-0149-5.

Rialp, A., J. Rialp, and G. A. Knight (2005). The phenomenon of early internationalizing firms: What do we know after a decade (1993–2003) of scientific inquiry? *International Business Review*, 14(2), 147–166, doi: 10.1016/j.ibusrev.2004.04.006.

Rugman, A. M. and A. Verbeke (2003). Extending the theory of the multinational enterprise: Internalization and strategic management perspectives. *Journal of International Business Studies*, 34(2), 125–137, doi: 10.1057/palgrave.jibs.8400012.

Schneider, B. R. (2010). Business groups and the state: The politics of expansion, restructuring, and collapse. In Colpan, A. M., T. Hikino, and J. R. Lincoln (eds.) *The Oxford Handbook of Business Groups*. Oxford: Oxford University Press, 650–669.

Turgut, P. (2008). Ambitious confectioner snaps up Belgium's Godiva, Financial Times, Available at: https://www.ft.com/content/f071969e-bcdb-11dd-af5a-0000779fd18c (Accessed: January 15, 2020).

Ülker (2018a). *Annual Report*. Available at: http://ulkerbiskuviyatirimciiliskileri.com/finansal-ve-operasyonel-veriler/faaliyet-raporlari.aspx.

Ülker (2018b). *History*. Available at: http://ulkerbiskuviinvestorrelations.com/en/about-ulker/history.aspx (accessed on January 31, 2020).

UNCTAD (2017). *World Investment Report 2017: Investment and Digital Economy*.

UNCTAD (2019). *World Investment Report 2019: Key Messages and Overview*, doi: 10.18356/a5d1dee8-en.

Verbeke, A. and L. Ciravegna (2018) International entrepreneurship research versus international business research: A false dichotomy? *Journal of International Business Studies*. Palgrave Macmillan UK, 49(4), 387–394, doi: 10.1057/s41267-018-0154-8.

Verma, S., K. Sanghi, H. Michaelis, P. Dupoux, D. Khanna, and P. Peters (2011). *Companies on the Move Rising Stars from Rapidly Developing Economies Are Reshaping Global Industries*. BCG Challengers, Boston Consulting Group.

Vissak, T. and X. Zhang (2014). Chinese immigrant entrepreneurs' involvement in internationalization and innovation: Three Canadian cases. *Journal of International Entrepreneurship*, 12(2), 183–201, doi: 10.1007/s10843-014-0128-2.

Whitley, R. (1998). Internationalization and varieties of capitalism: The limited effects of cross-national coordination of economic activities on the nature of business systems. *Review of International Political Economy*, 5(3), 445–481, doi: 10.1080/096922998347480.

Xia, J., X. Ma, J. W. Lu, and D. W. Yiu (2014). Outward foreign direct investment by emerging market firms: A resource dependence logic. *Strategic Management Journal*, 35, 1343–1363, doi: 10.1002/smj.

Yamak, S. and B. Üsdiken (2006). Economic liberalization and the antecedents of top management teams: Evidence from turkish "big" business. *British Journal of Management*, 17(3), 177–194, doi: 10.1111/j.1467-8551.2006.00491.x.

Yamakawa, Y, M. W. Peng, and D. L. Deeds (2008). What drives new ventures to internationalize from emerging to developed economies? *Entrepreneurship Theory and Practice*, 32(1), 59–82, doi: 10.1136/jcp.35.12.1388.

Yaprak, A. and B. Karademir (2010). The internationalization of emerging market business groups: An integrated literature review. *International Marketing Review*, 27(2), 245–262, doi: 10.1108/02651331011037548.

Yaprak, A. and B. Karademir (2011). Emerging market multinationals' role in facilitating developed country multinationals' regional expansion: A critical review of the literature and Turkish MNC examples. *Journal of World Business*, 46(4), 438–446, doi: 10.1016/j.jwb.2010.10.004.

Yaprak, A., B. Karademir and R. N. Osborn (2006). How do business groups function and evolve in emerging markets? The case of Turkish business groups. *Advances in International Marketing*, 17(06), 275–294, doi: 10.1016/S1474-7979(06)17010-6.

Yaprak, A., T. Yosun, and D. Cetindamar (2018). The influence of firm-specific and country-specific advantages in the internationalization of emerging market firms: Evidence from Turkey. *International Business Review*, 27(1), 198–207, doi: 10.1016/j.ibusrev.2017.07.001.

Yin, R. K. (2018). *Case Study Research and Applications: Design and Methods*. 6th ed. Los Angeles, USA: Sage Publications.

Yiu, D. W., Y. Lu, G. D. Bruton, and R. E. Hoskisson (2007). Business groups: An integrated model to focus future research. *Journal of Management Studies*, 44(8), 1551–1579, doi: 10.1111/j.1467-6486.2007.00735.x.

Yurtoglu, B. (2000). Ownership, control and performance of Turkish listed firms. *Empirica*, 27, 193–222. Available at: https://link.springer.com/article/10.1023/A:1026557203261.

https://doi.org/10.1142/9789811228445_0006

Chapter 6

Internationalisation and Competitive Strategies of Enterprises

Šárka Zapletalová

Department of Business Economics and Management,
School of Business Administration in Karviná,
Silesian University in Opava, Czechia
zapletalova@opf.slu.cz

Abstract

The internationalisation of entrepreneurial activities is a necessity for the majority of entrepreneurial subjects. The internationalisation of entrepreneurial activities is represented by the geographic expansion of entrepreneurial activities across national borders. Internationalisation is a phenomenon researched intensively over the last few decades from a variety of viewpoints. Issues such as the development of international activities and factors favouring or disfavouring internationalisation have been studied for both large enterprises as well as small and medium enterprises. The internationalisation of entrepreneurship activities counts among long-lasting strategic decisions; these decisions bring significant changes in running an enterprise and are conditioned by them as well. The entrance of an enterprise on the market itself allows for a significant opportunity, so long as the said enterprise possesses the proper readiness, which grants it the chance to develop entrepreneurial activities (business) in the foreign markets. Entrepreneurial activities in international markets bring significant changes in competitive strategy. The objective of this chapter is to identify a possible connection between competitive strategy and international activities in the internationalisation of the studied enterprises. The study is based on primary data collected from a recent survey of enterprises from the Czech Republic. The relationships of interest are analysed using relevant regression techniques.

Keywords: Internationalisation of entrepreneurial activities; Competitive strategies; Strategic decisions; International activities; Foreign markets.

Introduction

International entrepreneurship, which entails new managerial mindsets and ways of framing the challenges of organising and managing business activities with a global outlook, has received increased attention from a number of researchers over the last decade. A plethora of studies on enterprise internationalisation have been conducted in developed industrialised countries (Bell, 2005; Theodosiou and Morgan, 2007); however, only recently has research centred on the enterprises from Central Europe. Therefore, evidence from these countries is still lacking. The high rate of returns of enterprise internationalisation in developed countries (Raynard and Forstater, 2002) demonstrates the benefits countries from Central Europe can gain, so they are encouraged to follow the trend by their respective governments.

The internationalisation of the enterprise is a fundamental key for improving the competitiveness of firms and for decreasing the degree of vulnerability to the changes in demand conditions and the entry of new competitors. The internationalisation strategies are also diverse and depend on several factors such as firm characteristics (firm size, firm age, ownership, innovation and technological variables, resources and knowledge), management factors (factors like the qualifications and the age of the entrepreneurs) and business environment (Calof, 1994; Pereira, 2005; Higon and Driffield, 2007). It clear that internationalisation can bring a number of finance and non-financial benefits to enterprises. Although enterprises may benefit in the short term from taking advantage of international opportunities as they arise, the overall benefit of internationalisation is accruing in the medium to long term. Therefore, the owners/management must be willing to make a long-term commitment to internationalisation. Because internationalisation is a long-term strategy, enterprises intending to venture overseas, or aiming to increase their degree of internationalisation, need to engage in strategic planning. This often requires an organisational change, and the founders or management must be fully aware of what is required to develop a successful internationalised enterprise. Strategic planning addresses issues such as the fit between the owner/management's aspirations, the vision and objectives of the enterprise and the deliberate internationalisation strategy. It is also useful to recognise the resources and capabilities that would need to be acquired or developed in order to implement the intended internationalisation strategy, how they will be obtained and the organisational change that would need to occur to bring about this. A key part of the enterprise internationalisation is its strategic management where the strategic plans of the enterprise are compared with the outcomes so that corrective actions, where necessary, can be taken.

The existing theories assume implicitly that internationalisation is preceded by opportunity recognition, but provide little explanation about this process or the capabilities individuals need to identify these opportunities (Chandra *et al.*, 2009; Acedo and Jones, 2007). A related but distinct category is where entrepreneurs actively create opportunities that can be exploited using innovative approaches and products that promote faster market entry (Mort *et al.*, 2012). This opens up a novel and a much broader way of looking at opportunities incorporating marketing as well as environmental factors in order to understand it in its entirety.

To investigate how competitive strategies and internationalisation of entrepreneurial activities interact, this chapter reviews extant theories of this phenomenon. This chapter is not just another review of the field of international entrepreneurship but also a review of competitive strategies of enterprises from Central Europe, especially from the Czech enterprises, that operate internationally. Although we use a single small country, the Czech Republic, as a laboratory to test our theoretical propositions, our study is situated within the domain of business studies, since its focus is on the effects of strategy on the success of international activities. The Czech Republic is a country with a high share of exported and imported goods in its GDP, which is typical of small countries, of which we are one. The Czech entrepreneurial subjects have been increasingly taking part in the international market since the beginning of the 21st century, and this trend seems to be growing. A dominant factor that influences this process of the internalisation of entrepreneurship activities is globalisation. The necessity of active participation of Czech entrepreneurial subjects at international markets is conditioned primarily by the character of Czech economics and its foreign political orientation. One of the main reasons for the interest of Czech enterprises to expand to foreign markets nowadays is the limited market size of the Czech Republic and, consequently, the increasing competition in the domestic market. The growing interest in doing business in foreign markets gives rise to interests in internationalisation in a broader context. International activities have been realised by Czech enterprises, both large and small and medium-sized enterprises. The historical context of the centrally planned economy in the Czech Republic until 1989 suggests that internationalisation has been an innovation for almost all Czech enterprises after 1989. Until that time, foreign trade was a monopoly of the state, and only a limited number and type of state-owned enterprises referred to as "foreign trade enterprises" were privileged to operate directly abroad. As expected, some Czech enterprises have served in international markets before that time. However, they mainly exported to other socialist or ideologically similar countries, which was not such a challenge as it would have been when exporting to developed market economies. Moreover, the companies that wanted to operate in foreign markets before 1989 had to use official Czech Foreign Trade Enterprises as an intermediary. The opening of new markets such as in the Czech Republic has created the potential for enterprise expansion and investment. The internationalisation process of enterprises and an enterprise's decision to sell its products in international markets have been the subject of intense academic research in the past 40 years. Several theories and conceptual frameworks have been developed, outlining an enterprise's decision to initiate the internationalisation process. According to Lopez *et al.* (2009), studying the phenomenon of internationalisation in small, open economies (such as the Czech Republic) should be of growing interest because, given the limited potential of the local market, incentives to internationalise should be strong.

We offer a new angle on a business theory by focusing on the effects of the competitive strategy on the internationalisation process of studied enterprises from the Czech Republic. It also aims to comprehensively review the growth modalities and strategies applied in such organisations. Based on our review of models, our study helps to advance the theoretical development of the role of competitive strategy in international activities.

International Entrepreneurship

A series of varying themes and theoretical approaches can be found under the umbrella term of international entrepreneurship, and this is a field that can also be understood as an interdisciplinary one (Schultz *et al.*,

2009). The central themes in international entrepreneurship are the analysis of antecedents (Moen and Servais, 2002), management (Knight and Cavusgil, 2004) and the success features of internationalisation forms (Lu and Beamish, 2006). The term internationalisation of entrepreneurial activities refers to all those entrepreneurial activities which involve cross-border transactions of goods, services and resources between two or more nations. Transactions of economic resources include capital, skills and people for the international production of physical goods and services such as finance, banking, insurance or construction. The internationalisation of entrepreneurial activities is represented by the geographic expansion of entrepreneurial activities across national borders (Lopez *et al.*, 2009). Enterprises go international for a variety of reasons, but the common goal is the enterprise growth or expansion. The problems of the internationalisation of entrepreneurial activities have seen a considerable interest among a number of significant economists such as Johanson (2009, 1977, 1975), Andersen (1993), Ruzzier *et al.* (2006) and Lopez *et al.* (2009), who have fundamentally contributed to the rethinking of the concept of internationalisation theory (Baronchelli and Cassia, 2008). Internationalisation entails entry into new country markets. It may, therefore, be described as a process of innovation (Andersen, 1993; Casson, 2000). International new ventures have, in particular, been described as uniquely innovative in their internationalisation (Oviatt and McDougall, 1994; Knight and Cavusgil, 2004). Innovation is also central to the field of entrepreneurship (Schumpeter, 1934; Shane and Venkataraman, 2000). As defined by McDougall and Oviatt (2000), international entrepreneurship is "… a combination of innovative, proactive, and risk-seeking behaviour that crosses national borders and is intended to create value in organizations".

According to Zahra and George (2002), international entrepreneurship was first mentioned by Morrow (1988) in his article, which highlighted recent technological advances and cultural awareness for new ventures to exploit foreign markets. Morrow (1988) introduced the term International entrepreneurship in describing the evolving technological and international cultural environment, which was opening previously untapped foreign markets to new ventures. On the contrary, according to Reuber *et al.* (2018), international entrepreneurship as an area of scholarly inquiry dates from Oviatt and McDougall's (1994) paper identifying and explaining the phenomenon of "international new ventures", which received the 2004 *Journal of International Business Studies Decade*

Award. The emphasis on enterprises that, from inception, sought to gain a competitive advantage from resources and sales in multiple countries shifted attention from gradual internationalisation to the rapid internationalisation of young enterprises. In 2000, Oviatt and McDougall introduced a broader definition of international entrepreneurship, defined as a combination of innovative, proactive and risk-seeking behaviour that crosses or is compared across national borders and is intended to create value in business organisations (Zucchella and Scabini, 2007). Innovativeness reflects a tendency to support new ideas, experimentation and new processes, while proactiveness refers to the capacity to anticipate and act on future needs and desires. Lastly, risk-taking conduct indicates the will to commit large amounts of resources, fully aware that the potential for failure may be high. A decade on, a paper by Knight and Cavusgil (2004) described the capabilities of such "born global" enterprises, and received the 2014 *Journal of International Business Studies Decade Award*. A necessary consequence of these influential papers has been a focus on early and accelerated internationalisation, and a rich body of literature has emerged on the factors that enable enterprises to internationalise quickly, relatively soon after starting up (Knight and Liesch, 2016).

Over time, the scope of entrepreneurial internationalisation as a research domain has shifted. Alongside this body of literature, an alternative view of the domain of international entrepreneurship, centring on the opportunity, has emerged. International opportunity identification became an emergent theme in IE research from 2006 (Peiris *et al*., 2012), with many scholars contributing to comprehend the interplay between opportunity and variables such as commitment and knowledge (Johanson and Vahlne, 2006) to understand and define the IE domain (Styles and Seymour, 2006), rationalise accelerated/successful internationalisation (Mathews and Zander, 2007; Di Gregorio *et al*., 2008; Muzychenko, 2008) and introduce the opportunity-based view in understanding the IE process (Chandra *et al*., 2012). Another stream of research has focused on having the right mindset, its development and its impact on the choice of opportunities and value creation in foreign markets. Zahra *et al*. (2005) used the cognitive perspective (motivation and influence of experience, environment, self-efficacy mental models, heuristics and learning) to examine opportunity identification and exploitation to explain the born global phenomenon. This study signifies the value of knowing the minds of entrepreneurs and their mental models that can guide and shape internationalisation decisions.

Similarly, Butler *et al.* (2010) used the cognitive approach to explain why some individuals can notice opportunities in international environments, albeit with high levels of uncertainty, by focusing on the ability of the entrepreneur to absorb uncertainty and use creativity to take entrepreneurial actions. Offering a revised definition of international entrepreneurship, Oviatt and McDougall explicitly change the focus from the rapid internationalisation of new enterprises to the discovery, enactment, evaluation and exploitation of opportunities, across national borders, to create future goods and services (Oviatt and McDougall, 2005a, 2005b). Consistent with this perspective, Cavusgil and Knight point out that international entrepreneurship increasingly involves innovation across the value chain in terms of identifying and exploiting opportunities (Cavusgil and Knight, 2015). Autio argues that competitive advantage can ensue from establishment and exploitation of such cross-border positions (Autio, 2005), and reviews of the literature have recognised this as an essential theoretical construct (Jones *et al.*, 2011; Keupp and Gassmann, 2009; Mainela *et al.*, 2014; Mathews and Zander, 2007). The emergence of opportunity as theoretically important is also reflected in commentaries which note that a predominant focus in the international entrepreneurship literature on the enterprise-level antecedents of early and accelerated internationalisation has largely neglected consideration of the individual-level factors which enable or constrain the pursuit of opportunities, and the post-entry processes and outcomes through which the pursuit of opportunity is enacted (Autio, 2005; Coviello, 2015; Zahra, 2005; Zander *et al.*, 2015).

Over the past few decades, the international entrepreneurship research field has moved on from its early emphasis on international new ventures (Mainela *et al.*, 2014) towards studying a wider variety of international entrepreneurial behaviours. One contextual distinction merits discussion at the outset and relates to the nature of innovation associated with an opportunity. There has been much discussion in the entrepreneurship literature of alternative definitions of opportunity, differing views on how opportunities are pursued and debate on even whether opportunity is a meaningful theoretical construct (Alvarez *et al.*, 2013; Davidsson, 2015; Dimov, 2011; Garud *et al.*, 2014; Ramoglou and Tsang, 2016).

According to Mainela *et al.* (2014), the characterisation of opportunities builds on two claims about the nature of entrepreneurship. The first is that entrepreneurship is about the generation of new economic activity. The second claim is that entrepreneurship is behaviour. The concept of international opportunity has grown in importance in international entrepreneurship. Similarly, opportunity discovery and exploitation have been critical functions of entrepreneurship (Eckhart and Shane, 2003; Shane and Venkataraman, 2000; Short *et al*., 2010). Entrepreneurial innovation and opportunity identification have also been depicted as the core of MNEs (Casson *et al*., 2009; Casson and Godley, 2007). One of the most used definitions of entrepreneurial opportunities is that offered by Eckhardt and Shane (2003, p. 336) as "situations in which new goods, services, raw materials, markets, and organizing methods can be introduced through the formation of new means, ends, or means-ends relationships". Different opportunities arise from changes in different parts of the value chain. Another definition is presented by Sarasvathy *et al.* (2003, p. 79), who propose that the opportunity is "a set of ideas, beliefs, and actions that enable the creation of future goods and services in the absence of current markets for them". Hence, opportunity arises from perceptions and behaviours combined in an attempt to create new economic artefacts. Innovation opportunities move markets towards disequilibrium through creative destruction, at which point entrepreneurs innovate new solutions of higher value to the markets than the existing options (Schumpeter, 1934; Autio, 2005; Zahra, 2005). The opportunity arises from the entrepreneurial activity, which builds on the dissatisfaction of the entrepreneurs with the current options (McMullen and Shepherd, 2006). The development of innovation opportunities is primarily driven by the motivation, attitude and risk propensity of the entrepreneurs (McMullen and Shepherd, 2006). It focuses on an entrepreneurial idea of a venture that brings new economic value (Anokhin *et al*., 2011; Davidsson, 2004; Eckhardt and Shane, 2003; Shane, 2000). The innovation opportunity manifests as an innovation resource recombination (Shane, 2012), which has novelty value in the markets and whose realisation may need the crossing of national borders (Autio, 2005).

The notion of entrepreneurial opportunity gained prominence in entrepreneurship scholarship with the publication of an article by Shane and Venkataraman (2000). Following Casson (1982), Shane and Venkataraman (2000, p. 220) define an entrepreneurial opportunity as a situation in which the discovery of new means–ends relationships can result in the introduction of new goods, services, raw materials and organising methods which can be sold at rates higher than their cost of production. These new means–ends relationships, new resource combinations, underline the innovation that is inherent in the entrepreneurial pursuit of opportunities (Shane, 2012). Opportunity recognition involves a realisation that a market opportunity objectively exists for someone, labelled a third-person opportunity, and then an assessment of whether this market opportunity is both feasible and desirable for a particular person or enterprise to pursue, labelled a first-person opportunity (McMullen and Shepher, 2006). Opportunities tend to be conceptualised as product-market fit, where the market is defined by the type of customer in the target market, rather than by geography (Grégoire *et al.*, 2010; Grégoire and Shepherd, 2012; Wood *et al.*, 2014). For example, Williams and Grégoire (2015) view an opportunity as the first international market. They explore nuances in the distance construct by showing how executives' perceptions of commonalities and differences between a home and host market impact judgments related to which geographic market to enter, in what time frame and with what entry mode.

In contrast, opportunity in scholarship on internationalisation tends to describe possibilities for cross-border profit-seeking behaviour by enterprises. These tend to be conceptualised as market opportunities, especially new market entries. For example, Ellis (2011) defines an opportunity as an exchange agreement with new customers in new foreign markets. Chandra *et al.* (2012) define an opportunity as an enterprise's first international venture. Moreover, Karra *et al.* (2008) see opportunities as gaps in foreign markets that can be addressed by a local enterprise. While market opportunities imply a degree of innovation, innovation tends to be more closely circumscribed than in the entrepreneurship literature. It is enterprise-level innovation, usually associated with a new geographic market for an enterprise's existing products or services. The differences between the two domains in the conceptualisation of opportunity are unsurprising, given the emphasis on the creation of new technologies, enterprises and markets in the entrepreneurship literature and the emphasis on entering new geographic markets in the international business literature.

Factors Affecting International Entrepreneurship

According to Zucchella and Scabini (2007), international entrepreneurship is not in itself a novel orientation of enterprises and entrepreneurs. Schumpeter (1934) underlined the entry in new markets, also in geographic terms, as an expression of entrepreneurship. The majority of international entrepreneurship studies have looked at strategic orientations or mindsets of the entrepreneurs or the enterprise. Some of the most commonly used constructs include risk-taking, innovativeness and proactiveness which, when combined, are also called entrepreneurial orientation (Covin and Slevin, 1991; Lumpkin and Dess, 1996; Miller and Friesen, 1978). Entrepreneurial orientation is a behaviour that investigates enterprise-level strategic orientation as influencing various outcome variables such as performance and venture growth. However, some studies found evidence that all three dimensions were associated with rapid internationalisation (Dib *et al.*, 2010; Acedo and Jones, 2007; Acedo and Florin, 2006), opportunity identification (Chandra *et al.*, 2009) and international performance (Kropp *et al.*, 2006).

Through the internationalisation process, enterprises gradually spread their business operations and activities beyond their national boundaries (Ahmad and Kitchen, 2008). An enterprise has to prepare a marketing plan to penetrate the foreign market and set a control system to monitor its business performance (Koch, 2001). There are many possible driving forces behind an enterprise's internationalisation patterns. These factors are generally divided into two categories: proactive and reactive motivating factors (Czinkota and Ronkainen, 1998). The former group consists of the management's perceived benefits or opportunities. For instance, increased revenues or profits may motivate the enterprise to enter the international arena. The second group, the reactive motivators, refers to a set of motivators caused by the enterprise's response to environmental changes. For instance, overproduction, declining domestic sales, excess capacity and saturated domestic markets may cause the enterprise to turn to new markets, that is to foreign markets, to find new possibilities.

Competitive Strategy as a Driver of International Entrepreneurship

When an enterprise hires international employees or searches for new markets abroad, an international strategy can help diversify and expand the business (Twarowska and Kakol, 2013). The progress and speed of business activity internalisation depend on the importance and the role that are assigned to the international entrepreneurship within the entrepreneurship strategy of the particular company. The strategy is a process that can allow an organisation to concentrate its resources on optimal opportunities with the objectives of increasing sales and achieving a sustainable competitive advantage (Kotler, 2012). According to Chaffee (1985), the strategy is the determination of the primary long-term goals of the enterprises, and the adoption of courses of action and allocation of resources necessary for carrying out these goals. The strategy has been defined as the match an organisation makes between its internal resources and skills, and the opportunities and risks created by its external environment (Grant, 1991).

According to McDougall-Covin *et al.* (2014), international entrepreneurship is reported to be a research domain at the intersection of two fields, which are entrepreneurship and international business. Zucchella and Sciabini add one more fundamental pillar, which is strategic management. International entrepreneurship can be seen as an amalgamation of three fields: international business, entrepreneurship and strategic management.

A business strategy is then used as an umbrella term to denote the broad range of strategic options open to the company, including both organisational and functional management strategy, product/market strategies and diversification strategies (Barringer and Greening, 1998). It consists of integrated decisions, actions or plans that will help to achieve target goals. A business strategy is a set of fundamental choices that define its long-term objectives, its value proposition to the market, how it intends to build and sustain a competitive business system, and how it organises itself. In the competitive strategy framework, a successful business is one that sustains an attractive relative position for the company. The success of the process of internationalisation of an enterprise depends in large part on the formulation and implementation of competitive strategy (Knight, 2000). According to Sliwiński (2012), a permanent competitive strategy is obtained through synergy. When a company has a permanent competitive advantage, its resources and capabilities are durable, hard to identify and hard to copy. The organisation of domestic economic activity and the integration of the company in the domestic markets (Dunning, 2000) are essential factors for the definition and success of an internationally competitive business strategy (Feio, 1998). For companies seeking benefits from international markets, the type of competitive strategies they choose may represent an important vehicle by which they build a distinctive business position at the international level and achieve superior financial returns (Allred and Swan, 2004; Luo and Zhao, 2004). Competitive strategies can be classified according to their level and types. There are various competitive strategy typologies.

Michael Porter revolutionised the thinking about competitive strategies twenty years ago with the development of three generic strategies that the companies may adopt to outperform industry rivals: overall cost leadership, differentiation and focus (Porter, 1980a, 1980b, 1985, 1991). Porter (1980b) transformed the theory, practice and teaching of business strategy. He described competitive strategy as taking offensive or defensive actions to create a defendable position in the industry, to cope successfully with the five competitive forces and thereby yield a superior return on investment for the company. When engaging in cost leadership, the company produces products for a broad customer group with lower costs resulting from the economies of scale. When following a differentiation strategy, a company attempts to differentiate the offered product, to be perceived industry-wide, as unique, thereby increasing and capturing consumers with the relatively inelastic price sensitivity of demand. The third generic strategy is the focus strategy by which the company targets a particular buyer group, a segment of the product line or geographic market. Many companies have ignored any strategy (Porter, 2001; Barney, 1997); some companies only define price as the primary and, in many cases, the only competitive variable (Stark *et al.*, 2002). There are always external and internal factors behind the choice of the competitive strategy on international markets.

All competitive strategies appear to be sensible, logical and coherent, highlighting the advantages and benefits the company could gain if applying any of the approaches mentioned above. A more common approach is to differentiate where possible and reduce the cost where necessary. Besides that, Porter's thesis of "stuck in the middle" (Porter, 1980a, 1996) argues that these two strategies cannot be combined. While a company focusing on cost leadership has to maintain a certain standard of its products, thus reducing the possibility of creating economies of scope, a company focusing on differentiation may find it difficult to keep costs low and compete with other companies producing more standardised products for the same market. Unlike Porter, many suggest that a combination of cost leadership and differentiation is not only a feasible option (Hill, 1988; Miller and Friesen, 1986) but also a successful approach to improve competitive position and to cope with rapid and complex changes in the market environment (Acquaah and Yasai-Ardekani, 2008; Pertusa-Ortega *et al.*, 2009). Unlike Porter (1991), they argue that it is false to choose between two orientations (differentiation and cost leadership), and they advise to follow up both the cheaper and better strategies, which will be a sustainable competitive strategy. Chetty and Campbell-Hunt (2003) argue that companies must develop strategies that are capable of capturing as many economies of scale as they can, while also supporting multiple product variants. By this new, hybrid strategy, companies do not rely on a single generic strategy, but companies integrate the generic strategies and successfully pursue the cost leadership and differentiation strategies simultaneously. Differentiation enables the company to charge premium prices, and cost leadership allows the company to charge the lowest competitive price.

International Entrepreneurship and Competitive Strategies: Empirical Evidence from Central Europe

The objective of this research study is to identify a possible connection between competitive strategy and activities on international markets in the internationalisation of the studied enterprises. The analysis aimed at a better understanding of the relationship between competitive strategy and international activities of Czech enterprises. The direct and indirect relations between these variables are examined in the proposed conceptual model present in Figure 1.

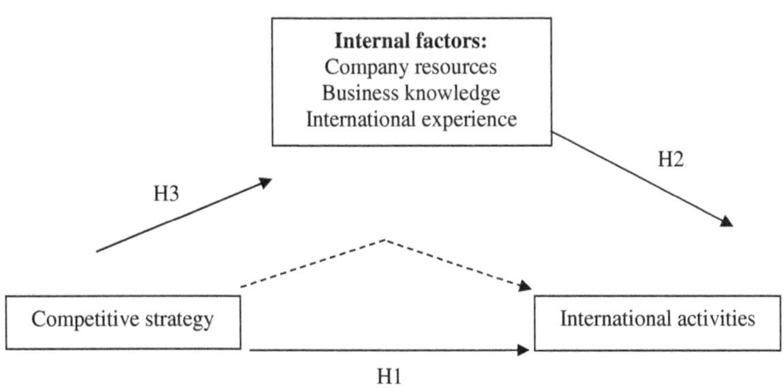

Figure 1: Conceptual Model

Source: Developed by the author.

In relation to the above mentioned, there are three hypotheses based on the theoretical basis and empirical studies:

H1: Competitive strategy is positively related to the activities on international markets.

H2: Internal factors (company resources, business knowledge and international experience) are positively related to the activities on international markets.

H3: Competitive strategy is positively related to the activities on international markets through the mediating effects of internal factors (company resources, business knowledge and international experience).

Based on the research results, the essential characteristics of the competitive strategy of Czech enterprises will be specified. The method of oral questioning and a questionnaire are the principal instruments utilised for researching the competitive strategies of Czech enterprises. The research was carried out in the Czech Republic in the period between May 2018 and May 2019. The research includes primary data collection from top managers of selected Czech enterprises. The sample consists of 450 Czech enterprises located in the Czech Republic. The selection of enterprises under research is based on the method of non-probability purposive sampling, by assumption and random selection. The researched enterprises have already started their internationalisation operations, all of them were incorporated in the Czech Republic and all of them are private enterprises.

The instrument used in the survey, a structured questionnaire, contains five fields of varying degrees of complexity relating to the area of internationalisation. The questionnaire consists of closed, semi-closed and open questions. The questions were designed based on the information gained from experts from business and universities and previous research. In some questions, particularly those related to the entry mode choice and market choice, simple and complex scales were used, mostly the Likert-type scale (5 = strongly agree to 1 = strongly disagree). Also, the questionnaire included four questions related to the enterprise background (the type of a business sector on the domestic market and international markets; the size of the enterprise measured by the number of employees and the revenue; the year of enterprise foundation; and the year of the first foreign market entry). The questionnaire was pre-tested for the instrument validity by 20 managers. In interviews, the managers were asked to respond to the items measuring the theoretical construct. They were also requested to identify any ambiguities revealed in the questionnaire draft. Based on the feedback, some minor changes in the wording were made. Because of the relatively low response rate in mail surveys in the Czech Republic, and sensitivity to Czech managers' concerns about industrial espionage, a high level of personal involvement consisting of telephone calls and personal delivery and pickup of questionnaires was necessary. First, telephone calls were made with general managers or CEOs of the Czech enterprises to explain the purpose of the study and to ask for their participation. The questionnaire was hand-distributed to the general managers and CEOs after a telephone appointment. Trained research assistants helped the managers and CEOs complete the questionnaire and explained any items that the respondents wished to have clarified. This procedure resulted in 600 matched questionnaires, out of which 150 were eliminated due to the incompleteness of responses. Thus, 450 (a response rate of 75.0%) questionnaires were used in the subsequent data analysis and statistical processing.

What follows is an overview of the question types used in the research. The dependent variable *international activities* was measured by subjective ratings. We asked the respondents to evaluate the present company's international activities and its performance 3 years ago, relative to other companies in the same industry, using a five-item, five-point Likert-type measure adopted for this study. The question was "The level of company performance of international activities has had a positive trend over the last 3 years: (1 = totally disagree; 5 = totally agree)". Cronbach's α of this measure was 0.84. The mean rating by top managers was 3.64, with a standard deviation of 1.042.

The independent variable *business strategy* was measured by subjective indicators included using a dichotomous variable, assigned 1 for receiving differentiation strategy and 0 for cost strategy. Competitive strategies can be classified according to their level and types. This research study focuses on Porter's (1980a, 1985, 1991) typology of competitive strategies. The findings show that most respondents (82.3%) are applying the differentiation approach, and only 17.7% apply cost leadership.

We have included mediating variables, referred to as internal factors. We have selected these moderating variables: company resources, business knowledge and international experience. *Company resources* are monitored in the categories tangible resources and intangible resources.

Respondents identified their most significant resources. The most important resources were resources of intangible character (81%). *Business knowledge* measures knowledge of international markets and knowledge of practices in international markets by company management. The knowledge of international markets plays a key role in the process of the realisation of international entrepreneurial activities. Knowledge contributes to increased competitiveness of entrepreneurial subjects in international markets. Questions on business knowledge of managers were presented in the form of five-point scales (5 = strongly agree, 4 = agree, 3 = neutral, 2 = disagree and 1 = strongly disagree) to ensure maximal respondent specificity. All multi-item measures achieved superior or adequate reliability scores in tests using Cronbach's alpha. The alpha values range from 0.74 to 0.82. As for *International experience* with international activities, we measured at the company level using prior work international experiences (by years) in keeping with prior management research. International experience includes prior work in a company with international entrepreneurial activities. The average rate of international experience as measured by the number of years was seven years (minimum 0 years, maximum 45 years).

Guided by current research and empirical evidence, we have included several control variables. Among the company-level determinants of company performance, the company's size and company age are the two widely used demographic characteristics of companies. Therefore, we include *company size* (which is measured as natural logarithm of the number of employees) and *company age* (in years). The enterprises differed as to their size, assessed by the number of employees so that 53% of the sample consists of small enterprises, 29% medium ones and large ones 18%. The EUROSTAT (2011) and the Czech Statistical Office (2013) classify enterprises by a wide range of variables such as sales revenues and the number of employees. This research study follows the conventional idea (European idea) that small and medium-sized enterprises have less than 250 employees (microenterprises have less than 10 employees, small enterprises have less than 50 employees and medium-sized enterprises have between 50 and 250 employees). The average company age of the respondents is 26 years. We also work with the *industry level* of the company: whether the company operates in manufacturing, the service sector or in other sectors. The final research sample consisted of 27% of companies representing manufacturing, 19% service enterprises and 54% commercial enterprises.

Table 1: Pearson Correlations

Variables	Mean	S.D.	1	2	3	4	5	6	7	8
Activities	3.64	1.04	1	—	—	—	—	—	—	—
Size	4540.15	34416.19	0.062	1	—	—	—	—	—	—
Age	28.59	41.97	−0.071	0.203*	1	—	—	—	—	—
Industry	9.73	5.18	0.052	0.045	−0.071	1	—	—	—	—
Strategy	4.02	0.91	0.371**	0.034	−0.192*	−0.091	1	—	—	—
Resources	2.21	0.46	−0.035	0.065	−0.004	−0.132	0.261**	1	—	—
Knowledge	3.88	0.88	−0.039	0.305**	0.052	0.107*	0.042	0.121	1	—
Experience	6.40	8.54	0.062	0.091	−0.102	−0.031	0.161**	0.111	0.242**	1

Notes: *Correlation is significant at the 0.05 level.
**Correlation is significant at the 0.01 level.
Source: Own research.

The analysis began by examining the correlation between variables. All variables were screened to reveal their distribution through Pearson correlation coefficients (Table 1).

Since the descriptive data revealed a promising variation as well as the correlation among the variables included in the model, the results seem to support the hypotheses. The second phase of research includes the analytical method: Hierarchical regression analysis.

Hierarchical regression has been used to test the hypotheses with international activities as the dependent variable. We tested the impact of competitive strategy and internal factors on international activities, controlling for company size, company age and industry type. The results of the analyses are presented in Table 2. We entered the control variables as the first block, Model 1. The regression equation in Model 1 is statistically significant (F = 2.724, $p < 0.05$). The control variables explain 17.1% of the variance in Model 1. Model 1 in Table 2 shows that control variables are not significantly associated with international activities of Czech enterprises.

The competitive strategy variable was entered into the regression as the second block, Model 2. The incremental explanatory prediction on international activities was significant in the regression; ΔR2 was 0.210. The regression equation in Model 2 is statistically significant (F = 4.701, $p < 0.01$). The independent variables explain 38.1% of the variance in Model 2. The multicollinearity test showed that the VIF of independent

Table 2: Regression Results for International Activities

	Model 1	Model 2	Model 3
Size	0.031(0.000)	0.032(0.000)	0.035(0.000)
Age	−0.001(0.001)	−0.01(0.001)	−0.002(0.001)
Industry	0.080(0.048)	0.095(0.048)	0.094(0.048)
Strategy H1	—	0.389(0.115)**	0.339(0.115)**
Resources H2a	—	—	−0.364(0.032)
Knowledge H2b	—	—	−0.0137(0.112)
Experience H2c	—	—	0.192(0.113)
Model R^2	0.171	0.381	0.563
ΔR^2	0.171	0.210	0.182
F	2.724*	4.701**	5.571**

Notes: [a] Unstandardised coefficients are reported, with standard errors in brackets. The changes in R^2 in Models 2–3 are in comparison with the value of R^2 in the model to their left.
Value of Durbin-Watson is 1.942.
*$p < 0.05$; **$p < 0.01$.
Source: Developed by the author.

variables in the final model ranged from 1.015 to 1.053 and the factor of tolerance ranged from 0.950 to 0.985. These values indicate no serious problems with multicollinearity. Hypothesis 1 claiming that the competitive strategy is positively related to international activities was supported. The internal factors (company resources, business knowledge and international experience) were then entered as the third block, Model 3. The change in model R^2 of 0.182 was significant. The regression equation in Model 3 is statistically significant ($F = 5.571, p < 0.01$). The independent variables explain 56.3% of the variance in Model 3. An examination of the variance inflation factor VIF of the independent variable (ranging from 1.015 to 1.065) and a factor of tolerance showed a range of 0.939 to 0.985 in the final model. These values indicate no serious problems with multicollinearity. Hypothesis 2 claiming that the internal factors are positively related to international activities was not supported.

To examine Hypothesis 3 claiming that internal factors (company resources, business knowledge and international experience) have a mediating role between competitive strategy and international activities, we entered the interaction terms into the hierarchical regression analysis. Table 3 shows these results.

Table 3: Regression Results for Multiple Mediation[a]

	Unstandard Coefficient B	Standard Coefficient Beta	*t*	95% Confidence Interval
Competitive strategy to mediators' internal factors H3	0.351(0.165)**	0.152**	3.365	(0.123; 0.656)
Mediators' internal factors to international activities H2	0.099(0.032)**	0.142**	3.105	(0.037; 0.162)
Competitive strategy to international activities H1	0.389(0.115)**	0.154**	3.375	(0.162; 0.615)
Sobel test z		**2.287****		

Notes: [a]Unstandardised coefficients are reported, with standard errors in brackets. Bootstrap results are provided for the lower and upper bounds of 95% confidence intervals.
*$p < 0.05$, ** $p < 0.01$.
Source: Developed by the author.

Table 4: Direct, Indirect and Total Effects for Mediation Model

	Estimate	95% Confidence Interval
Direct effect		
Strategy — international activities H1	0.389	(0.162; 0.615)**
Strategy — internal factors H3	0.351	(0.123; 0.656)**
Internal factors — international activities H2	0.099	(0.037; 0.162)**
Indirect effect		
Strategy — internal factors — international activities	0.032	(0.009; 0.074)**
Total effect		
Strategy — success	0.333	(0.130; 0.515)**

Notes: Bootstrap results are provided for the lower and upper bounds of 95% confidence intervals.
*$p < 0.05$, ** $p < 0.01$.
Source: Developed by the author.

While these results provide information about the association between the mediators and the dependent variables consistent with the results reported in Tables 2 and 3, they also provide information about the association between the independent variable and each mediator, controlling for the other mediators. Hypothesis 3 was confirmed.

Table 4 shows the results for the mediation model. In the model, the competitive strategy has a significant total effect on the international activities' variable. However, when the internal factors are introduced as mediator, the competitive strategy variable substantially reduces its direct effect on the international activities' construct, although it remains significant, while its indirect effect through the internal factors' variable achieves an important and significant point estimate of 0.032. We have additionally calculated the variance accounted for (VAF) index that determines the size of the indirect effect in relation to the total effect. A VAF value below 20% indicates a small mediation. In our case, the indirect effect achieves a VAF of 10%. When internal factors are introduced as mediator, the competitive strategy substantially reduces the direct effect on the international activities.

Conclusion

The competitive strategies of Czech companies on international markets were monitored in terms of Porter's competitive strategy (generic strategies). We found that Czech companies primarily used differentiation focus for international markets (Table 5).

The cost leadership strategy was most frequently reported by medium-sized enterprises (55%) from the manufacturing industry. Enterprises with a cost leadership strategy have declared their dominant tangible resources and below-common knowledge about international markets by their management. About half of the enterprises with cost leadership strategy reported that their managers had no experience with international activities, while the remaining managers had experience ranging from 5 to 18 years. The average number of years of experience with the international activities of managers in these enterprises is ten years.

Table 5: Competitive Strategy of Czech Companies on International Markets (%)

Strategy	**(%)**
Cost leadership	5.6
Cost focus	1.7
Differentiation	41.8
Differentiation focus	50.8

Source: Own research.

The cost focus strategy was most frequently reported by medium-sized enterprises (67%) from agriculture, manufacturing and retail trade. Enterprises with a cost focus strategy have declared their dominant intangible resources (specialised knowledge and knowledge of markets) and below-average level of knowledge about international markets by their management. Approximately one-third of the sample reported that their managers had no experience with international activities, while the remaining managers had experience ranging from 12 to 15 years. The average number of years of experience with the international activities of managers in these enterprises is 14 years.

The differentiation strategy was most frequently reported by large (34%) enterprises from manufacturing. Enterprises with differentiation strategies have declared their dominant tangible and intangible resources (specialised knowledge and international contacts) and above-average level of knowledge about international markets by their management. About 30% of the sample reported that their managers had no experience with international activities, while the remaining managers had experience ranging from 1 to 23 years. The average number of years of experience with the international activities of managers in these enterprises is nine years.

Mostly, microenterprises and small enterprises (34%) from manufacturing used the differentiation focus strategy. Enterprises with the differentiation focus strategy have declared their dominant intangible resources (specialised knowledge and international contacts) and the average level of knowledge about international markets by their management. Approximately 40% of the sample reported that their managers had no experience with international activities. Moreover, the remaining managers had experience ranging from 2 to 60 years. The average number of years of experience with the international activities of managers in these enterprises is 13 years.

The results indicate that the strategy of most Czech enterprises in international markets is driven by the differentiation strategy and differentiation focus strategy. A differentiation focus strategy is appropriate where the target customer segment is not price sensitive. The market is competitive or saturated, and customers have particular needs that are possibly under-served, and the enterprise has unique resources and capabilities which enable the enterprise to satisfy these needs in just those ways that are difficult to copy (Porter, 1985). The selection of the appropriate competitive strategy on international markets by Czech enterprises is affected by several variables: industry, resources and knowledge of international markets. The industry is a variable that is statistically significant only for cost leadership strategy. The variable is negatively related to the dependent variables, while the variables of resources and knowledge are statistically significant for the differentiation strategy and differentiation focus strategy. Resources and knowledge of international markets are positively related to the likelihood of a competitive strategy. The variable knowledge of international markets has the most significant projected impact. The remaining variables such as enterprise size and experience with international activities are not statistically significant for the selection of competitive strategy on foreign markets.

The globalisation of the economy offers new opportunities to enterprises, resulting from their access to more significant markets, scale economies and exposure to best practice management and technology. However, globalisation also poses and invites new competitive challenges, either by local and international competitors, with new production processes and innovative products and services. In response to these challenges, enterprises try to conquer new international markets and expand their present ones and operate in the global market (Pereira *et al.*, 2009). Internationalisation is a fundamental element of competitiveness for enterprises, reflecting on the performance, determined by own business, industry and environmental factors.

The term internationalisation of entrepreneurial activities refers to all those activities which involve cross-border transactions of goods, services and resources between two or more nations. The internationalisation of entrepreneurial activities is represented by a geographic expansion of activities across national borders (Lopez *et al.*, 2009). Enterprises go international for a variety of reasons, but the common goal is still the enterprise growth or expansion. The internationalisation of entrepreneurship activities ranks among long-lasting strategic decisions; these decisions result in significant changes, with the running of the enterprise being the most relevant. Studies of international entrepreneurship often focus on the pattern and speed with which new enterprises break into foreign markets (Jones *et al.*, 2011; McDougall *et al.*, 1994; Sapienza *et al.*, 2005; Zhou *et al.*, 2010). In the last decade, the strategies of internationalisation have been included among the most relevant topics in managerial literature. New perspectives are flourishing, and new approaches combine different methods, knowledge and competencies.

References

Acedo, F. J. and J. Florin (2006). An entrepreneurial cognition perspective on the internationalization of SME's. *Journal of International Entrepreneurship*, 4, 49–67.

Acedo, F. J. and M. V. Jones (2007). Speed of internationalization and entrepreneurial cognition: Insights and a comparison between international new ventures, exporters and domestic firms. *Journal of World Business*, 42(3), 236–252.

Acquaah, M. and M. Yasani-Ardekani (2007). Does the implementation of a combination competitive strategy yield incremental performance benefits? A new perspective from a transition economy in Sub-Saharan Africa. *Journal of Business Research*, 61, 346–354.

Ahmad, S. Z. and P. J. Kitchen (2008). Transnational corporations from Asian developing countries. The internationalization characteristics and business strategies of Sime Darby Berhad. *Internal Journal of Business Science and Applied Management*, 3(2), 21–36.

Allred, B. B. and K. S. Swan (2004). Contextual influences on international subsidiaries' product technology strategy. *Journal of International Management*, 10, 259–286.

Alvarez, S. A., J. B. BARNEY, and P. Anderson (2013). Forming and exploiting opportunities: The implications of discovery and creation processes for entrepreneurial and organizational research. *Organization Science*, 24(1), 301–317.

Anokhin, S., J. Wincent, and E. Autio (2011). Operationalizing opportunities in entrepreneurship research: Use of data envelopment analysis. *Small Business Economics*, 37, 39–57.

Autio, E. (2005). Creative tension: The significance of Ben Oviatt's and Patricia McDougall's article "Toward a Theory of International New Ventures". *Journal of International Business Studies*, 36(1), 9–19.

Barney, J. B. (1997). *Gaining and Sustaining Competitive Advantage*. New York: Addison-Wesley Publishing Company, Inc.

Baronchelli, G. and F. Cassia (2008). Internationalization of the firm: Stage approach vs. Global approach. In *8th Global Conference on Business & Economics*, pp. 1–33. Italy.

Barringer, B. R. and D. W. Greening (1998). Small business growth through geographic expansion: A comparative case study. *Journal of Business Venturing*, 13, 467–492.

Bell, J. (2005). The internationalization of small computer software firms a further challenge to stage theories. *European Journal of Marketing*, 29(8), 60–75.

Butler, J. E., R. Doktor, and F. A. Lins (2010). Linking international entrepreneurship to uncertainty, opportunity discovery, and cognition. *Journal of International Entrepreneurship*, 8(2), 121–134.

Calof, J. (1994). The relation between firm size and export behaviour revisited. *Journal of International Business Studies*, 25(2), 367–387.

Casson, M. C. (1982). *The Entrepreneur: An Economic Theory*. Oxford: Martin Robertson.

Casson, M. C. (2000). An entrepreneurial theory of the firm. In *Competence, Governance and Entrepreneurship: Advances in Economic Strategy Research*, N. J. Foss and V. Mahnke (ed.), Oxford: Oxford University Press, pp. 116–145.

Casson, M. and A. Godley (2007). Revisiting the emergence of the modern business enterprise: Entrepreneurship and the springer global distribution system. *Journal of Management Studies*, 44, 1064–1077.

Casson, M., K. Dark, and M. A. Gulamhussen (2009). Extending internalisation theory: From the multinational enterprise to the knowledge-based empire. *International Business Review*, 18, 236–256.

Cavusgil, C. T. and G. Knight (2015). The born global firm: An entrepreneurial and capabilities perspective on early and rapid internationalization. *Journal of International Business Studies*, 46(1), 3–16.

Chaffee, E. E. (1985). Three models of strategy. *The Academy of Management Review*, 10(1), 89–98.

Chandra, Y., C. Styles, and I. F. Wilkinson (2009). The recognition of first time international entrepreneurial opportunities: Evidence from firms in knowledge-based industries. *International Marketing Review*, 26(1), 30–61.

Chandra, Y., C. Styles, and I. F. Wilkinson (2012). An opportunity-based view of rapid internationalization. *Journal of International Marketing*, 20(1), 74–102.

Chetty, S. and C. Campbell-Hunt (2003). Paths to internationalization among small-to medium-sized firms: A global versus regional approach. *European Journal of Marketing*, 37(5/6), 796.

Coviello, N. E. (2015). Re-thinking research on born globals. *Journal of International Business Studies*, 46(1), 17–26.

Covin, J. G. and D. P. Slevin (1991). A conceptual model of entrepreneurship as a firm behaviour. *Entrepreneurship Theory Practice*, 16(1), 7–24.

Czech Statistical Office (2013). The Czech Republic since Year 1989 in the Numbers, http://www.czso.cz/csu/redakce.nsf/i/cr_od_roku_1989 (accessed on May 11, 2019).

Czinkota, M. R. and I. A. Ronkainen (1998). *International Marketing*. Chicago: The Dryden Press.

Davidsson, P. (2004). *Researching Entrepreneurship* (*International Studies in Entrepreneurship*), 5. New York: Springer.

Davidsson, P. (2015). Entrepreneurial opportunities and the entrepreneurship nexus: A re-conceptualization. *Journal of Business Venturing*, 30(5), 674–695.

Di Gregorio, D., M. Musteen, and D. E. Thomas (2008). International new ventures: The cross-border nexus of individuals and opportunities. *Journal of World Business*, 43(2), 186–196.

Dib, L. A., A. Rocha, and J. F. Silva (2010). The internationalization process of Brazilian software firms and the born global phenomenon: Examining firm, network, and entrepreneur variables. *Journal of International Entrepreneurship*, 8(3), 233–253.

Dimov, D. (2011). Grappling with the unbearable elusiveness of entrepreneurial opportunities. *Entrepreneurship Theory and Practice*, 35(1), 57–81.

Dunning, J. H. (2000). The eclectic pradigma as an envelope for economic and business theories of MNE activity. *International Business Review*, 9(2), 163–190.

Eckhardt, J. and S. Shane (2003). Opportunities and entrepreneurship. *Journal of Management*, 29, 333–349.

Ellis, P. D (2011). Social Ties and International Entrepreneurship: Opportunities and Constraints Affecting Firm Internationalization. *Journal of International Business Studies*, 38(7), 99–127.

EUROSTAT (2011). Summary Indicators — Employment Size Classes for EU25/EU27 (all NACE activities), https://appsso.eurostat.ec.europa.eu/nui/show.do?dataset=jvs_q_nace2&lang=en (accessed on May 10, 2019).

Feio, P. A. (1998). *Território e Competitividade: Uma perspectiva geográfica do processo de internacionalizacao do sector cerámico*. Lisbon: Edicores Colibri.

Garud, R., J. Gehman, and A. P. Giuliani (2014). Contextualizing entrepreneurial innovation: A narrative perspective. *Research Policy*, 43(7), 1177–1188.

Grant, R. M. (1991). The resource-based theory of competitive advantage: Implications for strategy formulation. *California Management Review*, 33(3), 114–135.

Grégoire, D. A. and D. A. Shepherd (2012). Technology-market combinations and the identification of entrepreneurial opportunities: An investigation of the opportunity-individual nexus. *Academy of Management Journal*, 55(4), 753–785.

Grégoire, D. A., P. S. Barr, and D. A. Shepherd (2010). Cognitive processes of opportunity recognition: The role of structural alignment. *Organization Science*, 21(2), 413–431.

Higon, D. and A. N. Driffield (2007). Exporting and innovation performance: Analysis of the annual small business survey in the UK. Economics and Strategy Group, Aston Business School, Aston University, https://www.etsg.org/ETSG2007/papers/higon.pdf, (accessed on May 10, 2019).

Hill, C. W. L. (1988). Differentiation versus low cost or differentiation and low cost: A contingency framework. *Academy of Management Review*, 13, 401–412.

Johanson, J. and J. E. Vahlne (1977). The internationalization process of the firm — A model of knowledge development and increasing foreign market commitments. *Journal of International Business Studies*, 8(1), 23–32.

Johanson, J. and J. E. Vahlne (2006). Commitment and opportunity development in the internationalization process: A note on the Uppsala internationalization process model. *Management International Review*, 46, 165–178.

Johanson, J. and J. E. Vahlne (2009). The Uppsala internationalization process model revisited: From liability of foreignness to liability of outsidership. *Journal of International Business Studies*, 40(9), 1411–1431.

Johanson, J. and F. Wiedersheim-Paul (1975). The internationalization of the firm — four Swedish case studies. *Journal of Management Studies*, 12, 305–322.

Jones, M. V. (2001). First steps in internationalization. Concepts and evidence from a sample of small high-technology firms. *Journal of International Management*, 7(2001), 191–210.

Jones, M. V., N. Coviello, and Y. K. Tang (2011). International entrepreneurship research (1989-2009): A domain ontology and thematic analysis. *Journal of Business Venturing*, 26(6), 632–659.

Karra, N., N. Philips, and P. Tracey (2008). Building the born global firm: Developing entrepreneurial capabilities for international new venture success. *Long Range Planning*, 41(4), 440–458.

Keupp, M. M. and O. Gassmann (2009). The past and the future of international entrepreneurship: A review and suggestions for developing the field. *Journal of Management*, 35(3), 600–633.

Knight, G. A. (2000). Entrepreneurship and marketing strategy: The SME under globalization. *Journal of International Marketing*, 8(2), 12–32.

Knight, G. A. and S. T. Cavusgil (2004). Innovation, organizational capabilities, and the born-global firm. *Journal of International Business Studies*, 8, 11–26.

Knight, G. A. and P. W. Liesch (2016). Internationalization: From incremental to born global. *Journal of World Business*, 51(1), 93–102.

Koch, A. J. (2001). Factors influencing market and entry mode selection: Developing the MEMS model. *Marketing Intelligence & Planning*, 19(5), 411–432.

Kotler, P. (2012). *Kotler on Marketing.* New York: Simon & Schuster.

Kropp, F., N. J. Lindasay, and A. Shoham (2006). Entrepreneurial, market, and learning orientations and international entrepreneurial — business venture performance in South African firms. *International Marketing Review*, 23(5), 504–523.

Lopez, L. E., S. K. Kundu, and L. Ciravegna (2009). Born global or born regional? Evidence from an exploratory study in the Costa Rican software industry. *Journal of International Business Studies*, 40(7), 1228–1238.

Lu, J. W. and P. W. Beamish (2006). Partnering strategies and performance of SMEs international joint ventures. *Journal of Business Venturing*, 21(4), 285–307.

Lumpkin, G. T. and G. G. Dess (1996). Clarifying the entrepreneurial orientation construct and linking it to performance. *Academy of Management Review*, 21, 135–172.

Luo, Y. D. and H. X. Zhao (2004). Corporate link and competitive strategy in multinational enterprises: A perspective from subsidiaries seeking host market penetration. *Journal of International Management*, 10, 77–105.

MacMullen, J. S. and D. A. Shepherd (2006). Entrepreneurial action and the role of uncertainty in the theory of the entrepreneur. *Academy of Management Review*, 31(1), 132–152.

Mainella, T., V. Puhakka, and P. Servais (2014). The concept of international opportunity in international entrepreneurship: A review and a research agenda. *International Journal of Management Reviews*, 16(1), 105–129.

Mathews, J. A. and I. Zander (2007). The international entrepreneurial dynamics of accelerated internationalization. *Journal of International Business Studies*, 38(3), 387–403.

McDougall, P. P. and B. M. Oviatt (2000). International entrepreneurship: The intersection of two research paths. *Academical Management Journal*, 43, 902–906.

McDougall, P. P., S. Shane, and B. M. Oviatt (1994). Explaining the formation of international new ventures: The limits of theories from international business research. *Journal of Business Venturing*, 9(6): 469–487.

McDougall-Covin, P., M. V. Jones, and M. G. Serapio (2014). High-potential concepts, phenomena, and theories for the advancement of entrepreneurship research. *Entrepreneurship Theory and Practice*, 38(1), 1–10.

Miller, D. and P. H. Friesen (1978). Archetypes of strategy formulation. *Management Science*, 24(9), 921–933.

Miller, D. and P. H. Friesen (1986). Porter's (1980) generic strategies and performance: An empirical examination with American data. Part II: Performance implications. *Organization Studies*, 7, 255–261.

Moen, O. and P. Servais (2002). Born global or gradual global? Examining the export behavior of small and medium-sized enterprises. *Journal of International Marketing*, 10, 49–72.

Morrow, J. F. (1988). International entrepreneurship. A new growth opportunity. *New Management*, 3, 59–61.

Mort, G., J. Weerawardena, and P. Liesch (2012). Advancing entrepreneurial marketing: Evidence from born global firms. *European Journal Marketing*, 46(3), 542–561.

Muzychenko, O. (2008). Cross-cultural entrepreneurial competence in identifying international business opportunities. *European Management Journal*, 26(6), 366–377.

Oviatt, B. M. and P. P. McDougall (1994). Toward a theory of international new ventures. *Journal of International Business Studies*, 25(1), 45–64.

Oviatt, B. M. and P. P. McDougall (2005a). Towards a theory of international new ventures. *Journal of International Business Studies*, 36(1), 29–41.

Oviatt, B. M. and P. P. McDougall (2005b). The internationalization of entrepreneurship. *Journal of International Business Studies*, 36, 2–8.

Peiris, I. K., M. E. M. Akoorie, and P. Sinha (2012). International entrepreneurship: A critical analysis of studies in the past two decades and future directions for research. *Journal of International Entrepreneurship*, 10(4), 279–324.

Pereira, E. T., A. J. Fernandes, and H. M. M. Diz (2009). Internationalization as a competitiveness factor: The case of the Portuguese ceramic firms. University of Aveiro, https://www.etsg.org/ETSG2009/papers/pereira.pdf (accessed on August 14, 2019).

Pertusa-Ortega, E. M., F. M.-A. José, and E.C.-C. Claver-Cortés (2008). Competitive strategies and firm performance: A comparative analysis of pure, hybrid and "Stuck-in-The-Middle" strategies in Spanish firms. *British Journal of Management*, 20(4), 508–523.

Porter, M. E. (1980a). *Competitive Strategy*. New York: Free Press.

Porter, M. E. (1980b). *Competitive Strategy: Techniques for Analyzing Industries and Competitors*. New York: Free Press.

Porter, M. E. (1985). *Competitive Advantage*. New York: Free Press

Porter, M. E. (1991). Towards a dynamic theory of strategy. *Strategy Management Journal*, 12, 95–117.

Porter, M. E. (1996). What is strategy? *Harvard Business Review*, 74(6), 61.

Porter, M. E. (2001). Strategy and the internet. *Harvard Business Review*, March, 66–78.

Ramoglou, S. and E. W. K. Tsang (2016). A realistic perspective of entrepreneurship: Opportunities as propensities. *Academy of Management Review*, 41(3), 410–434.

Raynard, P. and M. Forstater (2002). Corporate social responsibility: Implication for small and medium enterprises in developing countries. United Nations Industrial Development Organization UNIDO, Vienna.

Reuber, A. R., G. A. Knight, P. W. Liesch, and L. Zhou (2018). International entrepreneurship: The pursuit of entrepreneurial opportunities across national borders. *Journal of International Business Studies*, 49, 395–406.

Ruzzier, M., R. D. Hisrich, and B. Antoncic (2006). SME internationalization research: Past, present, and future. *Journal of Small Business and Enterprise Development*, 13, 476–497.

Sapienza, H. J., D. Declercq, and W. R. Sandberg (2005). Antecedents of international and domestic learning effort. *Journal of Business Venturing*, 20(4), 437–457.

Sarasvathy, S., N. Dew, S. Velamuri, and S. Venkataraman (2003). Three views of entrepreneurial opportunity. In *Handbook of Entrepreneurship Research: An Interdisciplinary Survey and Introduction*. Z. Acs, and D. Audretsch (ed.), New York: Springer, pp. 141–160.

Schulz, A., T. Borghoff, and S. Kraus (2009). International entrepreneurship: Towards a theory of SME internationalization. *International Journal of Business and Economics*, 9(1), 1–12.

Schumpeter, J. (1934). *The Theory of Economic Development*, 1st ed., Cambridge, Massachusets: Harvard University Press.

Shane, S. (2000). Prior knowledge and the discovery of entrepreneurial opportunities. *Organization Science*, 11, 448–469.

Shane, S. (2012). Reflections of the 2010 AMR decade award: Delivering on the promise on entrepreneurship as a field of research. *Academy of Management Review*, 37(1), 10–20.

Shane, S. and S. Venkataraman (2000). The promise of entrepreneurship as a field of research. *Academy of Management Review*, 25, 217–226.

Short, J., D. Ketchen, C. Shook, and R. D. Ireland (2010). The concept of “Opportunity” in entrepreneurship research: Past accomplishments and future challenges. *Journal of Management*, 36, 40–65.

Sliwiński, R. (2012). Internationalization strategies of Polish fast growing enterprises. *Poznań University of Economics Review*, 12(1), 17–39.

Stark, C. E., L. E. Moss, and D. E. Hahn (2002). Farm business goals and competitive advantage. In *Proceeding of American Agricultural Economics Association Annual Meeting,* California: American Agricultural Economics Association, pp. 28–31.

Styles, C. and R. G. Seymour (2006). Opportunities for marketing researchers in international entrepreneurship. *International Marketing Review*, 23(2), 126–145.

Theosidou, M. and E. R. Morgan (2007). Managerial, organizational and external drivers of sales effectiveness in export market ventures. *Journal of the Academy of Marketing Science*, 35(2), 270–283.

Twarowska, K. and M. Kakol (2013). International business strategy. reasons and forms of expansion into foreign markets. In *International Conference 2013 Active Citizenship by Knowledge Management & Innovation. Management, Knowledge and Learning*, Zadar, pp. 1005–1011.

Williams, D. W. and D. A. Grégoire (2015). Seeking commonalities or avoiding differences? Re-conceptualizing distance and its effects on internationalization decisions. *Journal of International Business Studies*, 46(3), 253–284.

Wood, M. S., A. McKelvie, and J. M. Haynie (2014). Making it personal: Opportunity individuation and the shaping of opportunity beliefs. *Journal of Business Venturing*, 29(2), 252–272.

Zahra, S. A. (2005). A theory of international new ventures: A decade of research. *Journal of International Business Studies*, 36(1), 20–28.

Zahra, S. A. and George, G. (2002). International entrepreneurship: The current status of the field and future research agenda. In Hitt, M., Ireland, D., Sexton, D., and Camp, M. (Eds.), Strategic entrepreneurship: Creating an integrated mindset (pp. 255–288). Malden, MA: Blackwell Publishers.

Zahra, S. A., J. S. Korn, and J. F. Yu (2005). Cognition and international entrepreneurship implications for research on international opportunity recognition and exploitation. *International Business Review*, 14(2), 129–149.

Zander, I., P. McDougall-Covin, and E. L. Rose (2015). Born globals and international business evolution of a field of research. *Journal of International Business Studies*, 46(1), 27–35.

Zhou, L., B. Barnes, and Y. Lu (2010). Entrepreneurial proclivity, capability upgrading, and performance advantage of newness among international new ventures. *Journal of International Business Studies*, 41(5), 882–905.

Zucchella, A. and P. Scabini (2007). *International Entrepreneurship — Theoretical Foundations and Practice*. New York: Palgrave MacMillan.

https://doi.org/10.1142/9789811228445_0007

Chapter 7

The Value of Talent Management to Entrepreneurial Spinoff Teams

Alexandra Kriz[*,†], Miriam Moeller[*,‡], Emily Russo[*,§] and Peter Liesch[*,¶]

[*]*University of Queensland, Brisbane, Queensland, Australia*

[†]*a.kriz@business.uq.edu.au*

[‡]*m.moeller@business.uq.edu.au*

[§]*e.russo@business.uq.edu.au*

[¶]*p.liesch@business.uq.edu.au*

If you want to go fast, go alone; if you want to go far, go together.

African Proverb

Abstract

Through this chapter, we explore the role of talent management in the context of entrepreneurial spinoff teams. Based on our conceptual model, we propose that understanding the complex talent dynamic in spinoffs during their incubation journey may facilitate more effective spinoff management and technology commercialisation success. We draw on Garnsey's *Theory of the Early Growth of the Firm*, Harper's *Theory of Entrepreneurial Teams* and Timmons' *Model of New Venture Creation* to highlight the potential value of talent management in supporting an entrepreneurial founder and their team to develop an early stage innovation for domestic and global markets. Our exploratory focus outlined in this chapter provides scope for further qualitative and quantitative research in this domain in order to apply and refine our model, and to further bridge together the talent management, entrepreneurship and spinoff literatures.

Keywords: Talent management; Spinoffs; Garnsey; Harper; Timmons; Entrepreneurial teams.

Introduction

Spinoffs facilitate commercialisation by taking or "spinning" a technology or novel concept out of a parent firm (such as a university, publicly funded research institute or corporate venture) (Parhankangas and Arenius, 2003). This process is designed to support the development of the technology or novel concept by enabling it to be managed relatively independently from the parent and to focus on its commercial development. However, the dynamic between the team and the "widget" to be commercialised is a complex one. In the words of respected Australian investor, Bill Bartee, "A great team can fix a broken technology, a great technology can't fix a broken team. So, people are a vital part of how we assess potential. They are probably an order of magnitude more important than the technology itself..."

Bartee's sentiments about the importance of the team are echoed within the entrepreneurship literature (e.g. Yusubova *et al.*, 2020). However, while significant research has been conducted on managing talent in large, established multinational companies, the talent management[1] (TM) literature has lacked an understanding of how "parent" firms manage a team of entrepreneurial talent as they grow the resource base for a spinoff venture. Given the importance that spinoffs play in facilitating the global diffusion of innovation, it is surprising we do not have a better

[1]Note that, given that the field of TM is still nascent (Scullion and Collings, 2011), we take a holistic approach to TM that encompasses both global talent management (GTM) and TM literatures. While GTM is likely to be more relevant for spinoffs at a later stage of their development (for example, if they mature into established multinational enterprises), there may be instances where global talent is involved in a spinoff's incubation and inception. Therefore, while we adopt the term "TM", we use this term in such a way that is inclusive of the concept of GTM and the associated literature.

understanding of how to successfully nurture entrepreneurial teams involved in spinning off a new venture from a parent. The TM literature discusses the importance of attracting, developing and retaining talent (Collings *et al.*, 2019; Tarique and Schuler, 2010), and in our context, we propose that the parent has an important role (albeit not an exclusive role) in attracting, selecting and developing the talent base of the spinoff's founding entrepreneurial team.

We apply Elizabeth Garnsey's Penrosean-inspired *Theory of the Early Growth of the Firm* (TEGF) to understand the early developmental phases that incubated firms with access to a parent (i.e. spinoffs) encounter. In doing so, we explore the parent's influence in managing the talent of the entrepreneurial spinoff team in the context of Garnsey's growth phases. Garnsey discusses several early growth phases that young firms typically experience on their path to independent growth. We build on Garnsey's theory by integrating a discussion of Harper's (2008) *Theory of Entrepreneurial Teams* (TET) to identify how the development of entrepreneurial teams, in conjunction with the development of the early growth spinoff, is a valuable component to examine in the context of TM during a spinoff's "gestation" period. Furthermore, since a spinoff represents the creation of a new venture separate to the parent, we draw on the emphasis placed upon entrepreneurial teams in Timmons' model of new venture creation. We focus on entrepreneurial teams specifically since Santos and Cardon (2019) explain that most entrepreneurial firms are founded by teams. Hence, understanding how teams in new firms, such as spinoffs, can function most effectively and yield desired outcomes is a vital and presumably worthwhile exercise.

In scoping this chapter, we have focused on the pre-founding period (in the spinoff's case, gestation), building on previous work on early firm development (Hewerdine and Welch, 2012). We have limited our focus to this phase as the parent has the most direct influence during this period of the firm's development compared to later phases of development when the firm is exposed to a wider range of influences (e.g. talent selection by the company board post-spinoff). When referring to the "parent", we take interest in the constituents of the complex system which operates within the parent including internal staff; consultants and advisory boards employed by or engaged by the parent to support strategic decision-making; and individuals involved in subsidiaries of the parent or in entities that are arms of the parent, and make decisions involving the parent. Furthermore, as previously acknowledged, while the parent does play a major role in terms of shaping the formation of the founding entrepreneurial spinoff team, the process of team formation can be decided by the entrepreneurs themselves as part of an organic process, and this should be considered when understanding talent decisions made during incubation.

We offer exploratory insights on the following puzzle: *How valuable is TM to entrepreneurial spinoff teams?* In responding to this puzzle, we first review the literature relating to spinoffs, and proceed to discuss the scope to apply Garnsey's TEGF to the spinoff context as an underutilised yet insightful lens to understand the early growth phases of firms with access to a parent during their gestation period. We then review the literature pertaining to TM, entrepreneurial talent and entrepreneurial teams, and this discussion of talent and entrepreneurship paves the way for our focus on Harper's TET and Timmons' model for holistically exploring the role of TM in entrepreneurial spinoff teams. We then present a model exploring TM during a spinoff's incubation and evaluate the potential for further development of the model through future empirical work. Finally, we discuss the contributions of our chapter.

Literature Review

Spinoffs

We focus on the importance of talent selection and development during the spinoff process, and therefore, providing a clear interpretation of the term "spinoff" is important. A spinoff refers to the situation when "founding takes the form of the departure of employees" (Ferriani *et al.*, 2012, p. 1012). Spinoffs have also been referred to as "(1) a new legal entity (company); (2) founded by one or more individuals seconded or transferred (sometimes part-time) from a parent organisation; (3) to exploit some kind of knowledge; (4) gained in the parent organisation and transferred to the new company" (De Cleyn and Braet, 2007, pp. 2–3). While the term spinoff suggests a relatively homogenous category, there is considerable heterogeneity among spinoffs (Druilhe and Garnsey, 2004; Woolley, 2017) and diversity in the environment and with parents from which they were spawned. The main source of diversity stems from whether the spinoff emerged from a parent that is research-oriented (e.g. university, publicly funded research institute) or commercially oriented (e.g. multinational). These differences in parents have a significant impact on the spinoff in terms of resource endowments, market orientation, the nature of the technology or new product the spinoff seeks to commercialise, and the experience and competencies of talent transferred from the parent.

While we acknowledge that these differences between spinoff genres are important, for the purposes of this chapter, which is exploratory, we do not confine our discussion to one spinoff type over another. Rather, we seek to initiate a broader and exploratory conceptual discussion in relation to spinoffs as a general family of firms, and thus, to encourage further research that delves into the nuances existing between specific spinoff types. The paucity of research investigating TM as part of the spinoff process suggests that there is a clear avenue to progress this domain given the theoretical and practical importance of understanding the role of talent in influencing how spinoffs can more effectively commercialise innovation.

Projects culminating in a spinoff are more likely to be "explorative" in nature and this is one reason why they may be spun off from a more risk-averse parent. However, a dominant emphasis on "exploring" can be detrimental to the new firm development process and may result in a failure trap of excessive exploration (Gupta *et al.*, 2006). In many ways, this parallels Timmons and Spinelli's (2007) arguments that there is a constant "balancing act" in terms of matching (or mismatching) opportunities, resources and the entrepreneurial team and its activities. Timmons and Spinelli (2007) highlight the "fragility" of this balancing act accompanying the new venture creation process. TM therefore potentially plays a role in overseeing the process by which opportunities, resources and the entrepreneurial team and their activities are matched, and to motivate and incentivise the new venture to avoid a failure trap by encouraging the implementation of disciplines and procedures in the emerging firm (i.e. exploitation) where necessary. The complexity of this balancing act reinforces the value of attracting complementary skillsets as part of a TM strategy that supports ambidexterity (i.e. the ability to undertake radical and incremental innovation) (Harmancioglu *et al.*, 2020). The next section explores the TEGF as a possible lens to assist in understanding the nature of resource base development in a spinoff.

Garnsey's Theory of the Early Growth of the Firm

The TEGF was proposed by Elizabeth Garnsey, who personally knew Edith Penrose (author of the *Theory of the Growth of the Firm*). The key distinction between Garnsey and Penrose in terms of their respective theories is that while Penrose focused on the more mature business that has an established resource base, Garnsey (1998) focuses on embryonic firms developing an early resource base as they progress through "critical junctures" during which decision are made and resources are required. The TEGF (Garnsey, 1998) is of considerable value in terms of understanding the nonlinear and complex growth processes associated with innovative, early growth firms. In particular, Garnsey's theory is of value to spinoffs, as she explicitly refers to situations in which young firms are incubated.

Garnsey's model is not a rigid phase-type model; rather, firms can go back and forward between phases as they develop, or as they regress. Phases may also overlap. Garnsey highlights that various growth phases such as resource access, resource mobilisation and resource generation may occur within a parent and are attributed to what she terms the "privileges" of incubation. While we acknowledge the range of Garnsey's phases depicted in her growth model, the key growth phases that spinoffs are likely to encounter during their gestation are resource access, resource mobilisation and resource generation. We therefore discuss these phases in more detail.

Resource access (Phase I)

Garnsey suggests resource access is the "early prospecting phase" (Garnsey, 1998, p. 531) when opportunities are explored. The founding team is critical in shaping decisions regarding potential opportunities and brings their experiences and knowledge to the prospecting process. The parent can play an important early role in supporting resource access by acting as an incubator and supporting early opportunity identification. An awareness of the market is developed regarding potential applications for the technology or product.

Resource mobilisation (Phase II)

Once resources are accessed and there is an initial awareness of the market, resources are deployed to facilitate the provision of productive services. A learned ability emerges about how to satisfy the needs of the market through services, and should market preferences change, addressing these needs by adapting the deployment of resources. If the deployment of resources fails to tap into a market opportunity, there may be a revisiting of the resource access phase to ensure a credible market opportunity exists.

Resource generation (*Phase III*)

During this phase, there is a level of establishment, since a market has been clearly identified. Revenue may be generated by this point and there is a level of experience accumulated, facilitating "routinization of problem-solving responses" (p. 537). A shift in market preferences may result in targeted niches no longer being viable for the firm. Changes in the market can therefore pose challenges for the firm, requiring an ongoing capacity to recognise these changes to ensure that the firm can respond.

Garnsey's model depicted in her 1998 paper is particularly suited to exploring TM in entrepreneurial spinoff teams as the team fabric develops as a function of the spinoff's growth journey. The non-deterministic assumptions of Garnsey's nonlinear growth model highlight the nature of resource base developments during incubation; and her model explicitly acknowledges the important role that parents play as incubators for the early development phases and who have the potential to provide an accelerated development journey. While Garnsey does not explore "talent" specifically, her model infers that a parent, through its resource base, may have a key role to play in managing the talent of the entrepreneurial spinoff team to facilitate rapid development of the spinoff during its gestation period. An explicit talent focus extends Garnsey's model by showing the role that talent can potentially play as a critical resource during the early developmental stages.

Having discussed the relevance of Garnsey's model, we now examine the literature exploring TM, entrepreneurship and entrepreneurial teams to elucidate the potential role TM plays in supporting entrepreneurial spinoff teams as part of the early resourcing phases during incubation. The sequencing of our discussion in the following sections provides the foundations for the model presented later in the chapter. Our model explores how access to talent as a key resource, and TM at "critical junctures" (Garnsey, 1998; Vohora *et al.*, 2004) during the spinoff's earliest stage of growth (i.e. during incubation), can support the development of the entrepreneurial founding team — ultimately increasing the chances of the spinoff's success.

Talent Management

The term "talent" was popularised following the release of a *McKinsey Quarterly* publication in the late 1990s on "talent" (see Chambers *et al.*, 1998) and following the release of a book in the early 2000s called *The War for Talent* (Michaels *et al.*, 2001) which prompted concerns by suggesting most firms were not well prepared for the competition for talent. There has been a core focus within the TM literature on the tasks of understanding, articulating, clarifying and reinforcing the definition of talent, and Al Ariss *et al.* (2014) assert that TM is a field with considerable potential in terms of both theory and practice. The TM literature discusses the importance of attracting, developing and retaining talent (Tarique and Schuler, 2010). We specifically define TM as follows:

> "activities and processes that involve the systematic identification of key positions which differentially contribute to the organisation's sustainable competitive advantage, the development of a talent pool of high potential and high performing incumbents to fill these roles, and the development of a differentiated human resource architecture to facilitate filling these positions with competent incumbents and to ensure their continued commitment to the organisation" (Collings and Mellahi, 2009, p. 304).

While TM represents an essential asset for organisations (Scullion and Collings, 2011), the literature currently lacks theoretical, conceptual and empirical contributions (Al Ariss *et al.*, 2014; Iles *et al.*, 2010; Tarique and Schuler, 2010) that confirm the contribution of talent to the firm's profitability and sustainability, and how talent is optimally managed. Collings (2014) suggests that there is scope to explore TM in a broader range of contextual settings and assess how stakeholders play a role in shaping TM. Similarly, Sparrow and Makram (2015) highlight that by exploring TM in diverse settings, we can further our understanding of the topic. For example, understanding the nuances of TM in smaller organisations due to their resourcing limitations and embryonic human resources processes (Festing *et al.*, 2013; Iles *et al.*, 2010) or recruitment challenges (Valverde *et al.*, 2013) adds depth to our understanding of the complex dimensions of TM. Except for a few papers (e.g. Festing *et al.*, 2013), there has been a dearth of research exploring TM in younger and less established ventures such as spinoffs, and Valverde *et al.* (2013) highlight that extant research has failed to adequately assess the role of TM in relation to embryonic firms. Our focus on understanding the value of TM to entrepreneurial spinoff teams during the spinoff's gestation provides greater insight in relation to TM in a unique yet important setting.

A major point of contention continues to be whether TM is reflective of an inclusive or an exclusive approach, and once determined, what implications arise from such an understanding of talent. Exclusive approaches refer to those approaches that place the focus on "a minority of employees not the entire workforce" and "focus on personal and career development not the full spectrum of HRM activities" (Swailes *et al.*, 2014, p. 531). On the contrary, inclusive approaches, as defined by Swailes *et al.* (2014) refer to one of two phenomena, the first being that "everyone has the opportunity to be included in a talent programme", and the other is that "everyone is deemed to have talent of some sort and should therefore have access to programmes that identify and locate their talent and put it to use" (p. 531). A further tension is over whether talent is something innate in an individual or whether it can be acquired (Meyers *et al.*, 2013), impacting the importance that may be placed on development opportunities for individuals. As Festing *et al.* (2013) suggest, approaches to TM can exhibit noticeable variations depending on the organisational type. This would suggest that there is scope to explore the extent the above-specified approaches play in harnessing a most effective entrepreneurial team in innovative settings such as spinoffs.

Managing entrepreneurial talent

Having introduced the various dimensions of TM, we now focus on entrepreneurial talent specifically. 97% of CEOs claim that the right talent is the most critical factor for their business's growth (PWC, 2013) and one would think this statement is even more relevant in the early growth phases associated with entrepreneurial activity. However, problematically, Cooke (2007) explains that talent, which could foster entrepreneurial activity, is in short supply nearly everywhere. Furthermore, Farndale and colleagues (2010) suggest entrepreneurial organisations need "talent pipelines" (Farndale *et al.*, 2010) that are responsive to the particular rhythms those firms encounter (i.e. rhythms in relation to time, place and context). These sentiments allude to the complexities accompanying the management of talent in entrepreneurial contexts. Harper (2008, p. 613) conceptualises entrepreneurship as "a profit-seeking problem-solving process that takes place under conditions of structural uncertainty" and this structural uncertainty brings with it challenges in the management of talent. While we do not delve into the nuances between entrepreneurial creation and entrepreneurial discovery (see for instance Alvarez and Barney, 2007), we acknowledge the complexity associated with developing an understanding of entrepreneurship and that contextual specificity needs to be accounted for in discussions relating to entrepreneurial spinoff teams.

Amit *et al.* (1990) define entrepreneurial talent as "the ability to combine tangible and intangible assets and to deploy them to meet customer needs in a manner that cannot be easily imitated" (p. 1233). Eesley and Roberts (2012) propose that entrepreneurial talent speaks to the "superior ability to consistently see viable entrepreneurial opportunities and effectively act upon them to generate greater venture performance" (p. 210). Literature from the early to mid-1990s offers some additional insight into what constitutes talent in the entrepreneurial context. Acemoglu (1995) comments that talent in entrepreneurship refers to someone who can be employed to harness productive activities for the firm. He observes that entrepreneurial talent as such allocates into activities through which entrepreneurs gain the highest levels of private returns, which does not inevitably equate with gaining the highest social returns. In 2010, Weitzel and colleagues spoke of entrepreneurial talent which they argue consists of two components: creative talent and business talent. The authors describe how individuals with a stronger business-oriented component of entrepreneurial talent are more likely to desire privately profitable activities at the expense of socially unproductive/destructive activities. At the team level, this suggests that individuals who are both more business-talented and less creative tend to behave more self-interestedly. Such an individualistic outlook may compromise team performance and highlights the potential role for TM to incentivise individual talent but not at the expense of the team's performance.

The discussion thus far also raises the issue as to whether all entrepreneurs can be considered as talent. Revisiting our earlier definition of TM as relating to selected positions that strategically influence the organisation and are undertaken by extremely competent individuals (Collings and Mellahi, 2009), this suggests an interpretive element and whether an entrepreneur is considered to be talent or not is specific to an organisational context. Indeed, Stahl *et al.* (2012) note the importance of context, and suggest that an organisation's strategy, situation and culture influence global talent management (GTM). Therefore, understanding whether an individual is considered entrepreneurial talent depends on what the spinoff requires strategically during its incubation. This suggests that a spinoff's parent plays a key role in determining who to select and how to develop the entrepreneurial founding team.

In further exploring the extent to which all entrepreneurs can be considered talent, we also build on the work of Bolton and Thompson (2004). They define an entrepreneur as an individual who "habitually creates and innovates to build something of recognised value around perceived opportunities" (p. 16). These authors suggest that entrepreneurial talent needs to be actively identified and encouraged or it may remain "buried"; however, only a small percentage of individuals can be considered to be genuine entrepreneurs. From this perspective, being able to identify entrepreneurs in the first place is understandably difficult, but once identified it would seem critical that their entrepreneurial skills be developed. Recognising these complexities is essential in setting the platform for the next part of our discussion which explores the literature pertaining to entrepreneurial teams.

Entrepreneurial team success and performance

The entrepreneurial literature suggests that there is a "myth of the lone entrepreneur", and that it is important to consider the role that entrepreneurial teams, as opposed to individuals, play in founding new ventures (Harper, 2008; Kamm *et al.*, 1990). While the literature acknowledges the debates surrounding the value of the "heroic entrepreneur" versus the role that multiple agents (versus a single agent) play to support the entrepreneurial process (Johnsen and Sorensen, 2017), we do not engage in these debates. However we do adopt a "both/and" perspective, and suggest that inevitably in some instances particular individuals will be naturally more "heroic" — consider the likes of Nikola Tesla or Marie Curie as historically famous individuals given their contributions to innovation (Schilling, 2018). But, we also acknowledge that as part of a system, multiple individuals in various capacities influence outcomes. Since our focus is on spinoffs, which as a unit of analysis typically comprises multiple individuals as part of a founding team, our discussion focuses more on TM in the context of an entrepreneurial talent team. However, we acknowledge the relatively more influential role that particular entrepreneurial talent (e.g. founder) may have in comparison to other talent within the team.

Santos and Cardon (2019) put into question whether simply having talent on board is enough or whether team entrepreneurial passion is a contributing factor in the success of an innovative firm. Team entrepreneurial passion is defined as "the level of shared intense positive feelings for a collective team identity that is high in identity-centrality for a new venture team" (Cardon *et al.*, 2017, p. 286). More specifically, the authors suggest that higher levels of team passion could be linked to better outcomes in general, as passion is a factor in collective identity. Therefore, the role of a parent in nurturing passion as part of a TM approach to support a team of founding entrepreneurs involved in the initiation of a spinoff would appear an important endeavour.

Harper (2008) suggests that entrepreneurial teams refer to "a group of entrepreneurs with a common goal that can only be achieved by appropriate combinations of individual entrepreneurial actions" (p. 614). A fundamental component of Harper's theory is the concept that teams may achieve outcomes superior to those that an individual can achieve, and it is therefore unlike the case of Prisoner's Dilemma where the ultimate outcome is to "cheat" and default to an "every individual for themselves" scenario. In some situations, the incentives are such that individuals are more inclined to cooperate. This situation is likely when there is a specific and desirable outcome that can only be achieved through cooperation and a mutual reliance shared by each team member. From a TM perspective in the spinoff context, one may suggest that a parent therefore plays a critical role in building incentives for team cooperation to bring the spinoff to fruition.

Several team styles are discussed by Harper (2008) that can reflect the situation for entrepreneurial teams, such as "hybrid entrepreneurial-economising teams", "nested entrepreneurial teams" and the "emergent entrepreneurial team". Each of these styles contains variations in terms of the roles that individuals play within the team. For example, the situation of a nested entrepreneurial team requires a minimum of two individuals to form the team with one individual representing the "lead entrepreneur" *vis-à-vis* the "sub-entrepreneur". This situation contrasts with the situation depicted in "emergent entrepreneurial teams", whereby entrepreneurs (again a minimum of two) hold equivalent roles, and therefore there is no such phenomenon as a "lead entrepreneur" in this situation.

For an entrepreneurial team to emerge, Harper (2008) identifies that "bounded structural uncertainty" is critical, as is a "perceived common interest". That is, the outcomes of entrepreneurial activities are not certain and depend on a range of factors (e.g. market preferences). However, there are elements that limit the degree of uncertainty, such as rules and regulations and existing market trends (Harper, 2008). These conditions provide for an appropriate level of risk such that there is an incentive for those who can envisage potential opportunities to carve out possibilities to generate value in the market (Harper, 2008). Harper (2008) identifies potential opportunities the team dynamic can generate, conditions under which this may occur and the nature of the teams that may emerge. A parent arguably has a role to play in terms of influencing the conditions of bounded structural uncertainty and perceived common interest as part of a TM approach to support a founding entrepreneurial team spinning off a venture.

The discussion of Harper's TET (2008) provides the platform for an analysis of how the concept of the entrepreneurial team is similarly fundamental to Timmons' *Model of New Venture Creation* (MNVC), further strengthening our understanding of entrepreneurial teams in the spinoff context and the role TM may play. Timmons' model highlights that lead entrepreneurs and entrepreneurial teams are key elements of the entrepreneurial process which helps drive the success of new ventures (Timmons and Spinelli, 2007). Furthermore, the entrepreneurial team is an element that can be controlled (Timmons and Spinelli, 2007) and can therefore be managed to promote more favourable outcomes, reinforcing the potential value of applying TM to support entrepreneurial teams as part of the spinoff process. Timmons (1975) long ago pointed out that rather than considering the new venture creation process as a complex landscape that is essentially random, elements such as careful and strategic management of the entrepreneurial team can reduce uncertainty in the entrepreneurial process.

Timmons (1975) identifies key team challenges that can hamper early venture creation efforts. These can include the existence of a power orientation; deficits in self-awareness, leadership and an achievement orientation; and disputes regarding the perceived appropriate strategic direction. As depicted in the MNVC, concrete activities can be employed which nurture the foundations for a strong entrepreneurial team (Timmons and Spinelli, 2007) and may include the presence of an entrepreneurial leader who is honest, resilient, has integrity, develops a culture and is both a learner and teacher (Timmons and Spinelli, 2007). The entrepreneurial leader is supported by a team that brings experience, motivation, is able to operate in environments involving risk, and can adapt and communicate (Timmons and Spinelli, 2007).

While in a *de novo* new venture model (Bates and Bradford, 1992) where the venture is not a spinoff from an existing institution, but rather is started "from nothing", the lead entrepreneur and founder of the venture is key to selecting and building the team, considering their desire to grow the enterprise and to determine the talent required to do so (Timmons and Spinelli, 2007). In the situation of a spinoff firm (i.e. a *de alio* — "from others" (Walsh and Bartunek, 2011)), the parent alongside the lead entrepreneur typically co-selects talent to support the formation of the founding team. This co-sharing of TM between parent and founder/lead entrepreneur is an interesting dynamic that warrants a deeper examination of the potential nuances of TM in entrepreneurial spinoff teams. Questions such as how parent and founder/lead entrepreneur navigate this new domain are important because rifts between parties due to differences of opinion and priorities, and miscommunication can occur. Therefore, understanding that such tensions are possible and how a TM plan may culminate in an agenda to support the team and promote common directions is important in managing talent in the new enterprise.

Finally, a discussion of entrepreneurial teams should consider the promotion of entrepreneurial talent policy beyond the firm. Keeping in mind the general promotion of entrepreneurship (Tyson *et al.*, 1993) as a matter of national interest, and more specifically the development and retention of entrepreneurial teams, we now outline some of the ideas currently advocated that speak to the philosophies and practices of increasing the supply of entrepreneurs (and entrepreneurial teams) as a means of increasing the national well-being. That is, any input into policy must be framed with the aim of convincing some percentage of the relevant labour force to engage in entrepreneurial careers more so than academic, civil service or non-entrepreneurial private sector career positions (Tyson *et al.*, 1993).

For entrepreneurial talent to thrive in team environments, this depends in part on the availability of inputs in an economy. As such, it is plausible to suggest that national policies targeted at macroeconomic stability and strengthening property rights, for example, are necessary but not sufficient for fostering productive entrepreneurship activity. To encourage and foster entrepreneurial talent in an economy is paramount, and policies and resulting programs must then target the development and channelling of entrepreneurial talent to a productive enterprise that increases the national well-being. Therefore, a deep understanding of the extent to which TM can support entrepreneurial teams involved in spinning off ventures requires an appreciation of the national context and of the nature of the institutional (and regulatory) environment within which this enterprise occurs.

Discussion

The discussion up to this point has identified that a talented entrepreneurial team, while a complex and context-dependent phenomenon, has the potential to be managed during the earliest resource development phases that occur during incubation as part of the spinoff's "gestation" journey. We propose a conceptual model (Figure 1) that explores the emergence of an entrepreneurial team as the firm progresses through Garnsey's phases of resource access, resource mobilisation and resource generation. The model focuses on the gestation period prior to spinoff and as highlighted in the model, a decision to form a team represents a "critical juncture" (CJ) in the firm's development, and we extend on this concept to identify this as a "TM critical juncture" (TMCJ). For the critical juncture to occur there must be conditions of "bounded structural uncertainty" and "perceived common interest" (Harper, 2008). Subsequent TMCJs are featured in the model, which highlight how TM can initially support the founder, and later the entrepreneurial team, as the resource base develops during incubation and up until the point of spinoff as new opportunities and challenges unfold on the growth journey.

As the model indicates, the parent and usually the entrepreneurial founder would co-share the responsibility of talent attraction, selection, development and retention of the entrepreneurial team during this early stage of the firm (and team's) development during incubation. The types of skills that the parent would support the entrepreneurial leader/founder to develop during this period would be those depicted by Timmons and Spinelli (2007), such as honesty, resilience and integrity. The parent and entrepreneurial leader/founder would also build the team by attracting, selecting and developing individuals with skills including experience, motivation and the ability to operate in environments involving risk (Timmons and Spinelli, 2007). Such an approach reinforces Garnsey's

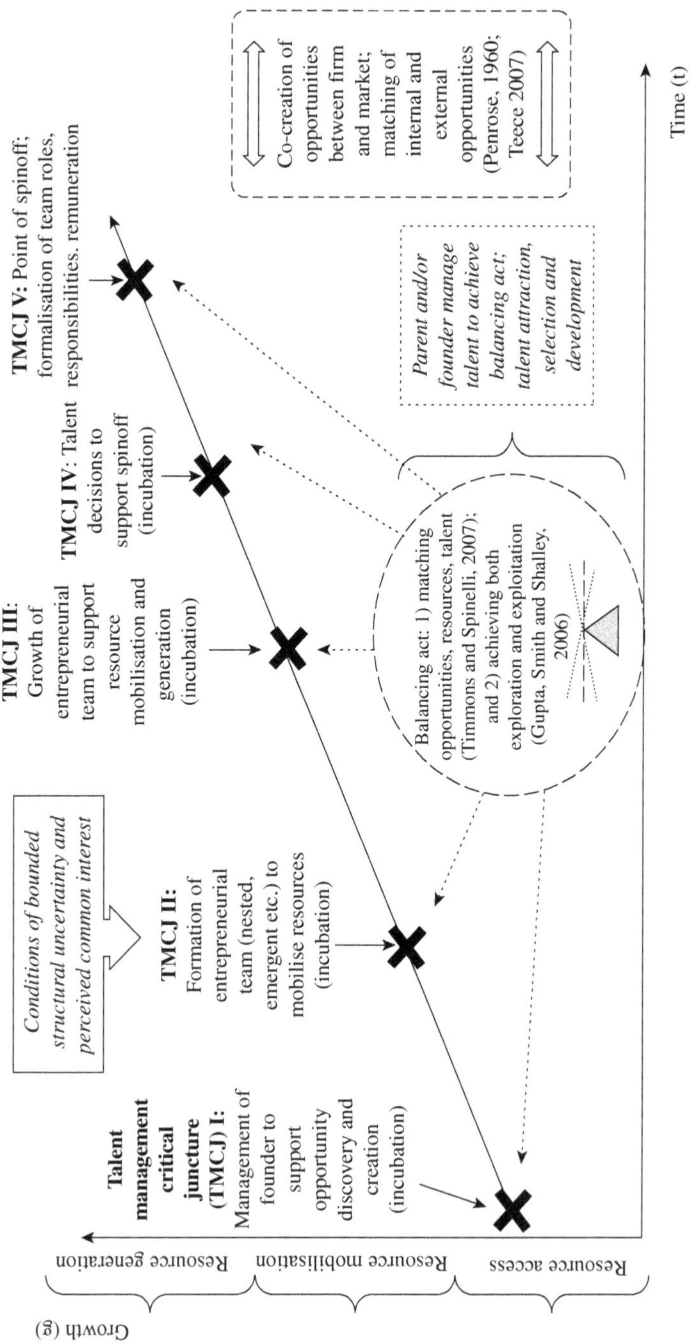

Figure 1: Model of TM in Early Growth Spinoffs During Gestation Period (Developed for Purposes of this Chapter)

(1998) sentiments that mentors (i.e. represented in this instance by experts the parent has access to, or the founder) are critical to provide important knowledge and development opportunities in incubated environments.

Understanding the nuances of teams here is important (e.g. Harper's (2008) nested entrepreneurial team versus an emergent entrepreneurial team). This nuancing is valuable in terms of understanding the precise balancing and complementarity of skills and talent required to maximise the chances of success. Furthermore, as depicted in Figure 1, balancing opportunities, resourcing and the team, while also striving for both exploration and exploitation, resembles the seesaw depicted in Timmons' MNVC. Part of a TM strategy we propose is to identify how to support the team to match resources and opportunities and to support the team to achieve both exploration and exploitation (Gupta *et al.*, 2006). It is also important to consider that this process is not operating within a vacuum, but as Garnsey's open-systems thinking suggests, actors and entities are part of an open system that both shapes and is shaped by the environment. This logic is consistent with the notion of resource development in the context of changes in the environment (Penrose, 1960; Teece, 2007).

Thunnissen *et al.* (2013) argue, "new perspectives are essential for a theoretical framework for TM in different contexts, for example in different branches of industry or in public or private organizations" (p. 1758). Our integration of Garnsey's TEGF, Harper's theory and Timmons' model moves the TM domain forward by highlighting the value of TM to entrepreneurial teams to support spinoffs in their gestation period. The specific skill sets required to support entrepreneurship in a spinoff are unique given the context and include the capacity to thrive in an environment characterised by considerable technological and market uncertainty (Kriz and Welch, 2018). Therefore, to build a team that is reflective of the types of skills Timmons prescribes requires entrepreneurial talent that already demonstrates these skills or can develop these skills with the support of ongoing TM efforts. We encourage future research to further explore the extent to which entrepreneurial talent is an exclusive versus inclusive concept, and also the role of potential in terms of whether talent is innate or is something that can be developed. Future empirical research could also provide more clarity with respect to specific spinoff contexts. Greater insight into such concepts could have implications for practice including the different TM philosophies and practices adopted by parent companies and entrepreneurial teams. We also encourage research which establishes a better understanding of the skills necessary to produce technological capacity in the new firm, but in addition that produce the internationalisation acumen to engage successfully with markets overseas (Kriz and Welch, 2018). It is not clear that these skill sets are the same, but it is clear that both skill sets are essential if the firm moves beyond national borders.

One may easily ponder the influence of TM on entrepreneurial founding spinoff teams with prospective opportunities that might be pursued at the global level. For this, we must consider the context of international entrepreneurship (IE). McDougall and Oviatt (2000) suggest that IE is a "combination of innovative, proactive, and risk-seeking behaviour that crosses national borders" (p. 903). These insights have been echoed by Zahra and George (2002) who conceptualise IE as "the process of creatively discovering and exploiting opportunities that lie outside a firm's domestic markets in the pursuit of competitive advantage" (p. 261). Not long after, Oviatt and McDougall (2005) succinctly defined IE as "the discovery, enactment, and exploitation of opportunities — across national borders — to create future goods and services" (p. 7).

The literature suggests two dominant branches in the study of IE; the first focusing on cross-national-border behaviour of entrepreneurial actors, and the second focusing on cross-national-border comparison of entrepreneurs, their behaviour and the entrepreneurial context (Oviatt and McDougall, 2005). While the authors refer to "behaviour", "actors" or generally "entrepreneurs" on numerous occasions, it remains elusive as to who these actors/entrepreneurs are, their geographic location and behaviour — better yet, contribution — relative to the discovery, enactment, evaluation and exploitation of opportunities. A discussion around the dynamics between actors is also concerningly absent, since the IE literature has tended to focus more on individual entrepreneurs and their assessment of risk (Liesch *et al.*, 2011). TM however focuses on a collection of actors working on a common purpose and such a perspective could add new insights for the IE domain.

These circumstances trigger the following series of questions: How does a parent and/or founder best attract, select, develop and retain talent suitable to support the process and desired outcomes of IE? What is the role of the parent and/or founder in attracting, selecting, developing and retaining talent in an IE spinoff context? What skills and capabilities does talent require in the discovery, enactment, evaluation and exploitation of opportunity phases and what type of TM approach is most suited for each phase? The global nature of work will demand an entrepreneurial talent team to work virtually, bearing much greater levels of uncertainty compared to domestic ventures (Butler *et al.*, 2010). It is plausible that being distant in space and time (Butler *et al.*, 2010) can provoke challenges and opportunities for TM in IE, as cultural differences and variations in space and time permeate into IE activities.

We therefore allude to the potential for IE which is "manifested in global ecosystems of actors pursuing opportunities" (Reuber *et al.*, 2018, p. 400) to add further depth to our understanding of how entrepreneurial spinoff teams can develop talent capable of recognising opportunities globally. While our broader discussion in this chapter does not specify whether the talent is focused on exploring domestic versus international opportunities, this is an area we would encourage future researchers to contemplate and explore how this adds complexity to the IE process. Related to this point, future research that explicitly adds an international dimension to our model may help to address calls regarding scope for further theory development in the IE field (Jones *et al.*, 2011).

Conclusion

Our chapter makes several contributions. We provide a more acute understanding of the potential for TM in entrepreneurial spinoff teams by drawing on Garnsey's TEGF, Harper's TET and Timmons' MNVC. In doing so, we extend these theories and frameworks by integrating them with TM principles, and respond to invitations by Garnsey (1998) to explore her model in new contexts. Furthermore, by adopting Garnsey's lens and through our pre-founding focus, we also acknowledge the critical role the parent plays in the development of young firms (Hewerdine and Welch, 2012). We suggest that future qualitative case studies would be particularly useful to refine our proposed model given the ability of the case study research design to focus on the processual and longitudinal dimensions of complex relationships between actors and institutions over time (Welch and Paavilainen-Mäntymäki, 2014; Welch *et al.*, 2011).

While our model explores the pre-founding/incubation period, it may be fruitful for further research to understand the role that the parent continues to play in terms of supporting the spinoff's ongoing TM following spinoff. It may also be useful to consider how TM approaches and capacities vary for entrepreneurial spinoff teams depending on the type of the parent (e.g. publicly funded research institute *vis-à-vis* corporate entity). Understanding the incentives and motivations of the founding talent base is also a key element that the parent should consider from the perspective of attracting and selecting the optimal talent for the spinoff. Therefore, this chapter provides scope for future research to empirically explore and test the value of TM in entrepreneurial spinoff teams and further develop the spinoff, TM and entrepreneurship literatures. These future research endeavours can build upon our proposed model by evaluating its applicability to various institutional and international spinoff contexts.

References

Acemoglu, D. (1995). Reward structures and the allocation of talent. *European Economic Review*, 39(1), 17–33.

Al Ariss, A., W. F. Cascio, and J. Paauwe (2014). Talent management: Current theories and future research directions. *Journal of World Business*, 49(2), 173–179.

Alvarez, S. A. and J. B. Barney (2007). Discovery and creation: Alternative theories of entrepreneurial action. *Strategic Entrepreneurship Journal*, 1(1–2), 11–26.

Amit, R., L. Glosten, and E. Muller (1990). Entrepreneurial ability, venture investments, and risk sharing. *Management Science*, 36(10), 1232–1245.

Bates, T. and W. D. Bradford (1992). Factors affecting new firm success and their use in venture capital financing. *The Journal of Entrepreneurial Finance*, 2(1), 23–38.

Bolton, B. and Thompson, J. (2004). *Entrepreneurs: Talent, Temperament, Technique*. 2nd ed. Oxford: Elsevier Butterworth-Heinemann.

Butler, J. E., E. Doktor, and F. A. Links (2010). Linking international entrepreneurship to uncertainty, opportunity discovery, and cognition. *Journal of International Entrepreneurship*, 8, 121–134.

Cardon, M. S., C. Post, and W. R. Forster (2017). Team entrepreneurial passion: Its emergence and influence in new venture teams. *Academy of Management Review*, 42(2), 283–305.

Chambers, E., M. Foulon, H. Handfield-Jones, S. Hankin, and E. Michaels (1998). The war for talent. *The McKinsey Quarterly*, (3), 44–57.

Collings, D. G. (2014). Integrating global mobility and global talent management: Exploring the challenges and strategic opportunities. *Journal of World Business*, 49(2), 253–261.

Collings, D. G. and K. Mellahi (2009). Strategic talent management: A review and research agenda. *Human Resource Management Review*, 19(4), 304–313.

Collings, D. G., K. Mellahi, and W. F. Cascio (2019). Global talent management and performance in multinational enterprises: A multilevel perspective. *Journal of Management*, 45(2), 540–566.

Cooke, P. (2007). Regional innovation, entrepreneurship and talent systems. *International Journal of Entrepreneurship and Innovation Management*, 7(2–5), 117–139.

De Cleyn, S. and J. Braet (2007). Research valorisation through spin-off ventures: Integration of existing concepts and typologies: Department of Environment, Technology and Technology Management University of Antwerp.

Druilhe, C. and E. Garnsey (2004). Do academic spin-outs differ and does it matter? *The Journal of Technology Transfer*, 29(3–4), 269–285.

Eesley, C. E. and E. B. Roberts (2012). Are you experienced or are you talented?: When does innate talent versus experience explain entrepreneurial performance? *Strategic Entrepreneurship Journal*, 6(3), 207–219.

Farndale, E., H. Scullion, and P. Sparrow (2010). The role of the corporate HR function in global talent management. *Journal of World Business*, 45(2), 161–168.

Ferrante, F. (2005). Revealing entrepreneurial talent. *Small Business Economics*, 25, 159–174.

Ferriani, S., E. Garnsey, and G. Lorenzoni (2012). Continuity and change in a spin-off venture: The process of reimprinting. *Industrial and Corporate Change*, 21(4), 1011–1048.

Festing, M., L. Schäfer, and H. Scullion (2013). Talent management in medium-sized German companies: An explorative study and agenda for future research. *The International Journal of Human Resource Management*, 24(9), 1872–1893.

Garnsey, E. (1998). A theory of the early growth of the firm. *Industrial and Corporate Change*, 7(3), 523–556.

Gupta, A. K., K. G. Smith, and C. E. Shalley (2006). The interplay between exploration and exploitation. *Academy of Management Journal*, 49(4), 693–706.

Harmancioglu, N., M. Sääksjärvi, and E. J. Hultink (2020). Cannibalize and combine? The impact of ambidextrous innovation on organizational outcomes under market competition. *Industrial Marketing Management*, 85, 44–57.

Harper, D. A. (2008). Towards a theory of entrepreneurial teams. *Journal of Business Venturing*, 23(6), 613–626.

Hewerdine, L. and C. Welch (2012). Are international new ventures really new? A process study of organizational emergence and internationalization. *Journal of World Business*, 48(4), 466–477.

Iles, P., D. Preece, and X. Chuai (2010). Talent management as a management fashion in HRD: Towards a research agenda. *Human Resource Development International*, 13(2), 125–145.

Johnsen, C. G. and B. M. Sorensen (2017). Traversing the fantasy of the heroic entrepreneur. *International Journal of Entrepreneurial Behavior & Research*, 23(2), 228–244.

Jones, M. V., N. Coviello, and Y. K. Tang (2011). International entrepreneurship research (1989–2009): A domain ontology and thematic analysis. *Journal of Business Venturing*, 26(6), 632–659.

Kamm, J., J. Shuman, J. Seegar, and A. Nurick (1990). Entrepreneurial teams in new venture creation: A research agenda. *Entrepreneurship Theory and Practice*, 14(4), 7–17.

Kriz, A. and C. Welch (2018). Innovation and internationalisation processes of firms with new-to-the-world technologies. *Journal of International Business Studies*, 49(4), 496–522.

Liesch, P. W., L. S. Welch, and P. J. Buckley (2011). Risk and uncertainty in internationalisation and international entrepreneurship studies: Review and conceptual development. *Management International Review*, 51, 851–873.

McDougall, P. P. and B. M. Oviatt (2000). International entrepreneurship: The intersection of two research paths. *Academy of Management Journal*, 43(5), 902–906.

Meyers, M., M. Van Woerkom, and N. Dries (2013). Talent — Innate or acquired? Theoretical considerations and their implications for talent management. *Human Resource Management Review*, 23(4), 305–321.

Michaels, E., H. Handfield-Jones, and B. Axelrod (2001). *The War for Talent*. Boston: Harvard Business School Press.

Oviatt, B. M. and P. P. McDougall (2005). Defining international entrepreneurship and modelling the speed of internationalization. *Entrepreneurship Theory and Practice*, 29(5), 537–553.

Parhankangas, A. and P. Arenius (2003). From a corporate venture to an independent company: A base for a taxonomy for corporate spin-off firms. *Research Policy*, 32(3), 463–481.

Penrose, E. (1960). The growth of the firm — a case study: The Hercules Powder Company. *Business History Review*, 34(1), 1–23.

PWC (2013). *Talent Mobility 2020: The Next Generation of International Assignments*, https://www.pwc.com/gx/en/managing-tomorrows-people/future-of-work/pdf/talent-mobility-2020.pdf.

Reuber, A. R., G. A. Knight, P. W. Liesch, and L. Zhou (2018). International entrepreneurship: The pursuit of entrepreneurial opportunities across national borders. *Journal of International Business Studies*, 49(4), 395–406.

Santos, S. and M. Cardon (2019). What's love got to do with it? Team entrepreneurial passion and performance in new venture teams. *Entrepreneurship Theory and Practice*, 43(3), 475–504.

Schilling, M. A. (2018). *Quirky: The Remarkable Story of the Traits, Foibles, and Genius of Breakthrough Innovators who Changed the World.* New York: Public Affairs.

Scullion, H. and D. G. Collings (2011). Global talent management: Introduction. In *Global Talent Management*, H. Scullion and D. G. Collings (ed.). New York: Routledge.

Sparrow, P. R. and H. Makram (2015). What is the value of talent management? Building value-driven processes within a talent management architecture. *Human Resource Management Review*, 25(3), 249–263.

Stahl, G. K., I. Bjorkman, E. Farndale, S. S. Morris, J. Paauwe, P. Stiles, J. Trevor, and P. Wright (2012). Six principles of effective global talent management. *MIT Sloan Management Review*, 53(2), 24–32.

Swailes, S., Y. Downs, and K. Orr (2014). Conceptualising inclusive talent management: Potential, possibilities and practicalities. *Human Resource Development International*, 17(5), 529–544.

Tarique, I. and R. S. Schuler (2010). Global talent management: Literature review, integrative framework, and suggestions for further research. *Journal of World Business*, 45(2), 122–133.

Teece, D. (2007). Explicating dynamic capabilities: The nature and microfoundations of (sustainable) enterprise performance. *Strategic Management Journal*, 28(13), 1319–1350.

Thunnissen, M., P. Boselie, and B. Fruytier (2013). Talent management and the relevance of context: Towards a pluralistic approach. *Human Resource Management Review*, 23(4), 326–336.

Timmons, J. A. (1975). The entrepreneurial team: An American dream or nightmare? *Journal of Small Business Management (pre-1986)*, 13(4) (October 1975), 33.

Timmons, J. and S. Spinelli (2007). *New Venture Creation: Entrepreneurship for the 21st Century*. New York: McGraw Hill.

Tyson, L., T. Petrin, and H. Rogers (1993). Promoting entrepreneurship in Eastern Europe. *Small Business Economics*, 6, 165–184.

Valverde, M., H. Scullion, and G. Ryan (2013). Talent management in Spanish medium-sized organisations. *The International Journal of Human Resource Management*, 24(9), 1832–1852.

Vohora, A., M. Wright and A. Lockett (2004). Critical junctures in the development of university high-tech spinout companies. *Research Policy*, 33(1), 147–175.

Walsh, I. and J. Bartunek (2011). Cheating the fates: Organizational foundings in the wake of demise. *Academy of Management Journal*, 54(5), 1017–1044.

Weitzel, U., D. Urbig, S. Desai, M. Sanders, and Z. Acs (2010). The good, the bad, and the talented: Entrepreneurial talent and selfish behavior. *Journal of Economic Behavior and Organization*, 76(1), 64–81.

Welch, C. and E. Paavilainen-Mäntymäki (2014). Putting process (back) in: Research on the internationalization process of the firm. *International Journal of Management Reviews*, 16(1), 2–23.

Welch, C., R. Piekkari, E. Plakoyiannaki, and E. Paavilainen-Mantymaki (2011). Theorising from case studies: Towards a pluralist future for international business research. *Journal of International Business Studies*, 42(5), 740–762.

Woolley, J. L. (2017). Origins and Outcomes: The roles of spin-off founders and intellectual property in high-technology venture outcomes. *Academy of Management Discoveries*, 3(1), 64–90.

Yusubova, A., P. Andries, and B. Clarysse (2020). Entrepreneurial team formation and evolution in technology ventures: Looking beyond the top management team. *Journal of Small Business Management*, 1–30. https://doi.org/10.1111/jsbm.12539.

Zahra, S. A. and G. George (eds.) (2002). *International Entrepreneurship: The Current Status of the Field and Future Research Agenda.* United Kingdom: Blackwell Publishers.

Part 3

Social and Environmental Characteristics of International Entrepreneurship

https://doi.org/10.1142/9789811228445_0008

Chapter 8

Importance of Green Investment and Entrepreneurship for Economic Development

Gordana Djukic*,‡ and Biljana Ilic†,§

**Faculty of Economics, University of Belgrade, Beograd, Serbia*

†Megatrend University Belgrade, Faculty of Management Zajecar, Serbia

‡gordanadkc048@gmail.com

§biljana.ilic@fmz.edu.rs

Abstract

Nowadays, many banks in Europe, as well as many financial institutions in general, have realised the need to change their business activities, and must pay attention to "how to invest". A new approach to investing money is green investments. Green investments are part of the green economy that contributes to the sustainable development concept. This study provides a detailed description of the terms of green investments, green finance and green bonds. This is used to compare countries at different levels of sustainable development. Malaysia is a country that is much more on the road to economic sustainability, and it will be compared to Serbia, North Macedonia, and Bosnia and Herzegovina, as countries that are in the process of transition. We aim to present the best practices of green investment in developed countries and provide suggestions for these practices to be adopted and the actions required to implement them in less developed economies.

Keywords: Green investment; Entrepreneurship; Keynesian theory; Empirical model; GGEI; ASEAN; Western Balkans.

Introduction

Green finance policies are in the domain of green investment or can be seen as part of green funding and the green economy. The green economics concept, which was first prompted 80 years ago, emphasises protection of nature and life (eco-design in all spheres of life). Looking back on the year 1992 and the UN (1993) Conference on Environment and Development in Rio, it can be concluded that the main emphasis was placed on sustainability in economic, social and environmental terms. According to the 2010 United Nations Environment Program, the green economy minimises the "burden" on the environment and provides opportunities for different and sustainable growth. The Head of the EU Integration Sector of the EU Delegation to Serbia, Frejk Janmat pointed to Chapter 27, to encourage investment that provides environmental benefits, said that the basic tasks of green funding are to protect the environment and to reduce the risk on the environment (Janmat, 2014).

Economic progress must be reconciled with the social and environmental component; in other words, it must reduce the negative impact on the environment by using resources that are not harmful to the natural environment and increase employment (Stojanovic *et al.*, 2014). This explains why, today, the green economy represents a proactive approach, contributing to sustainability in profit areas, greening business and improving the quality of life of people. Green funding is a positive step in the transition of the global economy (Kalkan, 2018), and part of sustainable development. The Sustainable development (SD) concept consists of three pillars that are united for the common good of humanity and the survival of the planet. In the case of sustainability, the economy takes on a different connotation and becomes green in the sense that the size of the economy is not the only way to make a profit, but that economic development is in line with social and ecological development (Ilic *et al.*, 2018). As a form of financing, it is carried out through public funds, private green investments and public policies that support green initiatives. According to the European Union, the green economy should be understood as a sort of "aid" to further development, the possibility of the new job creation and reduction of poverty through investment in natural capital, with maximum conservation of that natural capital (Ilic *et al.*, 2019). Considering the above, the green economy opens up new opportunities basing its growth on the utilisation of renewable energy resources, accelerating the growth of green industrial directions/lines.

Green industrial lines refer to activities that emit minimum (harmful) greenhouse gases into the atmosphere, reducing the consumption of non-renewable resources that contribute to the social dimension of development. The focus of a green economy is not only on economically unlimited and "booming" growth but also on providing an impetus to a different growth that involves human-worthy jobs, i.e. jobs that will help to reduce poverty and to increase well-being. The concept of "green" is often considered and attributed to the richest countries of the world, as an opportunity to make those countries even richer by using the resources of the poor countries and their cheap labour. Certain examples in the sectors of economies that are in the process of development or the transition processes indicate that the establishment of the green economy concept can provide great benefits and can be applied in almost all parts of the world. Green economy through green investments supports the social dimension of development with the possibility of new job creation, uses renewable energy sources and reduces the negative impact on the environment (protecting biodiversity) (Stojanovic and Ilic, 2018).

Sustainable financing of green growth requires continued investments. Although the state budget finances green infrastructure, the funds are not sufficient for long-term investments. For this reason, governments use private capital to research green growth, with an appropriate international environment. The main factors affecting the development of green funding are banks, institutional investors and international financial institutions, such as the central bank and financial regulators. In the following sections, we describe some of the financial green systems (financial green system and green economy) in detail, and then, using a comparative method, explain the sustainable development process followed in Malaysia, and the Western Balkan countries, Serbia, North Macedonia, and Bosnia and Herzegovina.

Entrepreneurship

Today's modern global market is characterised not only by the dynamics of numerous competitions, rapid and frequent changes but also by high unemployment, especially among young people. There are a small number of young people in Serbia who "dare" to start and develop their own business. There is a lack of a positive climate and incentives from the state, along with numerous problems faced by entrepreneurs as well as factors that affect the establishment and survival of small and medium enterprises. Development strategies, numerous documents, acts and provisions indicate the need to develop a positive environment for entrepreneurship in general, and among young people in particular. One of the world's biggest economic problems is rising unemployment. By encouraging new business ventures, governments can create new employment opportunities.

In recent years, there have been many discussions about entrepreneurship and the importance of starting small and medium enterprises. Attention is increasingly focused on small business growth as industrial giants are disappearing. Entrepreneurs become innovators, initiators and creators. Successful entrepreneurs are important not only for bringing better financial changes to the society in which they live and the economy in which they operate but they are also the bearers of overall progress and create multiple benefits both locally and nationally. Entrepreneurs are considered key players in sustaining the global economy because of their approach, way of working and commitment. Innovations are characteristic of entrepreneurs, and creative ideas and the desire to be noticeable in the market lead them to success. Hence, through their unique business ideas, entrepreneurs attempt to increase the number of people who consume their products or services, even during times of instability in the global economy.

Over the last few years, the effects of a diverse and vibrant entrepreneurial spirit have been reflected in the prosperity not only of the entrepreneurs' family and them personally but also of all the people they employ and the local economy. Entrepreneurs pay taxes to the state budget, and those funds are later used to improve the quality of life of the people and are directed to where they are most needed. In addition to influencing the growth of the economy, entrepreneurs create new jobs. Successful entrepreneurship requires a variety of production and service activities, which increase the production and trade chain and reduce unemployment. The growth of entrepreneurial activity often affects the flourishing and emergence of new service activities, be it suppliers, retail chains, warehousing or logistics. All this affects the purchasing power and makes the economic situation of the local community more stable. Corporate social responsibility is an integral part of any successful business, and the relationship with the community in which the entrepreneur operates is one of the key factors of business success. It is necessary to emphasise that the success of every entrepreneur is an integral part of the success of society as a whole. The safety of employees and their families, the competitiveness of all market participants, consumer satisfaction as well as the favourable economic climate of the environment are related factors in the development of the economy of each country.

In recent years, due to changes in living conditions, as well as climate factors at the global level, it has been important to trace the path to a new economy, the so-called green economy. The green economy encourages development, is inclusive and encourages social equality, and takes care of the environment. It is an economy that contributes to the common good and social equality while at the same time significantly reducing risks to the environment and further exploitation of natural resources (United Nations Environment Program — (UNEP)). Thus, a green economy can create a better quality of life for everyone within the ecological boundaries of the planet (Green Economy Coalition). New trends in the green economy also apply to green entrepreneurship. Green entrepreneurship has emerged as a result of climate change, overexploitation of natural resources and environmental pollution. It deals with the realisation of entrepreneurial ideas that do not have a negative impact on the environment and at the same time are financially sustainable.

As green entrepreneurship grows worldwide, there are many incentives and support systems for such projects, including grants that can help entrepreneurs initiate such investments, reduce risks and increase the success of ventures to the satisfaction of investors and the communities in which they operate. Green entrepreneurship is characterised by business that respects and does not endanger the environment. In this regard, there is a significant mechanism for overcoming the crisis in underdeveloped and isolated rural areas to achieve economic development.

In rural areas, green entrepreneurship takes place mainly through organic agriculture and production, cultivation of indigenous varieties and breeds, rural tourism, fishing tourism, adventure and educational tourism, organic fish and shellfish farming, and other innovative business activities inspired by nature, tradition, local resources and their sustainable use (FORS Montenegro, 2020). From the example of developed countries, it can be concluded that creating an environment that encourages and supports entrepreneurship requires the involvement of all participants, especially the state. That is to say, the state should be a system in which all elements will have a common goal related to entrepreneurial incentives. It is very important to educate future entrepreneurs, nurture entrepreneurial potential, provide adequate training and development, as well as inform young people (Stanisavljev *et al.*, 2019).

Green Elements in Variations of Financial Green System and Green Economy

Green elements, or in other words, green finance elements, are subject to certain negative oscillations. To reduce the "oscillations" of the financial system, actors in the green finance domain carry out various development policies, taking different measures to regulate the harmful phenomena. Some of the significant measures of regulation are credit conditions, financing, subsidies with lower credit rates, interest rates and the possibility of refinancing (Stojanovic and Ilic, 2018). Based on the fact that estimates of the actual needs of green investment financing vary significantly between different sources, it requires a large amount of private capital. To increase the flow of private equity for green investments, it is necessary to form positive effects in the business environment, laws and investment regime that facilitate green funding.

It is necessary to implement certain standards with the aim of promoting development funds. These imply that voluntary principles and guidelines for green financial assistance should be implemented and monitored regularly. However, when voluntary principles are not enough, they must be supplemented with financial and regulatory incentives. To achieve the positive effects of these principles, actors in financial, environmental and regulatory policies must cooperate better with each other (Berensmann and Lindenberg, 2016). Based on the fact that environmental development requires large capital and long-term return on invested capital, each country must have a unique way of financing. Therefore, the mobilisation of capital for green investments is limited to different microeconomic levels.

Important challenges at the microeconomic levels include environmental internalisation problems, association data, analytical capacity and a lack of clear definition of "what the term of green means". These facts lead to certain problems in the development of green funds. Today, there is a mismatch between the maturity of long-term green investments and the relatively short period of anticipation, i.e. the investment and investors' expectations (that the invested funds will be returned as soon as possible). Globally, finance and ecology policies are not sufficiently aligned. Many governments provide poor information that does not support the promotion of a green transition. The conclusion is that aligning green financing policies with reforms and innovative financial resources contributes to mitigating the problems of green investment.

A green finance policy includes several aspects (Ilic *et al.*, 2019): financial reform, research of good fiscal policy practices and possible ways to raise money for green finance development. It is evident that business processes are a dominant source of "pressure" on the environment, and large business companies must play an active role in protecting the environment, as well as in mobilising green international capital for developing a green economy at the global level.

Green Bonds as a Part of the Green Investment

Green investment includes green bonds. Green bonds are defined as modern securities that are named after the method in which they "raise" monetary funds. They contribute to the achievement of sustainability goals because the financial funds that they collect are spent on the development of environmental projects and reducing environmental pollution. Green bonds, as securities that are already traded in markets in the world, not only bring investors a positive image but also significant profits. The private sector has a major role in solving the problems of the environment, i.e. climate change, while green finance sectors are channelling money into green investment.

Capital markets also play an important role, mobilising private funds to mitigate climate change damage and directing projects towards sustainable development. Based on this fact, the green financial market is composed of market mechanisms or financial products aimed at controlling the emission of harmful gases into the atmosphere. It is also one of the features of financial sustainability made up of diversified financial products that promote reduced carbon pollution and support ecology-related projects. Thus, carbon and atmospheric pollution are the products that are most traded in the green market, while green bonds are the most famous product for such trade (Stojanovic and Ilic, 2018).

Green bonds are significant because they support project financing in the area of climate change mitigation. Their value lies in the fact that their owner tries to channel funds to finance projects that have a positive environmental impact. Thus, green bonds oblige the use of funds to finance or refinance "green projects", or green business activities. Following the principles of green bonds, the "raised" funds are directed to the following (Vella, 2018): (1) renewable energy, (2) energy efficiency, (3) sustainable waste management, (4) sustainable forestry and agriculture, (5) conservation of biodiversity, (6) clean, sustainable transport, (7) sustainable water management (including clean and/or drinking water) and (8) adaptation to climate change.

Green bonds are a relatively new financial instrument used to protect against climate change, but their market has grown tremendously since 2007 (Blumberg, 2019). The real expansion of the green bond trade began in 2014 when the principles for trading these securities were established. The market is constantly growing; in 2015, the total green bond bonus was worth $42,000,000,000, while in 2016, it was worth $80,000,000,000. Specifically, the European Bank for Reconstruction and Development (EBRD) raised €1,640,000,000 in 2016, through 57 bonds in eight different currencies (Ilic *et al.*, 2019).

The Paris Agreement paved the way for the green trend. Green bond issuance fosters a corporate reputation for sustainability and creates new "green thinking" in financial markets (Chiesa, 2017). Unlike conventional bonds, green bonds are used to fund specific "green" investments that have no additional risk for investors. Compared to bank deposits, green bonds provide greater profitability, liquidity and stability for the most diversified investors. Green funding must be spent on renewable energy and sustainable development projects. Green bonds are experimental proof that capital markets can be a source of financial initiatives for climate change adaptation. The main objective of green bonds is not only to offer investors a product that is in line with their goals but also to support the financing of projects that reduce greenhouse gas emissions on the one hand and help countries adapt to the effects of climate change on the other (Knezevic *et al.*, 2013).

According to the OECD report (2015), there are six types of green bonds: (1) Corporate bond: "Use of proceeds" bond issued by a corporate entity with recourse to the issuer in the case of default on interest payments or the return of principal; Earmarked for green projects; Debt recourse (to the issuer): same credit rating applies as issuer's other bonds. This category includes bonds issued by "YieldCo" vehicles to finance asset acquisitions. Example: EIB "Climate Awareness Bond" (backed by EIB); Barclays Green Bond"; (2) Project bonds: the funds that support one or more specific green projects for which the investor has direct exposure to risk; Debt recourse is only to the project`s assets and balance sheet; Example is Invenergy Wind Farm (backed by Invenergy Campo Palomas wind farm); (3) Asset-backed security (ABS): "Use of Proceeds" Revenue bond; the link was in the case of one or more specific projects, which usually provide access only to funds, of the green category; Earmarked for green projects or go directly into the underlying green projects; Debt recourse are revenue streams from the issuers through fees, taxes, etc. are collateral for the debt; Example is Hawaii State (backed by fees on electricity bills of the state utilities); (4) Covered bonds — Supranational, sub-sovereign and agency (SSA) bond; issued by international financial institutions (IFIs) such as the World Bank and the European Investment Bank (i.e. "supranational issuers"); have similar corporate bonds in terms of "use of revenue" (brokering agencies are covered by this category Export-Import Banks and the National Development Bank, for example, German KfV); Proceeds are assigned to eligible green projects; Debt recourse to the issuer, if the issuer is unable to repay the bond to the covered pool; Example: Berli Hy green Pfandbrief; Sparebank 1 Bolligkredit green covered bond; (5) Municipal bonds: bonds issued by the municipal government, region or city; municipalities issue green bonds to finance infrastructure or other green projects of local communities; it is a fixed income bond for raising capital through the debt capital market. During the bond maturity period, the agreed amount of "coupons" is paid, and (6) Financial sector bonds: type of corporate of a bond issued by a financial institution to specifically raise capital to finance the "balanced lending" of green activities. "This type of bond is considered separately for the purposes of OECD scenario modelling to retain a distinction between financial sector bond issuances which finance lending and those which directly finance green investments" (OECD, 2015).

Global Green Economy Index

The Global Green Economy Index (GGEI) provides aggregate results of four main economic and environmental indicators of the green economy: (1) leadership and climate change (the president of the state, media, international forums, climate change performances), (2) sector efficiency (urbanism, transport, energy, tourism), (3) market and investments (investments in renewable energy sources, "clean tech" innovations, "clean tech" commercialisation, green investment improvement) and (4) ecological

Table 1: Global Green Economy Index 2018

Rank (141) Countries	ASEAN and Western Balkans	GGEI*	Year
24	Singapore	0.6154	2018
38	Thailand	0.5551	2014–2018
62	Philippines	0.5078	2014–2018
63	Slovenia	0.5058	2018
65	Cambodia	0.5022	2014–2018
66	Malaysia	0.4990	2014–2018
67	Croatia	0.4912	2018
73	Vietnam	0.4827	2014–2018
94	Indonesia	0.4527	2014–2018
96	Myanmar	0.4515	2018
108	Macedonia	0.4322	2018
126	Serbia	0.3927	2018
138	Bosnia–Herzegovina	0.3441	2018

Note: GGEI* — Aggregate index (leadership, climate change, sector efficiency and the market, investment and the environment).
Source: Global Green Economy Index 2018.

environment and natural capital (agriculture, air and water quality, biodiversity, habitats, fish, forests). Successful green economy finance depends on many factors. Digital and social communication and knowledge exchange in some market segments play an important role. Marketing agencies must place on the web portals of their country promotional information on the attractiveness of investments in green jobs, with sophisticated "country data" to provide investment and interactive connection to international investors and entrepreneurs (Citizen, 2018).

The results of the GGEI (2018) (from the best to the worst) in Table 1, present four main dimensions: (1) markets and investment, (2) leadership and climate change, (3) efficiency sectors and (4) environment. Based on the GGGI Report 2018, it is observed that Singapore has the most favourable performance in the ASEAN Association in terms of financial market and investment, leadership and climate change, sector efficiency and the environment. The Global Green Economy Index for Singapore is 0.6154, ranked 24. Out of the observed countries, Malaysia has the best GGEI,

0.4990, and the best rank of 66; Macedonia a GGEI of 0.4322, with a rank of 108; Serbia GGEI, 0.3927, with the rank 126; and Bosnia and Herzegovina with the worst GGEI 0.3441 and the worst rank 138, in 2018. A key factor for the rapid development of the financial market in ASEAN countries and green bonds is the adoption of the ASEAN Green Bond Standards in November 2017. Promotional activities have contributed to the faster development and integrity of the 2018 green bond market.

Crucial to the development of the green bond market is the government's political decisions: (1) Broadcasting of Green Sukuk by "Nasional Berhad Malaysia"; (2) "Segi Astana Financial Corporation Malaysia", which has produced MTN (Green Medium Term Note), a medium-term program note to increase successfully the financing of green-certified buildings in the green infrastructure sector; and (3) (Sindicatum Renewable Energy" company in Singapore has issued $60 million of green shares in 2018. In this way, ASEAN countries gained benefits in terms of green action activities in the wider region.

Empirical Model — Tax Burden and FDI Inflows

Kiburi *et al.* (2017) study on the relationship between FDI and tax burden, and the study of numerous empirical literature, came to the following conclusion: that there are negative, i.e. inverse, relationships between tax burden (tax system, types of taxes, tax rates, tax base, and tax structure) and FDI inflows, and these were confirmed as the most dominant relations. A theoretical concept on the relationship between tax burden and FDI inflows assumes that there is a ratio of the tax burden and FDI inflow. The following model was developed:

$$FDI_{it} = \alpha_{it} + \beta T_{it} TAXB_{it} + \varepsilon_{it},$$

where
α – the model constant,
FDI – FDI inflows,
TAXB – tax burden (tax system, types of taxes, tax rates, tax base and tax structure),
βT_{it} – regression coefficients,
i – country,
t – time.

A negative or no relationship in the empirical model indicates that the tax burden may not be affected by the foreign direct investment inflows. However, relationships are not applied universally to all countries. Each country should make decisions based on its empirical research. The study recommends empirical research — a ratio of the tax burden and FDI inflow as well a survey of the country and economic region on the relationship between tax burden and FDI outflow.

Modern Green Keynesian Theory

According to Harris (2019), there is a significant overlap between the economic theory and politics, or in other words, between the Keynesian economy and the environmental concern, underlying the modern green economy. The green approach implements Keynes's economic approach with the new radical Keynesian environmental analysis and environmental priorities (Harris, 2019). According to Jacobs (2012), Keynesian theory and the contention that governments of countries should maintain aggregate demand in the economy instead of driving the economic demand of the private sector and the demand for public expenditure are radically linked to the environment, i.e. with a green economy. This creates a multiplier effect that results in further growth in income and employment. Governments should target aggregate spending in areas where green investment is needed, such as replacing old power plants or upgrading transmission lines. Therefore, the investment would be carried forward from the future.

A Keynesian stimulus would affect terms of cheap labour, materials and financing costs (Jacobs, 2012). The global macroeconomic model that applies is the Energy Environment-Economy Global Macro-Economic (E3ME) model, developed by Cambridge Econometrics, with exogenous inputs: associated investment costs and different policy assumptions. E3ME simulates an economy based on post-Keynesian principles.

Based on the parameters of the historical time series and the ratio of inputs and outputs from national statistics, data are estimated. The inputs to the model (left side of Figure 1) are data: (1) REmap energy sector costs (such as investments in electricity generation, energy efficiency, transmission and distribution (T&D) of the grid, and energy flexibility), and (2) Coal taxes and the abolition of fossil fuel subsidies. A representation of the country's energy sector, obtained from REmap analysis, is given in the model (right side of Figure 1).

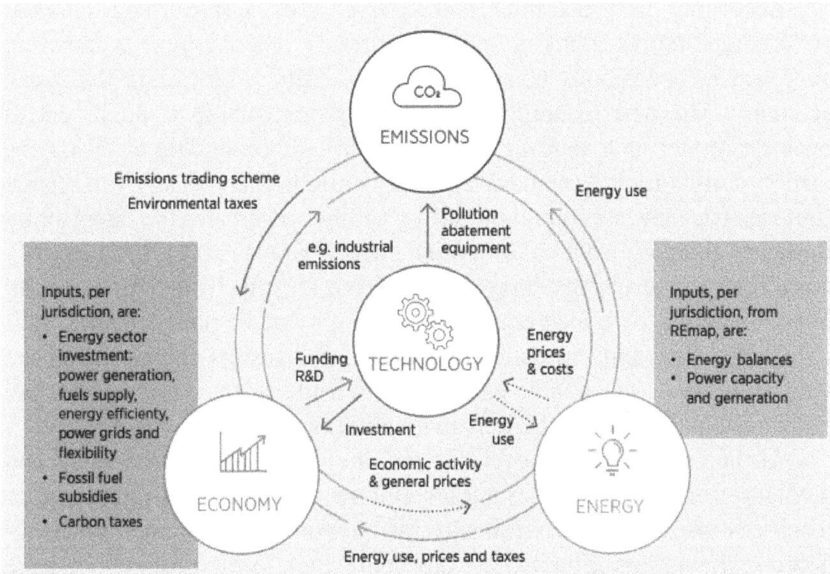

Figure 1: IRENA's Macroeconomic Analysis Methodology: REmap Results Feeding into the E3ME Model

Source: IRENA (2019, p. 124).

The dashed arrows show the installed energy capacities, i.e. exogenous components, outside the REmap model. The projects in the model include the official assessments of the EU 2030 climate and energy targets and the long-term green investment economic targets for climate change mitigation.

Entrepreneurship for the Green Investment

The Keynesian green model is committed to an entrepreneurial state that should support the investment in innovations in the public interest. The state is the driver of economic growth and a modest increase in investment and capital (Goldstein and Tyfield, 2019). To apply Green Creative Entrepreneurship, the state should direct its activities towards creating a competitive and profitable product, an appropriate policy for attracting foreign green investment and negotiating with foreign countries and foreign investors to regulate and adequately channel financial resources.

According to Benammar and Cressel (2015), local and regional government representatives, as entrepreneurs, should have a coherent approach to continuous coordination to identify priorities in the green economy. The best example of green entrepreneurship is an inventive business model such as Elon Musk's "Tesla". By producing electric cars, carbon emissions are reduced, and the cars are charged at fixed-charge stations. The newest production line of family cars creates the opportunity for home charging from solar or wind energy. Kraus *et al.* (2018) identify three relevant levels that they believe have an effect on the successful implementation of managerial sustainable practices; these are the individual, the firm and the contextual levels. The results show that on the individual level, sustainable entrepreneurs tend to derive their will to act more sustainably from their personal values or traits.

At the organisational level, though, they concluded that a small and medium-sized enterprise's internal culture and the reconfiguration of resources are critical determinants for adopting a sustainable entrepreneurial orientation. Finally, on the contextual level, researchers have focused on a better understanding of how entrepreneurs can help society and the environment through sustainable entrepreneurship, and how they can act as role models or change agents because the choice of investing or financing based on sustainability is still in its infancy (Kraus *et al.*, 2018). When we consider business opportunities in a green economy, we can point out that entrepreneurship has the potential to be a catalyst for a positive change in both the economic and environmental spheres.

In many countries, including Serbia, more attention has been paid to profit creation than to environmental protection in the context of tourist offers. Managing these impacts is a core function of the investment promotion process outlined here (Radovic-Markovic and Zivanovic, 2019; Shahidullah and Haque, 2014; Azevedo *et al.*, 2010). Demirel and Danisman (2019) examine the impact of circular eco-innovations and external funding available for CE activities on the growth of European SMEs using a dataset of 5,100 SMEs across 28 European countries in 2016. Findings reveal that a significant threshold investment (i.e. higher than 10% of revenues) into circular eco-innovations is required for SMEs to benefit from investing in the CE. Moreover, the majority of circular eco-innovations fail to boost the growth rates of SMEs, except for investments into eco-design innovations.

Although traditional forms of debt and grant finance targeted to CE activities are found to have no or negative impact on the growth of SMEs, equity finance (i.e. angel and venture capital investments) contributes positively to their growth (Demirel and Danisman, 2019). Sunny and Shu (2019) develop cross-cluster hypotheses regarding the firm formation and geographic clustering of clean-technology companies. They test them using a negative binomial random effects model in a panel sample of US clean-technology start-up firms and find general support (Sunny and Shu, 2019).

Green Investment in Malaysia

In Malaysia, based on the Malaysia Plan 2016–2020, a program of advanced economic development has been created for five years. Strategic goals have been defined for Malaysia to achieve sustainable green growth by 2020 in a sustainable low-carbon environment (Yatim *et al.*, 2017). The importance of the relationship between Islamic and green finance was emphasised at the conference (IOSCO, 2018) as a sustainable way of investing. Financing investments in innovative green technologies by integrating Islamic finance with green financing emphasised the importance of allocating basic principles of risk and responsibility (WB and SCM, 2019).

According to the UN Environment Program and DBS, ASEAN's demand for additional green investment in 2016–2030 is $3 trillion. The Conference Asia Pacific Hub Conference, themed "Harnessing Islamic Finance for a Green Future", gave an overview of green technology development projects that could be potentially invested through green Sukuk: (1) climate-friendly affordable housing in Perumnas, Indonesia, (2) integrated waste management in Cenviro, Malaysia, and clean energy projects in Energi, Malaysia.

Green Sukuk is significant because it attracts diversified investors: conventional, Islamic and green investors. Both Islamic and green investors apply common principles and values such as social responsibility, sustainable development and prosperity. Green Sukuk provides great opportunities for green investment goals and financing. Malaysia is the first country in the world to issue green Sukuk bonds (SRD, by Tadau Energy) in July 2017. The following year, 2018, saw the issuance of five green Sukuk bonds, RM 3.7 billion, of which RM 2.4 billion (five issues) was allocated for renewable energy and green projects.

In the process of transition to a sustainable economy with a low-carbon footprint and an inclusive economy, investments are needed. The

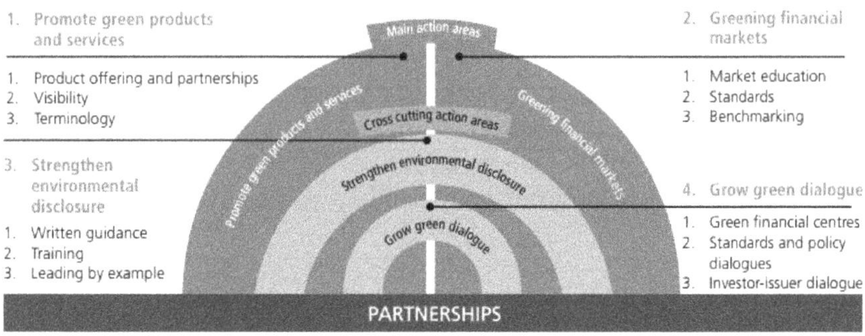

Figure 2: UN SSE Model on Green Finance Action Plan

Source: WB and SCM (2019, p. 51).

involvement of investment institutions is a key factor in achieving a green economy, considering the key environmental and societal challenges our planet faces (https://www.unepfi.org/investment/investment). At the same time, stock exchanges are also actively participating in the UN Sustainable Exchange Initiative (UN SSE). The goal of the UN SSE is to develop the securities market, increase the capacity of stock exchanges and promote responsible investment (Figure 2).

The UNSEE presents a basis for discussions. The model serves as a platform for learning models for investors and issuers to guide directions in the investment process. Investment information about green financial centres, standards, policy, market education, terminology, promotional visibility, etc. is provided to achieve transparency and data efficiency. As Malaysia's government is actively promoting a green agenda via policy and incentives, the participation of the private sector is now even more imperative.

Green funding is supported through The Japan Green Fund, through the Australian Clean Energy Financing Corporation and GBN, which is a platform for green banks and institutions where the promotion of green investment and international cooperation in terms of information, knowledge and experience is encouraged. GBN is a platform for green banks and institutions to cooperate, share knowledge, information and experience to promote green finance and investment. Malaysia is the only ASEAN country which is included in the Green Bank Network (GBN) and the only one to play a major role in promoting and financing green growth.

The private sector in Malaysia, which is largely controlled by institutional investors, has been actively streamlining ESG factors in their investment portfolios. They serve as excellent examples of actors with a strong internal drive to move towards SRI. What is more rewarding to learn is that their strategies involve not only building capabilities from within but also developing knowledge capacity and disseminating key information with stakeholders outside their organisation. Government entrepreneurship is important in terms of enacting regulatory measures and financial incentives such as tax incentives, price guarantees, subsidies and public investment, and eco-taxes are especially important for green investment and job creation (ILO, 2013). The government has popularised the green concept and has a decisive role in all initiatives to finance green growth, to spread knowledge and to acquire skills for green entrepreneurship.

It is important to have sustainable orientation and education of entrepreneurs in Malaysia, as this would enable sustainable living conditions for future generations in Malaysia and around the world (Ahmad, Halim and Rahman, 2015).

Green Investment in Europe (and Western Balkans)

Global UN goals in Sustainable development strategy for the green economy by 2030 are to do the following: "ensure universal access to affordable, reliable and modern energy services, increase substantially the share of renewable energy in the global energy mix — double the global rate of improvement in energy efficiency — enhance international cooperation to facilitate access to clean energy research and technology — including renewable energy, energy efficiency and advanced and cleaner fossil-fuel technology, and promote investment in energy infrastructure and clean energy technology — expand infrastructure and upgrade technology for supplying modern and sustainable energy services for all in developing countries, in particular, least developed countries, small island developing States, — and land-locked developing countries, following their respective programs of support".

Western Balkan countries have great potential for the use of renewable energy sources and the implementation of green energy efficiency measures. The Regional Energy Efficiency Program (REEP, 2019) aims to support the energy efficiency of the green economy in the Western Balkans through funding and through various financial instruments. This provides energy efficiency for the green economy. In July 2019, the European Commission, at the Western Balkans Summit in Poznań, published a set of concrete measures to strengthen the EU and the Western

Balkans in the energy, transport and digital sectors and cooperate with the regions. In the areas of environment and climate, the European Commission supported the Report on "Transition of Clean Energy in the Western Balkans", signed on February 21, 2019.

The Commission stressed the need for the region's efforts to develop a green agenda for the Western Balkan countries to harness the potential of a green, low-carbon and circular economy. Poland is the first sovereign publisher in the world, with € 750 million green bonds invested in renewable energy, clean transport, land use and low-CO_2 emissions. A significant Polish issuer is Bank Zachodni VBK, a subsidiary of BBVA, which has borrowed funds for clean energy, green buildings and climate-smart equipment (The CBI, 2018). In the Western Balkan countries, only Slovenia, as a small bond market, issued green bonds with the setting of ad hoc conditions for financing and issuing green bonds. The company that first aired green bonds in the Slovenian financial market is the "Gen-I Sun" for €14 million (euros) for the financing of energy efficiency and micro-solar energy.

IRENA (2019) assesses energy transition and green investment using a macroeconomic approach. The countries of Southeast Europe and the Western Balkans are provided with investment from several international donors and multilateral banks, including the European Commission Instrument for the pre-accession procedure, CEB, EBRD, EIB, KfV and the World Bank. The Western Balkans Investment Framework (VBIF) provided $426.2 million in renewable energy projects in the period covering 2010–2016 for coverage cost of feasibility and other technical studies (REN21 & UNECE, 2017). The Green for Growth Fund (GGF) makes direct investments in non-financial institutions with projects in these areas. Germany's KfV is a Financing Development Bank for renewable energy projects. Since 2010, KfV has financed the Podvelezje wind farms in Bosnia and Herzegovina with a loan of €65 million ($70 million) and a wind farm in Bogdanci in former Macedonia with a loan of €33 million ($35 million).

In the former Yugoslav Republic Macedonia, KfV also provided €32 million ($34 million for the rehabilitation of six hydropower plants (REN21 & UNECE, 2017)). The UNDP supports the Government of Serbia in the implementation of Goal 7 in the green economy: affordable and clean energy with biogas projects. The UNDP (2019) and the Global Environmental Facility (GEF) have concluded a five-year, $3 million project for new biogas projects in Serbia. The project is expected to provide CO_2 emission reductions of around 1 million tonnes over a 20-year green investment life cycle. New Power Plants (CHP) provided 100 new green jobs, increased the local tax base (corporate income tax) and reduced waste and wastewater from agricultural production.

Renewable energy is crucial for Serbia to cut CO_2 emissions and reach its environmental targets. The EBRD is co-financing the Cibuk and Kovacica wind farms, which will produce electricity for close to 180,000 households while reducing CO_2 emissions by more than 600,000 tonnes annually. To harness the potential of renewables, a program was launched in January 2019 by the EBRD and the Austrian Government for €4 million for development projects in solar thermal, geothermal technology and heat pumps. In Serbia, there has not been much implementation of investment in green projects with only feed-in tariffs for RE and only some favourable credits from IFIs, i.e. commercial banks. All green projects are financed from IPA. Other financing schemes are budgetary funds and the ESCO mechanism.

North Macedonia has refined its energy strategy and introduced a new energy data collection methodology that is in line with EUROSTAT. The result of the improved energy strategy brought about better government planning for the country's energy needs, energy resource management and diversification of energy supply. The process of harmonisation and collecting energy data began with a collaboration of two USAID projects: EC-LEDS Regional Program and USAID Macedonia's Clean Energy Project.

The project was realised as a result of good cooperation with the Cabinet of the Government of the Republic of Serbia. A working group introduced the EUROSTAT methodology for the MoE energy balance and to enable the Ministry of Economy to use the energy data that were already collected by the State Statistical Office, to support the development of national policies and meet reporting requirements to the Energy Community.

Bosnia and Herzegovina has great potential for environmental protection and green energy. Observed in the medium term, it has the conditions for sustainable economic development based on improvements in energy efficiency measures. Since 2013, it has been implementing a five-year Green Economic Development project. This project has been funded by Sweden and by the Environmental and Energy Efficiency Fund RS, ministries and other partners (UNDP).

According to a United Nations study (2019), Bosnia and Herzegovina had in the Western Balkan countries the best approach to investment project IPA CBC Alternergy. Small rural municipalities have the capacity and knowledge to develop and implement the projects in the following areas: replacement of the heating system, switching to wooden biomass, window and insulation replacement, and lighting. During 2016, the Fund realised financial commitments for the planned projects from the Government for environmental protection. By public competition on March 16, 2015, the financial obligations of KM 604,500 were realised. The planned investment was 350,000 KM, but investments in the amount of 106,962 KM were realised (Environmental and Energy Efficiency Fund RS — EEEF RS, 2017).

Recommendations

Based on a study by the World Bank (WB) and Securities Commission Malaysia (SCM) (2019), raising awareness of the green capital market would result in greater demand for sustainable financial services aimed at a sustainable green economy. Continuous cooperation at the global and local level in terms of reporting, innovation, implementation of standards, etc. would reduce transnational barriers in the green investment process. This would reduce costs for publishers and, on the contrary, would increase transparency and awareness for green investors. Continued demand for green investment products would create conditions for the continued growth of Islamic green finance and for Malaysia to become a catalyst for the sustainable growth of a green economy globally.

To be effective, the green economy and financing policies should be predictable and consistent over time, consistent with the existing energy market structure and coordinated with other policies. The governments of the countries of Southeast Europe (and the Western Balkans) play a key role in the investment activities regarding legal regulations and green economy investment policy. Recommendations for the types of activities in selected countries of the Western Balkans are given to raise awareness of energy efficiency and renewable energy sources nationally and locally, which implies green financing: Bosnia and Herzegovina needs to take actions at all levels from national to state to local. That includes workshops, seminars and conferences on varied topics, implementation of various projects and green investing in EE (energy efficiency) and RE (renewable energy). The result of raising awareness is increased interest of the public in introducing EE measures and using RE.

North Macedonia needs to take action to raise awareness at the national level: media marketing campaign about saving household energy on TV, flyers, billboards, etc.; publishing guidelines for development and financing green projects.

Private firms, local consultancy firms and the banking sector are also missing the required knowledge on the development of EE and RE. The results which are expected are reduction of household energy consumption and reduction of energy costs of the national economy. Raising awareness at the national and local levels in Serbia includes participation in various events that explain EE and RE policy to the general public, providing relevant information on web portals to the general public and investors about the prepared EE and RE guidelines for investors, providing advisory assistance on improvement of EE of buildings to the citizens/housing communities, and educational and training programs for professional managers to maintain multi-family buildings. The project documentation is of poor quality. The Ministry of Energy and Mining in Serbia has no financial capacity to organise and finance a program. The result of raising awareness is increased investments in EE and RE.

Conclusion

Green investments are very important especially for countries in transition, such as Serbia, North Macedonia, and Bosnia and Herzegovina. Green investments could reduce unemployment, increase exports and develop the entire SME sector in such economies. It can be stated that foreign investors "bringing green investment" in the Western Balkans opened the countries to the world. The policymakers, however, are aware of the facts and ground realities in the mentioned countries, and believe that green investments (such as greenfield investments) are "necessary" and that every effort will be made to attract them (in particular, in Serbia). However, this phrase is worn out from overuse, and the results achieved in "attracting green capital" are more than devastating.

On the contrary, some of the country's neighbours in the Balkans, such as Bulgaria and Romania, as well as the Croatia, had a much larger influx of green investments and investments in the green economy. These countries as members of the European Union, due to higher legal and economic security, create a motivating base for foreign investors to invest in green investments. Serbia is not at the top of the most attractive destination for green investments, but instead of increasing, as is the usual trend in Southeast Europe, green investments in Serbia are reduced. Investors who want to invest in Serbia and countries like it are wondering how safe it is to invest in a country that is still politically unstable. In Serbia, there is no clear national strategy as well as in other developed countries of the Balkans, where it is known that these are the areas in which it is advisable to invest in green energy and where the investors are encouraged in various ways to invest in certain sectors. There are issues related to the weak intersectoral cooperation between the Ministry of Economy and Regional Development, and this cooperation should be enhanced.

Green investment is pouring the most money into a country, because it starts from scratch, employing a complete workforce and moving production, which implies greater investment than, for example privatisation or brownfield investment. Green investments directly and unequivocally affect the growth of domestic employment and exports, which is another advantage for the host state. In addition, Serbia, like other countries that are still in the process of transition or have passed through it, such as North Macedonia and Bosnia and Herzegovina, does not have capital or modern production technologies, as well as domestic savings from which it could finance its development.

The practice of observing a closed and further-away environment (such as Malaysia and other ASEAN countries) shows how green investing has impacted economic growth and how this form of investment has directly (increasing employment, exports, paying taxes), but also indirectly, affected the economic development of a country. With these investments, subcontracting chains are formed and at the same time, small and medium-sized enterprises that are necessary for the development of the economies of transition countries are developing. However, at the end of this paper, we want to mention once more that countries that have associated a single market such as the EU and ASEAN Association come to sustainable development much easier because their economy is strengthened unlike small countries (Serbia, North Macedonia, Bosnia and Herzegovina), which have a far less developed economy and are alone. Smaller countries are forced to fend for themselves, waiting for better days for all, including for sustainable development, as well as green investment, hoping that they will also become full members of a strong Union. They have to put pressure on their customers to change their behaviour. And, they must also disclose information to its investors, who contribute to the pension funds, take deposits and buy insurance policies, because investors want to understand the level of risk of investment.

In this chapter, we have provided clear examples from Malaysia and the Balkan countries. It can be concluded that the Balkan countries have investments in sustainability such as green investments, while in Malaysia, the emphasis is on Islamic financial tools and government entrepreneurship to ensure financial stability. In this context, the importance of financial support from the state and of government entrepreneurship stands out when it comes to green investment and economic sustainability. Policymakers or entrepreneurs from the government have an important role to play in adopting strategies and mechanisms for financing green growth, promotion and technological innovation. Cooperation of government agencies is necessary through efficient partnerships and entrepreneurship and networking with domestic and international partners in the field of green growth for economic development.

References

Ahmad, N. H., H. A. Halim, T. Ramayah, and S. A. Rahman (2015). Green entrepreneurship inclination among Generation Y: The road towards a green economy. *Problems and Perspectives in Management*, 13(2–1), 211–218.

Azevedo, R., D. C. Moos, A. M. Johnson, and A. D. Chauncey (2010). Measuring cognitive and metacognitive regulatory processes during hypermedia learning: Issues and challenges. *Educational Psychologist*, 45(4), 210–223.

Berensmann, K. and N. Lindenberg (2016). Green finance: Actors, challenges and policy recommendations). *Briefing Paper* 23/2016. German development institute/Deutsches Institut für Entwicklungspolitik (DIE).

Benammar, K. and N. Cressel (2015). Forget sustainability: Go for green entrepreneurship. https://www.thnk.org/insights/go-for-green-entrepreneurship/.

CBI (2018). The Green bond market in Europe, The Climate Bonds Initiative, 15. https://www.climatebonds.net/files/files/The%20Green%20Bond%20Market%20in%20Europe.pdf.

Chiesa, M. (2017). The Green Bond Market: A new green trend. https://www.quadrantefuturo.it/settori/the-green-bond-market-a-new-green-trend.html.

Citizen (2018). Global Green Economy Index (GGEI): Dual citizen. https://dualcitizeninc.com/global-green-economy-index/.

Demirel, P. and G. O. Danisman (2019). Eco-innovation and firm growth in the circular economy: Evidence from European small- and medium-sized enterprises. *Business Strategy and Environment*, 28(8), 1608–1618.

Environmental and Energy Efficiency Fund RS (EEEF RS) (2017). Report on the implementation of the work plan and financial plan of the Environmental Protection and Energy Efficiency Fund of the Republic Srpska for the period January to December 2016. Banja Luka: EEEF RS, 51–52.

FORS Montenegro (2020). Handbook for green economy and green entrepreneurship. http://forsmontenegro.org/wp-content/uploads/2020/02/Zelena-ekonomija-prirucnik-4mail.pdf.

Goldstein, J. and D. Tyfield (2019). Green keynesianism: Bringing the entrepreneurial state back in? 32–33. https://nanopdf.com/download/article-about-green-keynesianism_pdf.

Harris, J. M. (2019). Ecological economics of the green. *GDAE Climate Policy Brief*, No.11. Somerville: Tufts University, 1–3. https://sites.tufts.edu/gdae/files/2019/10/ClimatePolicyBrief11_GreenNewDeal.pdf.

Ilic, B., D. Stojanović, and G. Djukic (2019). Green economy: Mobilization of international capital for financing projects of renewable energy sources. *Green Finance,* 1(2), 94–109. https://www.aimspress.com/fileOther/PDF/GF/GF-01-02-094.pdf.

Ilic, B., D. Stojanovic, and N. Pavicevic (2018). Green financing for environmental protection and sustainable economic growth — a comparison of Indonesia and Serbia. *Progress in Economic Sciences*. No. 5, 181–200, doi: 10.14595/PEW/05/012.

Ilic, B., G. Djukic, and M. Balaban (2019a). Management of green finance on the global level. In *Scientific Conference Accounting and Audit in Theory and Practice.* Banja Luka: Banja Luka College, 205–220, doi: 10.7251/BLCZB0119205I.

Jacobs, M. (2012). Green growth: Economic theory and political discourse. *Working Paper, No. 108*. Centre for Climate Change Economics and Policy, p. 9. https://pdfs.semanticscholar.org/6b16/d0d91baa816f2c9db42c20acff2927c84918.pdf.

Janmat, F. (2014) Social policy and employment reforms on the road to the EU, https://www.blic.rs/vesti/politika/frejk-janmat-reforme-socijalne-politike-i-zaposljavanja-na-putu-ka-eu/vpj2spt.

Kalkan, D. (2018). What is green financing and why it is more and more important? https://www.industrija.rs/vesti/clanak/sta-predstavlja-zeleno-finansiranje-i-zasto-je-sve-vaznije.

Kiburi, W. W., M. W. Mirie, K. O. Okiro, and G. M. Ruigu (2017). The Relationship between tax burden and foreign direct investment inflows: A review of the empirical literature. *European Journal of Accounting, Auditing and Finance Research*, 5(5). European Centre for Research Training and Development UK, p. 74.

Knezevic, S., B. Ilic, and Z. Babic (2013). Problems of modern times of global character — environmental protection and securing investments in the conditions of economic crisis. *Management in Hotel and Tourism*, Vol. 1, Vrnjacka Banja: Faculty of Hotel and Tourism, pp. 41–54.

Kraus, S., J. Burtscher, C. Vallaster, and M. Angerer (2018). Sustainable entrepreneurship orientation: A reflection on *status-quo* research on factors facilitating responsible managerial practices. *Sustainability*, MDPI, 10(2), 444, 1–21.

OECD (2015). Green Bonds Mobilising the Debt Capital Markets for a Low-Carbon Transition. Paris: OECD Publishing, pp. 13–28.

Radovic-Markovic, M. and B. Zivanovic (2019). Fostering green entrepreneurship and women's empowerment through education and banks' investments in tourism: Evidence from Serbia. *Sustainability*, MDPI, 11(23), 6826, 1–16.

Shahidullah, A. K. M. and C. E. Haque (2014). Environmental orientation of small enterprises: Can microcredit-assisted microenterprises be "Green"? *Sustainability*, 6, 3232–3251.

Stanisavljev, S., D. Djordjevic and D. Z. Cockalo (2019). Development of entrepreneurship among young people — significance and impact factors. https://www.researchgate.net/publication/333429184_Razvoj_preduzetnistva_kod_mladih_-_znacaj_i_faktori_uticaja_Development_of_entrepreneurship_among_young_people_-_significance_and_impact_factors.

Stojanovic, D. and B. Ilic (2018). Green financing in the function of risk management environment and sustainable economic growth. In *30th International Scientific Conference on Economic and Social Development*. Belgrade: John Naisbitt University Belgrade, pp. 69–76.

Stojanovic, D., B. Ilic, and B. Djordjevic (2014). Green economy — risks and challenges of sustainable economic growth. In *4th International Symposium on Natural Resources Management, Sustainable Development and Green Economy in Transition Countries — Challenges and Perspectives*. Zajecar: Megatrend University Belgrade, Faculty of Management Zajecar, pp. 103–111.

Sunny, S. A. and C. Shu (2019). Investments, incentives, and innovation: Geographical clustering dynamics as drivers of sustainable entrepreneurship. *Small Business Economics*, 52(4), 905–927.

Sustainable Development, Decent Work and Green Jobs, International Labour Conference, 102nd Session (2013). International labour office, Geneva, p. 8.

Vella, H. (2018). Global green bond partnership: Reinvigorating green energy investment, again. https://www.power-technology.com/features/global-green-bond-partnership/.

World Bank (WB) and Securities Commission Malaysia (SCM) (2019). Islamic green finance: Development, ecosystem and prospects, Malaysia: Suruhanjaya Sekuriti, p. 12.

Yatim, P., L. Ngan, and H. L. Lam (2017). Chapter: Financing green growth in Malaysia: Enabling conditions and challenges: Chapter, Publication of AIDC, *Chemical Engineering Transactions*, (eds.) Petar, S., P. S. Varbanov, R. Rongxin Su, H. L. Lam, X. Liu and J. J. Klemeš, 61, 1579–1584.

https://doi.org/10.1142/9789811228445_0009

Chapter 9

The State of Enterprises in West Africa: Psychological, Managerial and Environmental Perspectives

Rexford Owusu Okyireh[*,‡] and Marijke A. A. Okyireh[†,§]

[*]*Department of Marketing, Procurement and Supply Chain Management, University of Education, Winneba, Ghana*

[†]*Department of Business Administration, University of Professional Studies, Accra, Ghana*

[‡]*okyirehjoe@yahoo.co.uk*

[§]*marijke.okyireh@upsamail.edu.gh*

Abstract

This chapter evaluates the outcome of several studies undertaken in selected countries in West Africa on international entrepreneurship. Published works on venture creation and start-ups have been on the front burner for several decades on the best tactics in dealing with concerns. Entrepreneurial issues differ from one continent to another; however, there seems to be a common thread that weaves the fabric of the various continents including Africa. Studies on international entrepreneurship published between 2003 and 2019 were reviewed, and we concluded that entrepreneurship begins from small-scale businesses in West African societies and migrates into medium to large scales. Though several motives can be attributed to the reasons why people engage in entrepreneurship in West Africa, the success rate largely depends on one's self, family as well as government policies. The pivot of the research can be classified into psychological, management and environmental factors. We propose a model to capture the findings of the studies reviewed. Implications from this study are discussed for practice and future research.

Introduction

International Entrepreneurship (*IE*) is a concept that has been widely researched across the globe due to its relation with international business. As such, several researchers have proposed and continuously expanded the definition of *IE* to suit the discourse. One of the revised definitions as described by McDougall-Covin *et al.* (2014) states that international entrepreneurship is the discovery, enactment, evaluation and exploitation of opportunities across national borders in order to create future goods and services. The nature of *IE* cannot be examined without first identifying the concepts of entrepreneurship and factors that propel it.

In the recent past, entrepreneurial activity has received much attention because it is a behaviour that cuts across several societies. These activities enable people to develop their potentials and create wealth for themselves and their communities (Zahra and Wright, 2016). Inhabitants of these societies possess varied beliefs about how ventures are created, hence reducing unemployment in varied forms and ways. Welter (2011) argues that it is important for people to understand when or why businesses are created and who partakes in such ventures as well as the management of them. Reports from studies in West Africa have shown that three key factors drive entrepreneurial activities. These are psychological, management and environmental factors (e.g. Boso *et al.*, 2019; Quargarine, 2018).

Motivation and Purpose

The main objective of this study is to ascertain how and why people are inspired to set up businesses and create livelihoods for themselves and their societies. To achieve this, we selected published studies that lead to concepts like entrepreneurial behaviours, intentions and cognitions in two West African countries: Ghana and Nigeria. We chose these two countries because English is widely spoken and the authors are familiar with the entrepreneurial developments within the region.

Our review of the studies was grouped into three categories. We found that certain in-built characteristics make people susceptible to entrepreneurial activities and so we described these characteristics as *psychological factors*. The second set showed that processes for operating businesses have implications for the *performance of enterprises*. In the third set of papers, there was an indication that *situational factors* influence the intention to develop enterprises.

Our review enabled us develop a model to capture the opportunity sources in *IE* in West Africa.

Highlighting the Factors that Serve as Opportunity Sources

Psychological Drivers

First, it was gleaned from the papers that concepts such as personality traits, mental structures (cognitions) and intrinsic motives affect the performance of entrepreneurial activities. Personality traits in this case suggest that specific attributes of people predispose them to entrepreneurial activities. Also, the phenomenon of cognitions justifies how and why entrepreneurs make decisions in venture creation (Krueger, 2003). Furthermore, intrinsic motives are also described as the internal interest of an individual towards an entrepreneurial task (Kwarteng and Li, 2015). Evidence from start-up enterprises alludes to the fact that psychological factors have significant influence on entrepreneurial behaviour. Research by Okyireh (2018) examined two types of styles of thinking — analytical and intuitive, cultural orientations and psychological empowerment — and how it affects decision-making in Ghanaian enterprises. The results showed that both styles of thinking have a direct effect on entrepreneurial decision-making, whilst cultural orientations and psychological empowerment moderated the relationship between the two variables. The styles of thinking, analytical and intuitive, also connote rigid and flexible thinking techniques, respectively, and this implies that individuals with any of the two thinking styles have the potential to make decisions that can affect the performance of their enterprises. Hence, it is imperative for international entrepreneurship scholars to find ways of identifying types of information processing in potential entrepreneurs. Also, business owners who have devised strategies to assess entrepreneurial traits in the employees have found the results useful in enhancing positive outcomes in their businesses. Another paper by Mainela *et al.* (2014) assessed the various mediums through which innovation opportunities are enhanced and outlined some personal characteristics such as motivation, risk propensity and attitudes. The report also shows that some individuals possess traits that trigger inspiration, resilience to negative circumstances and these are likely to increase their intentions to create businesses. This report debunks the findings of Gartner (1985) who indicated that a multidimensional approach comprising individual, environment and organisational factors is the key determinant of an individual's orientation towards entrepreneurship.

In addition, Ekpe *et al.* (2014) assessed the role of gender role stereotypes, personality characteristics and other related variables in the entrepreneurial abilities of students in a theological seminary. A total number of 45 students were selected for the study and it was reported that there was a negative relationship between the combined factors of personality traits, gender role stereotypes and entrepreneurial behaviour. This implies that the more a student possesses the independent variables, the lesser its effect on entrepreneurial behaviour. The findings of Ekpe *et al.* (2014) affirm that in Ghana and Nigeria, much attention is given to characteristics of people who initiate enterprises and there is the belief that these may influence the outcome or performance of the business. Furthermore, Asamani and Opoku Mensah (2013) also examined the determinants of entrepreneurial inclination amongst Ghanaian university students. The study revealed that 520 students were potentially inclined to be entrepreneurial regardless of the presence of personality traits (leadership attributes, task performance attitude, achievement attitude and risk-taking attributes). The findings of this research also create awareness about how students are oriented to understand the discourse of entrepreneurship as well as the attitudes that enhance the development of small-scale enterprises. From the reviews, the findings of the studies are essential for building a concept on the genesis of *IE* in West Africa, which is that it is mainly initiated from a single unit, i.e. the individual.

Management Drivers

The second category of papers that was reviewed suggested that *IE* in West Africa is centred on how entrepreneurial activities are executed. In view of this, the sustenance of small- and medium-scale businesses determines the extent to which they are managed. Studies from Africa have shown that the way and manner in which businesses are initiated and sustained accounts for the growth of a country's economy (Abor and Quartey, 2010). The first paper reviewed from this category placed emphasis on the essence of skills development and entrepreneurial education. Entrepreneurial education is the process of acquiring the skills and knowledge needed in operating an enterprise (van Gelderen *et al.*, 2008).

Across the African continent, reports from the Global Entrepreneurship Report (GEM, 2018) indicate that the media have not shown enough effort in the entrepreneurial discourse compared to Asia and Europe. This phenomenon has an adverse effect on how entrepreneurship is seen and perceived, resulting in low levels of motivations across the continent. Notwithstanding the fact that entrepreneurship careers are introduced into the educational system at the tertiary level, several studies have reported that the nature of these career programs enhances entrepreneurial capacities through experiential learning (Dzisi and Odoom, 2017). A review of this paper by Nyadu-Addo *et al.* (2017) shows that Africans generally have entrepreneurial skills which help them develop and become more efficient in the management of their ventures. Their study brings to the fore the need for entrepreneurs to continuously organise and develop the skills of their employees for maximum performance in their organisations. This implies that, in order for international businesses to expand, the aspect of education should not be undermined.

Bamfo *et al.* (2015) also highlight the essence of management training for employees and affirm the case that job training exposes an individual to current trends in international business. The paper also discusses other managerial factors such as planning how business owners make decisions on the location, form, the use of resources and other organisational activities that aid in the achievement of the goals of business ventures (Bamfo *et al.*, 2015). Abdulsaleh and Worthington (2013) elaborate further on other managerial factors such as the use of financial resources. They explain financial management as the way the capital is used in operating the business efficiently as well as securing external funds for boosting the enterprise such as bank loans. In their view, an entrepreneur equipped with financial management means he or she has specific skills such as self-regulation, financial risk-taking, tolerance for managing business and operating capital that are beneficial or detrimental to the sustenance of the business. This paper brings to light that in Ghana, immense efforts are being made through management training to boost the financial resources of entrepreneurs. Despite these efforts, contrary reports from Nigeria tend to show that entrepreneurs, especially businesswomen, have challenges with the ability to save and secure loans for their business (Akanji, 2006). These contradictory findings in both countries show that, financial resources pose a challenge and when researchers in IE focus their attention on such key areas of management, it will boost the sector.

Another paper reviewed focused on entrepreneurial skills and that customer service has been shown to impact the performance of enterprises in Africa in varied ways. Customer service entails the activities (tangibility, reliability, responsiveness, empathy and assurance) that culminate in giving the best of service to customers. These characteristics do not work in isolation due to the complex nature of service (Baidoo and Odum-Awuakye, 2017) and, therefore, the success of a business largely depends on how customers are treated (Amah, 2017). Evidence from studies has reported that customers are not given the kind of treatment they deserve and, in most cases, it is as though the small business is doing the customer a favour (e.g. Abor and Biekpe, 2007). For example, aspects of the managerial process such as entrepreneurship education, planning, financial resources, logistics and customer care and the management of employees had implications for the performance of a business.

The implications of the findings in this category of papers show that the scope of *IE* encapsulates the activities that facilitate the management of the businesses in order to have an optimal performance. Therefore, these issues are quiet dominant in West African countries and it forms the core for future expansion of international businesses.

Environmental Drivers

There are also external factors which determine the growth and survival of enterprises in Ghana and Nigeria. These are culture and social capital. As enterprises are not established in isolation but within some cultural environments, entrepreneurship researchers have argued greatly for the role culture plays in the management and sustenance of a business. For instance, some cultural beliefs about women in entrepreneurship have impacted their level of productivity. Mordi *et al.* (2010) reiterate the notion that some Ghanaian societies still hold the view that a woman's primary role is being a family and child caregiver, which has formed the basis for gender inequality when it comes to allocation of resources for operating their businesses. The GEM (2019/20) survey results indicate that entrepreneurial activity takes place within a specific environment with unique cultural, social and economic characteristics. The report further shows that an individual's interaction within the environment determines the type of entrepreneurial activities to engage in. Additionally, some cultural orientations such as acknowledging the way power is distributed in society (power distance) and taking steps to reduce ambiguous situations (uncertainty avoidance and the extent to which a society values group interactions) have significant influences on entrepreneurial decision-making strategies (Okyireh, 2018).

The existence of social capital, that is the availability of social connections where information can be acquired on entrepreneurship skills, technical and financial capital can be obtained, also affects business in Ghana and Nigeria. For example, social capital is vital for start-ups and growing firms run by women entrepreneurs in Nigeria. Again, social capital has been widely measured and found to have a positive impact on the performance of women enterprises in developing countries (e.g. Ekpe *et al.*, 2010: Lawal *et al.*, 2009: Okyireh and Okyireh, 2018). In some Ghanaian tertiary institutions, the use of a mental process called arrangement scripts is very essential for potential student entrepreneurs as they believe that the use of networks provides emotional support and assistance during the operation of a venture (Okyireh and Okyireh, 2017).

Igwe *et al.* (2018) explored the entrepreneurial behaviour among Igbos in Nigeria. The study sought to understand some of the factors that affect entrepreneurial behaviour and concludes that extended family provides support for individuals within the community. In addition, the study makes an emphatic assertion that apprenticeship paves the way for young people to be entrepreneurial as they are taken through different types of training. It is worth understanding that Igbos in Nigeria are believed to be naturally inclined to entrepreneurial activities just like the Ashantis in Ghana. Ashantis believe strongly that they are the most endowed when it comes to entrepreneurship and this can be observed within several industries in Ghana.

Similar to Igwe *et al.* (2018) and Ugwa *et al.* (2019) concluded in a study that culture plays a vital role in the success of entrepreneurial ventures among women in Nigeria. The authors further opine that, though education is important, the heart of entrepreneurship rests solely in cultural dynamics (food, language, dress, etc.) as these help to have a targeted audience. Though these plausible indicators exist, there are some challenges expressed by Ofili (2014), which state that basic infrastructure such as water, power and the transport system impedes the fortunes of entrepreneurs in Nigeria. The work of Ofili (2014) continues to orate that these aforementioned challenges increase costs potentially on the overall outlook of the business environment and have the tendency also to discourage young people from engaging in a venture.

In the Ghanaian perspective, Adams and Quagraine (2018) investigated the narratives of some selected youth situated in Madina that cultural values can pose a challenge to setting up businesses. The findings of the paper showed that the dreams of some youth who set up their own businesses were thwarted by cultural practices of stereotyping, criticism, defying social expectations and rejection. The issues in Nigeria seem to be common with the Ghanaian outlook when it comes to the business environment, probably due to similar demographic characteristics. Again, the issues that have been described above imply that international enterprises ought to be aware of the situational factors as these may affect productivity in businesses. For instance, societies that value group interaction will encourage social capital or networks amongst entrepreneurs so that those who face challenges can seek assistance. Also, cultural practices such as stereotyping and discrimination can affect cross-border business participation as it will slow the economic growth of the destination country as well as remittances sent to home countries. Finally, some of the papers reviewed suggest that views about traditional roles assigned to men and women have some consequences on the participation in entrepreneurship activities. This is because these perceptions affect the quantum of opportunities available to both genders.

Methodology

We reviewed a total of thirty four (34) research papers from Nigeria and Ghana with a bit of perspective across the world. A majority of the studies used quantitative research procedures, whilst others used exploratory methods like interviews to understand the variables that sought to determine opportunity sources in International Entrepreneurship. Most of these studies employed students, women entrepreneurs and community participants or ethnic groups for the research. The studies conducted in both countries show that the target groups for entrepreneurial businesses are largely students, women and employees of organisations. The proliferative use of students for such studies implies that unemployment after school is a topical issue in West Africa and, therefore, governments and other stakeholders have tried to mitigate the effect on the economy with minimum success. Additionally, the women sampled also portray the significant role they play in enhancing the economic resources of their families and the shift in the caregiving role to others. Some of the studies also sought to understand the management of employees in the success of businesses in West Africa. The research variables investigated in the both countries (Nigeria and Ghana) show that the urgency attached to entrepreneurial discourse is very similar.

Observed Model of the Study

The model presented in Figure 1 shows how the three main factors, namely psychological, management and environmental, influence the

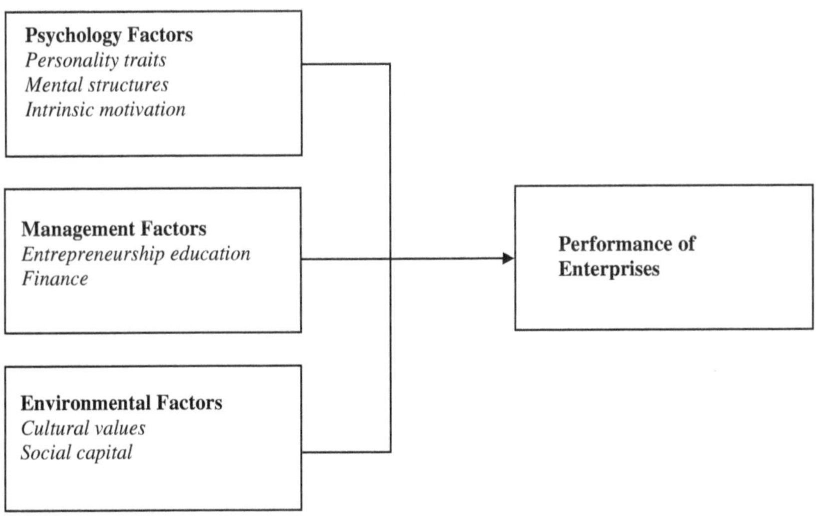

Figure 1: Conceptual Framework

Source: Adapted from the findings of Ekpe *et al.* (2010, 2014), Asamani and Opoku Mensah (2013), Okyireh (2018), Bamfo *et al.* (2015), Nyadu-Addo *et al.* (2017), Baidoo and Odum-Awuakye (2017), Okyireh and Okyireh (2017) and Adams and Quagraine (2018).

performance of enterprises in West Africa. Given the extant literature on entrepreneurship, it is evident that when these three factors are managed well, the fortune of enterprises will change for the better and can also help reduce the alarming rate of unemployment.

Implications for Practice and Research

Countries in West Africa have similar trends of unemployment and these are a result of numerous factors ranging from psychological, managerial and environmental. Several authors over the years have attempted to define entrepreneurship and its related areas in varied forms and concepts. In this study, we categorised the factors for having an effective enterprise in three forms with the first being psychological factors. According to the literature, personality traits, mental structures and intrinsic motivation have an effect on the performance of businesses. These effects can be negative or positive and hence it is important for enterprises to really determine through hiring processes the characteristics of individuals before they are hired. In addition, gender roles and stereotypes must be of prior importance to human resource practitioners who seek to break barriers within a given society. Many studies are of the view that entrepreneurship is a sure way to break out from poverty, and therefore, the ability to take risks, the change in attitudes and leadership styles are important in the survival of enterprises.

Second, the managerial factors according the literature are centred mainly on entrepreneurship education, finance and customer satisfaction. The ability of enterprises to perform better is largely dependent on availability of financial resource and agile mindset which ultimately ensure customer satisfaction. Moreover, the success of the business hugely depends on the customer service and satisfaction that is derived from patronising from a business entity. Customers generally must be treated well in order to have a lifetime value from them. Enterprises with poor customer orientations have the tendency to ruin an otherwise successful venture.

Lastly, environmental factors which consist of cultural values, social capital and its related concepts largely thwart the efforts of entrepreneurial intentions and activity. These are predominant with West African countries due to the cultural issues that pertain in these geographical setting. It is not uncommon to see a high rate of unemployment partly due to saturated educational programs and the upsurge in rural to urban migration. Moving on, these characteristics that have been outlined are paramount in addressing the issues raised and hence a solution ought to be found to address them.

Conclusion

The issues that confront enterprises in West Africa have some semblance with the global phenomenon as the variables being discussed are similar and, in some cases, the same as seen in Table 1. Issues in the entrepreneurship discourse are still being fine-tuned in order to address pertinent questions well. The current paper seeks to bring to light the psychological, management and environmental factors that seek to hamper the progress of enterprises in West Africa. The triad of factors is unique in terms of the perspectives shared within the West African region as a lot of works cited within the last ten years have scrutinised the factors individually and in advanced economies.

Furthermore, it is gleaned from the literature that there exist similar characteristics in starting a business in West Africa. The reasons that account for venture creation such as financial freedom, being a boss and solving societal problems are very similar across the sub-region. In addition, challenges faced in managing SMEs appear to be comparable as the socio-economic status is similar; hence, movement of goods, services and people across the West African states is much easier. The psychological drivers also show that apart from the unique characteristics that potential entrepreneurs may possess, flexible and rigid decision-making strategies also affect the sustenance of these businesses. Hence, the use of laid down business plans cannot be the ultimate criteria for achieving success in a business, but it should be blended with experimental methods until the desired goals are achieved.

One critical observation from the study is how the environment shapes cultural inclinations as well as traits of people wanting to be entrepreneurs. Individuals have goals and motivations, but the environment shapes the thoughts and experiences of such people, and hence, cultural dynamics and myths cannot be relegated to the background. African countries in general believe in mythology, which to a large extent influences decision-making, leadership styles as well as the type of venture to engage in. For example, Ashantis in Ghana believe entrepreneurship is a birthright for them just like the Igbos in Nigeria. These claims tend to subtly influence the business and the type of recruitment that is done.

Table 1: Summary of Entrepreneurial Issues in Developing Countries

Author	Variables	Findings
Abor and Biekpe (2007)	Credit and SMEs	Older and larger SMEs depend largely on bank loans and have relationship which helps both businesses to grow.
Abor and Quartey (2010)	SME development in Africa	Limited access to international markets and lack of finance.
Ekpe, Mat and Razak (2010)	Financing Small Business	Women entrepreneurs find it difficult to access finance which culminates in low productivity in developing countries.
Asamani and Opoku Mensah (2013)	Leadership attributes, task performance attitude, achievement attitude and risk-taking attributes	Students are exposed to these personality traits; however, the ability to be successful depends solely on finance and environmental factors.
Nwekeaku (2013)	Environmental factors and education	The lack of proper training has adverse effect on the mindset of students. These young minds are the future entrepreneurs, hence the right environment would give birth to a lot of potential business owners.
McDougall–Covin *et al.* (2014)	Concepts and theories in International entrepreneurship	Contextualising the issues as well as cross-cultural studies is key in international entrepreneurship.
Ofili (2014)	Challenges entrepreneurs face	The environment issues are enormous and may discourage any young mind wanting to be entrepreneurial, but persistence can break the ice.
Okyireh and Okyireh (2017)	Mental process (arrangement scripts)	Networks provided emotional support and assistance during the operation of a venture.
Adams and Quagraine (2018)	Culture and entrepreneurship	Businesses were thwarted by cultural practices of stereotyping, criticism, defying social expectations and rejection.
Igwe *et al.* (2018)	Family business	Apprenticeship helps in making a venture succeed due to the skills that are gained during the training period.

From the management perspective, there exists the Herculean task of West African states merging businesses to be competitive on the global market. Mergers and acquisitions are topics that are not discussed because, each business owner wants to carry the tag of being a boss or manager, but the bigger picture is that they are not competitive in most cases. The banking sector in Ghana for example has seen some cleanup whereby the Government was forced to merge some medium- and large-scale enterprises to be competitive whilst closing some of the small-scale businesses. The reforms have sanitised the sector and it is believed to be doing well. Managerial capacities have been a bane in moving businesses one step ahead and this paper seeks to bring to light the state of enterprises in West Africa.

References

Abor, J. and N. Biekpe (2007). Small business reliance on bank financing in Ghana. *Emerging Markets Finance and Trade*, 43(4), 93–102.

Abor, J. and P. Quartey (2010). Issues in SME development in Ghana and South Africa. *International Research Journal of Finance and Economics*, 39(6), 215–228.

Abdulsaleh, A. M. and A. C. Worthington (2013). Small and medium-sized enterprises financing: A review of literature. *International Journal of Business and Management*, 8(14), 36–54.

Adams, S. and F. A. Quagrainie (2018). Journey into entrepreneurship: Access and challenges of Ghanaian youths. *International Journal of Business & Economics*, 17(3), 239–253.

Adom, K., I. T. Asare-Yeboa, D. M. Quaye, and A. O. Ampomah (2018). A critical assessment of work and family life of female entrepreneurs in Sub-Saharan Africa: Some fresh evidence from Ghana. *Journal of Small Business and Enterprise Development*, 25(3), 405–427.

Amah, E. (2017). Pro-activeness and survival of small and medium scale enterprises in Nigeria. *Journal of Small Business and Entrepreneurship Development*, 5(2), 67–72.

Akanji, O. O. (2006). Microfinance as a strategy for poverty reduction. *Central Bank of Nigeria Economic and Financial Review*, 39(4), 111–134.

Asamani, L. and A. Opoku Mensah (2013). Entrepreneurial inclination among Ghanaian university students: *European Journal of Business and Management*, 5(19), 113–125.

Baidoo, F. and G. A. Odum-Awuakye (2017). Assessing customer satisfaction levels in the SMEs automobile vehicle maintenance and repairs service delivery system in Cape Coast–Ghana. *African Journal of Applied Research* (*AJAR*), 3(1), 82–94.

Bamfo, B. A., F. Asiedu-Appiah, and P. K. Oppong-Boakye (2015). Capacity building for entrepreneurship development in Ghana: The perspectives of owner-managers. *International Journal of Arts & Sciences*, 8(5), 481–498.

Boso, N., I. Adeleye, F. Donbesuur, and M. Gyensare (2019). Do entrepreneurs always benefit from business failure experience? *Journal of Business Research*, 98, 370–379.

Dzisi, S. and F. Odoom (2017). Entrepreneurship education and training in higher educational institutions in Ghana. *Journal of International Entrepreneurship*, 15(4), 436–452.

Ekpe, I., N. B. Mat, and R. C. Razak (2010). The effect of microfinance factors on women entrepreneurs' performance in Nigeria: A conceptual framework. *International Journal of Business and Social Science*, 1(2), 255–263

Ekpe, I., R. C. Razak, M. Ismail, and Z. Abdullah (2016). Entrepreneurial skill acquisition, psycho-social factors and youth's self-employment in Malaysia. *Journal of Entrepreneurship Education*, 19(2), 78–88

Gartner, W. B. (1985). A conceptual framework for describing the phenomenon of new venture creation. *Academy of Management Review*, 10(4), 696–706.

Global Entrepreneurship Report (2018). https://www.gemconsortium.org/report/gem-2018-2019-global-report.

Global Entrepreneurship Monitor Report (2020). https://www.gemconsortium.org/report/gem-2019-2020-global-report.

Igwe, P. A., R. Newbery, N. Amoncar, G. R. White, and N. O. Madichie (2018). Keeping it in the family: Exploring Igbo ethnic entrepreneurial behaviour in Nigeria. *International Journal of Entrepreneurial Behavior & Research*, 26(1), 34–53.

Lawal, J. O., B. T. Omonona, O. I. Y. Ajani, and A.O. Oni (2009). Effects of social capital on credit access among cocoa farming households in Osun State, Nigeria. *Agricultural Journal*, 4(4), 184–191.

Kwarteng, F. S. and Y. Li (2015). SMEs growth influencers: An exploratory study on the impact of entrepreneur character traits on SMEs growth in Ghana. *Journal of Economics, Management and Trade*, 9(4), 1–14.

Krueger, N. F. (2003). The cognitive psychology of entrepreneurship, In Acs, D. and D. Audretsch (Eds.), *Handbook of Entrepreneurship Research: An Interdisciplinary Survey and Introduction*, New York: Springer, pp. 105–140.

Mainela, T., V. Puhakka, and P. Servais (2014). The concept of international opportunity in international entrepreneurship: A review and a research agenda. *International Journal of Management Reviews*, 16(1), 105–129.

McDougall-Covin, P., M. V. Jones, and M. G. Serapio (2014). High-potential concepts, phenomena, and theories for the advancement of international

entrepreneurship research. *Entrepreneurship Theory and Practice*, 38: 1–10.
Mordi, C., R. Simpson, S. Singh, and C. Okafor (2010). The role of cultural values in understanding the challenges faced by female entrepreneurs in Nigeria. *Gender in Management*, 25(1), 5–21.
Nwekeaku, C. (2013). Entrepreneurship education and challenges to Nigerian universities. *Journal of Education and Practice*, 4(3), 51–56.
Nyadu-Addo, R. and M. S. B. Mensah (2018). Entrepreneurship education in Ghana — the case of the KNUST entrepreneurship clinic. *Journal of Small Business and Enterprise Development*, 25(4), 573–590.
Ofili, O. U. (2014). Challenges facing entrepreneurship in Nigeria. *International Journal of Business and Management*, 9(12), 258–274.
Okyireh, M. A. A. (2018). Entrepreneurial cognitions: Assessing the influence of cognitive styles and psychosocial factors on entrepreneurial decision making. University of Ghana. PhD Thesis.
Okyireh, M. A. A. and R. Okyireh (2017). Determinants of entrepreneurial decision-making among final year students in tertiary institutions. A Qualitative Study. *International Journal of Research in Computer Applications and Management*, 7(9), 74–77.
Okyireh, R. O., M. A. A. Okyireh, and I. Nyako Adu (2018). Dare to be entrepreneurial: A student's nightmare. *International Journal of Small Business and Entrepreneurship Research,* 6(5),16–30.
Quagrainie, F. A. (2018). Family values and practices promoting entrepreneurial competencies among Ghanaian women. *International Journal of Entrepreneurship and Small Business*, 33(2), 202–219.
van Gelderen, M., M. Brand, M. van Praag, W. Bodewes, E. Poutsma, and A. van Gils (2008). Explaining entrepreneurial intentions by means of the theory of planned behavior. *Career Development International*, 13(6), 538–559.
Welter, F. (2011). Contextualizing entrepreneurship — conceptual challenges and ways forward. *Entrepreneurship Theory and Practice*, 35(1), 165–184.
Zahra, S. A. and M. Wright (2016). Understanding the social role of entrepreneurship. *Journal of Management Studies*, 53(4), 610–629.

https://doi.org/10.1142/9789811228445_0010

Chapter 10

What Causes Social Entrepreneurship at a Societal Level? Emancipation Theory as an Explanatory Framework

Santiago A. Sena[*,‡] and Ricardo A. Pasquini[†,§]

[*]*IEEM Business School, University of Montevideo, Uruguay*

[†]*Universidad Austral, Faculty of Business, Argentina & Universidad Torcuato Di Tella, School of Government, Argentina*

[‡]*sasena@um.edu.uy*

[§]*rpasquini@austral.edu.ar*

Abstract

What causes the emergence of social entrepreneurship at a societal level? This chapter proposes that emancipatory theory provides an adequate theoretical framework in which to comprehensively understand the emergence of social entrepreneurship as an emancipatory phenomenon. We theoretically identify the elements of the human empowerment process (action resources, emancipative values and civic entitlements, in this sequence) that drive the emergence of social entrepreneurship.

Keywords: Social entrepreneurship; Emancipation theory; Social value.

Introduction

According to the United Nations Sustainable Development Goals Report (2017), despite having cut by half extreme poverty rates between 1990 and 2015, one in five people in developing regions still lives with less than 1.90 dollars a day, coverage of social protection systems for vulnerable populations is still very low, almost 800 million people around the world are undernourished and over 70% of victims of trafficking were women and girls, in 2014, among many other social and environmental problems that we still need to tackle. These "grandest" Challenges (Colquitt and George, 2011), defined as highly significant yet potentially solvable problems, affecting vast numbers of individuals in profound and various ways (Eisenhardt *et al.*, 2016) call for innovative solutions and approaches. Debates regarding the most effective ways to tackle social problems are held worldwide (Banerjee and Duflo, 2011). Social entrepreneurship has been acknowledged for its potential to solve complex and long-lasting social problems. Therefore, understanding what drives the phenomenon and clearly stating how it can be promoted are relevant issues both for the academy and for policymakers.

What causes the emergence of social entrepreneurship at a societal level? While the "embryonic" stage of development of social entrepreneurship as a research field (Short *et al.*, 2009; Hoogendoorn *et al.*, 2010; Choi and Majumdar, 2014) has allowed myriads of definitions to coexist, a good understanding of the causes for the emergence of such a pervasive global phenomenon (Bacq and Janssen, 2011; Defourny and Nyssens, 2010) at a societal level still seems to be missing. Despite important advances in the literature identifying potential drivers — both at the theoretical and empirical levels (Estrin *et al.*, 2013; Griffiths *et al.*, 2013; Hoogendoorn, 2016) — these contributions remain somehow conceptually isolated. With few exceptions, such as that of Stephan, Uhlaner and Stride (2015), studies seem to have motivated their drivers from different theories which are not always mutually aligned or conceptually harmonised. Accordingly, and following research calls from various entrepreneurial fields (Terjensen *et al.*, 2013), we understand that research on social entrepreneurship requires a coherent theoretical framework able to articulate and comprehensively explain its emergence. Comparative international entrepreneurship requires comprehensive frameworks in which to give sense to data (Jones *et al.*, 2011). This paper provides a conceptual contribution by theoretically framing social entrepreneurship as an emancipatory process.

The emancipation theory describes the processes by which human beings become free from the conditions that hinder their development (Alvesson and Willmott, 1992) and the pursuit of their values (Sen, 1999). Previous research introduced the idea of emancipation in the entrepreneurship literature by reconceptualising entrepreneurial activity as a means of emancipation (Rindova *et al.*, 2009). Moreover, another strand of the literature has proposed empowerment as the dominant logic of action of social entrepreneurs (Santos, 2012), and social entrepreneurship has been identified as a potentially emancipatory activity (Chandra, 2017). Building on Welzel's (2013) evolutionary theory of emancipation, we propose an explanatory framework for the emergence of social entrepreneurship that identifies the sets of elements of the human empowerment process (action resources, emancipative values and civic entitlements, in this sequence) as the drivers behind social entrepreneurial initiatives. We believe this theory serves to organise several drivers of a complex phenomenon such as social entrepreneurship, and it includes a dynamic perspective to the object of study, by understanding its elements as a sequence.

The contributions of this paper are relevant for emancipation theory and both for IE and social entrepreneurship research. First, at a theoretical level, we harmonise social entrepreneurship with individualism by building upon the concept of benign individualism (Welzel, 2013), a pro-civic form of individualism that encourages "other-regarding" initiatives. The intuition here is that emancipative values are a byproduct of individualism but have an orientation towards others, seeking to give them a voice and equalise the living conditions and opportunities of the others, the marginalised, the excluded and the poor. Second, we relate social entrepreneurship with the emancipation theory, providing a theoretical foundation and an explanatory framework for the emergence of the phenomenon, a necessary milestone for the further understanding of social entrepreneurship in an IE perspective. A unified conceptual framework contributes to the literature of comparative international entrepreneurship by providing a coherent theoretical foundation to comprehensibly understand the emergence of the phenomenon in different societies. Provided with such a theoretical approach, future research will be able to empirically corroborate the potential hypotheses derived from the framework, stimulate further studies in the field and give sense to contributions in the field that are not theoretically aligned. The emancipatory theory we propose can frame social entrepreneurship as an emancipatory process

(Rindova *et al.*, 2009) and sheds light on the reasons why some societies might be more socially entrepreneurial than others. Third, we contribute to Welzel's evolutionary theory of emancipation. Social entrepreneurship constantly reinforces the emancipation cycle since it is the result of emancipated individuals and societies and is, simultaneously, one of the ways by which underprivileged populations are promoted and empowered towards emancipation.

The remainder of the chapter proceeds as follows. In the next section, we introduce social entrepreneurship, Welzel's emancipation theory and "entrepreneurship as emancipation" perspective to reach our theoretical propositions. Discussion and Conclusion section discusses the relevance of the theory and its implications in light of the literature. We conclude by signalling the research limitations and future research directions.

Theory

Social Entrepreneurship

New streams of research have proposed to rethink and redefine the social value added by entrepreneurship to society (Zahra and Wright, 2016). Social Entrepreneurship has been acknowledged for potentially bringing innovative solutions to complex and neglected social problems. This is the reason why it has attracted the attention of governments (Lundstrom and Zhou, 2014), international organisations (e.g. World Bank, International Development Bank; Nicholls, 2010), the media and foundations, such as Ashoka or Schwab, that promote the work of social entrepreneurs.

As a field of research in an infant stage of development (Hoogendoorn *et al.*, 2010), most of the literature has focused on defining the construct and understanding which phenomena should be included under it (Short *et al.*, 2009). The phenomena included within the construct vary from "community-based entrepreneurship" (Peredo and Christman, 2006) to the "use of business knowledge in the social sector" (Porter and Kramer, 2011), including "social innovation" (Alvord *et al.*, 2004), "social reproduction" (Kenny *et al.*, 2020) and "the mobilisation of 'all-good' and politically neutral discourses" (Dey and Steyaert, 2018). Similar to the earliest stages of the field International Entrepreneurship (IE), when it was considered fragmented, inconsistent and lacking unifying paradigms (Keupp and Gassmann, 2009), several debates are open in the field of social entrepreneurship. Even the scope of the field and the relation of social entrepreneurs to profit-seeking activities are discussed, as presented by Austin *et al.* (2006) in a continuum that includes, in the extremes, from non-profits to traditional firms.

Despite the broadness of the approaches, there is generalised consensus in the field regarding the purpose for which social entrepreneurs work and innovate: to generate social change (Dees, 1998; Mair and Martí, 2004; Mair and Noboa, 2006), social impact (Nicholls, 2008) or social transformation (Alvord *et al.*, 2004; Roberts and Woods, 2005), and to create social value (Austin *et al.*, 2006; Weerawardena and Sullivan Mort, 2006; Zahra *et al.*, 2009). Social entrepreneurs want to alleviate poverty, include those that are excluded and regenerate the planet. They focus their attention and mobilise resources towards others. Social "change", "transformation", "impact" or "value" refers to an exogenous initiative towards something beyond the entrepreneur's self-interest (Santos, 2012). For social entrepreneurs, the provision of goods and services is not an end in itself but a means to achieve social objectives, thereby contributing to social change (Mair *et al.*, 2014).

According to GEM (2009), differences in the prevalence of social entrepreneurship cannot be explained exclusively by the level of economic development and are better attributed to the combined influence of regional variations in geographic, social and institutional backgrounds. Several authors (Estrin *et al.*, 2013; Griffiths *et al.*, 2013; Stephan *et al.*, 2015) have focused their attention on the drivers of the phenomenon at a societal level. Nevertheless, their conclusions vary and diverse variables had been identified as potential drivers of the phenomenon. Hitherto, many of these variables correspond to various theories and are not always mutually aligned nor conceptually harmonised. Broadly, most of the literature focuses on analysing the impact of economic, cultural and institutional variables on social entrepreneurship emergence. Different theories, which range from social capital theory (Estrin *et al.*, 2013) to the institutional void perspective (Hoogendoorn, 2016), coexist. The conclusions to which this set of studies reaches also vary, and recommendations for policymakers include dissimilar lines of action, such as, among others, augmenting women's participation in the labour force (Griffiths *et al.*, 2013), redistributing income and lowering levels of corruption (Méndez-Picazo *et al.*, 2015), giving visibility and legitimacy to social entrepreneurs (Estrin *et al.*, 2013), including cultural awareness and value-based issues in entrepreneurship education (Puumalainen *et al.*, 2015), or having a strong public sector expenditure (Hoogendoorn, 2016). This situation is coherent with the fact that this is an on-going conversation on a new topic where harmonised international datasets are the exception, rather than the rule. Although there are certain consensuses regarding the impact of some variables in social entrepreneurial activity, as self-expressive values (Hoogendoorn, 2016; Puumalainen *et al.*, 2015; Stephan *et al.*, 2015), there is still a way to go towards the objective of simply and elegantly explaining the reasons for social entrepreneurship to emerge at a societal level.

Emancipation

Emancipation describes the process through which individuals and groups become freed from repressive social and ideological conditions, in particular those that place socially unnecessary restrictions upon the development and articulation of human consciousness (Alvesson and Willmott, 1992). The idea of a life free from external domination where people can pursue their values is a universal desire (Sen, 1999). However, as the quest for freedom is adaptive, this desire flourishes or is hindered depending on the circumstances and contexts of a given person or group (Welzel, 2013). For centuries, inequality (Galor, 2011), miserable living conditions (Morris, 2010) and oppression of freedom (Diamond, 1997), among other factors, impeded development and emancipation from arising. Fortunately, although poverty traps and pockets (Sachs, 2005) continue to be the daily reality for millions of people worldwide, global indicators show that peace (Human Security Report Project, 2006), human rights, prosperity (UNDP, 2011), life expectancy at birth (World Bank Indicators), trust and even happiness and well-being (Inglehart, 2008) have been continuously rising for the past decades, particularly in post-industrial knowledge-based societies (Drucker, 1993). According to Beck (2002), people in these cosmopolitan societies experience both a process of globalisation and individualisation. Building upon these premises, Welzel (2013) affirms that emancipative values emerge as a psychological byproduct of individualisation. These values are particularly important as they constitute the motivational source of a broad process of human empowerment. Welzel (2013) presents a human empowerment framework based on an evolutionary theory of emancipation. This framework is connected to some of the factors that have been identified as drivers of social entrepreneurship, as emancipative values encourage a pro-social form of individualism that favours unselfish orientations that involve a concern for others and the environment.

Welzel's Theory of Emancipation

In 2013, Christian Welzel developed an *evolutionary* theory of emancipation affirming that human empowerment is the freedom to pursue valued utilities. For individuals, this means the development of personal agency, and for societies, the extent to which people are capable, motivated and entitled to exercise universal freedoms.

The human empowerment process has three constituent elements: action resources, emancipative values and civic entitlements. Action resources empower people by enhancing their capabilities. Motivations that encourage people to master their own life are catalogued as "emancipative values". Finally, civic entitlements empower people by guaranteeing their freedoms with a legal institutional framework, which includes personal autonomy rights, political participation rights and compensation rights.

All the empowerment process originates in an emancipatory desire to live free from any external domination. The desire for freedoms is adaptive: it drives people's efforts only as far as existential constraints allow. When these constraints decrease, freedoms grow and people gain control over their lives: the utility of freedoms increases, and people value freedoms accordingly. The sequence thesis of the emancipation theory suggests that whenever freedoms can arise, they will and that freedoms grow in a utility-value-guarantee sequence. Figure 1 summarises this thesis. This process seems to happen only at the individual level. However, a personal attribute's inherent impulse is amplified when the attribute's prevalence in a given society is high. The more people share the same

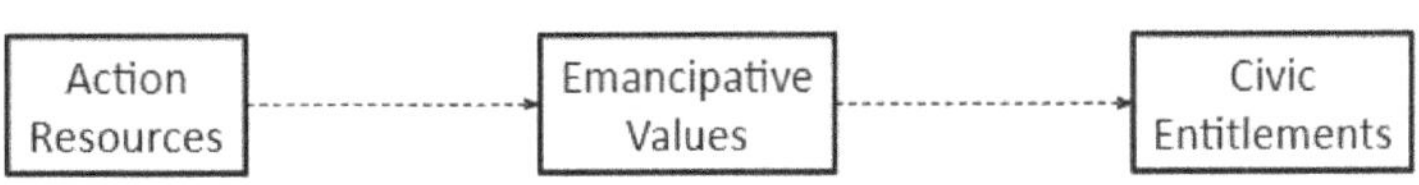

Figure 1: Welzel's Sequence Thesis

Table 1: Orientations and Domains of Emancipative Values.

	Orientations	Domains
Emancipative Values	Liberating orientation (emphasis on freedom of choice)	Autonomy Choice
	Egalitarian orientation (emphasis on equality of opportunities)	Equality Voice (postmaterialism)

values in a given society, the stronger each individual will affirm these values: this pattern is called *cross-fertilization*. The sequence is, therefore, collective: universal freedoms grow from joint utilities to shared values to general guarantees. Inclusive human empowerment implies that resources and values are common to the majority of society providing, thus, the basis for solidarity and the capacity of collective action, in the form of civic agency.

The cultural element of the empowerment process is related to *values*. "Emancipative values" is a construct that was built inspired in Inglehart and Welzel´s (2005) "self-expression values". Welzel argues that a new conceptualisation is needed since self-expression values are a necessary but insufficient condition for emancipation.[1] Emancipative values are a combination of two different orientations, comprising two domains each. On the one hand, the liberating orientation emphasises the possibility of making autonomous and free choices, and it is constituted by the domains of Choice and Autonomy, constructed using the World Values Survey answers. On the other hand, an egalitarian qualification of that liberating orientation translates into the search for "equality of opportunities", and its two constituting domains are Equality and Voice. Table 1 summarises the different elements that constitute the theoretical construct of "emancipative values" in Welzel (2013).

Emancipative values are a consequence of a process of individualisation that frees people from their dependence on narrow, uniform and close

[1] Welzel considers that emancipation is the process by which people internalise authority over their own life. To do so, the authority should be demystified and no external sources of authority should coerce people's freedoms. Internalising authority is necessary and, therefore, secular values are a necessary part of the process of emancipation. However, to be truly empowered people need other tools, such as action resources. Secular values by themselves do not lead to emancipation. For this reason, they are not sufficient conditions for empowerment.

support groups that they have not chosen. Despite individualism having been generally associated with a selfish or anti-civic orientation, emancipative values represent a benign form of individualism that is pro-civic and that stimulates caring for other people and the environment, trust and openness towards diverse groups of people. According to Welzel (2013), while these values unambiguously favour generalised trust and a humanistic orientation that welcomes diverse collectives, they also increase unselfishness and "other caring". Moreover, this "other caring" principle is applied to the environment, since the stronger emancipative values are in a given society, the easier environmental awareness translates into environmental activism.

Entrepreneurship as emancipation

The emancipation theory is not new to entrepreneurship literature. Several authors have proposed to apply the idea of emancipation in the context of management studies (Willmott and Alvesson, 1992) and, particularly, in entrepreneurship research (Rindova *et al.*, 2009). According to Rindova *et al.* (2009), entrepreneurship research "requires a bit of emancipation", since it has become too narrowly focused on wealth creation via new ventures, by assuming that wealth creation is the fundamental goal of entrepreneurial efforts. The authors questioned this assumption by proposing entrepreneurship as a change creation activity and by introducing the term *entrepreneuring* to draw attention to actions and processes geared towards change creation. *Entrepreneuring* is defined as the efforts of individuals or groups to bring new economic, social, institutional and cultural environments through their actions. This emancipatory perspective of entrepreneurship generated a new conversation within entrepreneurship research and, particularly, with social entrepreneurship. However, although there are several connections and potential bridges between this nascent research stream and the elements of the human empowerment process proposed by Welzel's emancipation theory, the latter have remained absent in this debate.

Rindova *et al.* (2009) point out that an emancipatory perspective on *entrepreneuring* should focus on the social change agenda that is inherent to every entrepreneurial project. From that perspective, the distinction between regular and social entrepreneurship blurs, since many entrepreneurs seek to improve their economic positions through the impact of broader social change. Building upon this paradigm-shifting paper, different studies deepened and empirically tested insights from the entrepreneurship-as-emancipation perspective. While Chandra (2017) explored the emancipatory potential of social entrepreneurship as a means to disengage individuals enthralled in ideology by allowing them both to escape constraints and to build new meaning for their life, Martí, Courpasson and Barbosa (2013) situated the phenomenon of *entrepreneurisation* of a local community at the cross-section of social entrepreneurship, community entrepreneurship and *entrepreneuring* as emancipation. Besides case study research, another prominent example is that of Mair *et al.* (2012), who derived different models of social *entrepreneuring* from texts generated by 200 social entrepreneurs who had been selected as fellows either by Ashoka or by the Schwab Foundation. They concluded that four different — and not mutually exclusive — models of social *entrepreneuring* exist, differentiated by the type of capital that each leverages: political, economic, human and social. Many of the papers in this literature focus on the processes by which certain collectives are empowered and pursue emancipation and are, consequently, qualitative and case-centred. Some prominent examples include cases of a local community in the south of Argentina (Martí *et al.*, 2013); women cooperatives (Datta and Gailey, 2012) and a social enterprise (Pless and Appel, 2012), both in India; displaced Palestinian women in East Amman, Jordan (Al-Dajani *et al.*, 2015); three social movements in the Netherlands (Montesano Montessori, 2016); or former religious terrorists in two social businesses in Indonesia (Chandra, 2017). None focuses on the drivers of social entrepreneurship at a societal level nor intends to explain the emergence of the phenomenon by building upon the emancipation theory.

There are many conceptual synergies between Rindova *et al.*'s (2009) call to introduce emancipation in entrepreneurship research and Welzel's evolutionary emancipation theory. New avenues in the existing conversation between entrepreneurship research and emancipation theory can be opened by introducing Welzel's emancipation theory as a possible explanatory framework for social entrepreneurship.

Emancipation and Social Entrepreneurship

We introduce Welzel's theory of emancipation by proposing a set of theoretical propositions that derive from his human empowerment framework. By doing so, we frame the phenomenon of social entrepreneurship in an integrative theoretical framework that coherently scaffolds it and that explains its emergence in an articulated manner. The sequence thesis of the emancipation theory suggests that emancipative values emerge in response to people's growing control over action resources. Action resources are material, intellectual and connective. All three types of resources have been highlighted as affecting social entrepreneurship in previous research. Regarding the material action resources, the better resources a society has, the better fitted it will be to address social problems. In places where people have enough money, social initiatives might flourish, since consumers are able to buy products and use services that in poorer conditions would not be purchasable: "fair trade" products could serve as an example. Additionally, better material resources mean better equipment, tools and higher income. Wealthier people reduce the cost of failure if their social businesses do not flourish better than poorer people, and can also leverage their organisation's growth with personal funding. Regarding intellectual action resources, several studies have linked the capabilities of people to the propensity of starting up social businesses (Shaw and Carter, 2007; Bravo Monge, 2018). Better skilled people, with better access to information and knowledge, will probably be more able to identify opportunities and think of innovative solutions to social problems than people that are unskilled or that do not have relevant information or knowledge. Nga and Shamuganathan (2010) show that certain (educable) personality traits have a positive impact on social entrepreneurial dimensions. Social entrepreneurs benefit from environments that boost appropriate levels of human capital (Méndez Picazo *et al.*, 2015). Moreover, Levie and Bosma (2009) observe that the education levels of individuals are positively linked to the propensities of being engaged in social entrepreneurial activity, across all phases of economic development, meaning that the more educated people are, the better the chances of them of becoming social entrepreneurs. Regarding connective action resources, Huybretchs and Nicholls (2012) affirmed the following: "making rise of global connectedness has improved the ability of citizens to identify and respond to social and environmental needs. The rise of new social media has also accelerated and intensified the interactions among social entrepreneurs, funders and other stakeholders. The involvement of individuals as social actors can be linked to the development of a 'pro-am' culture (Leadbeater, 2006) and the emergence of ′new localism′ (Murray *et al.*, 2010)". The better connected people are, the more conscious they are regarding other people's unsatisfied needs, and the more resources they 9ncreasinise to attend these unmet social demands since social capital lowers transaction costs by enabling resource access through collaboration and cooperation (Meyskens *et al.*, 2010). Connected people have a rich social capital and are part of networks of exchange and contact interfaces that boost their ability to gather resources and to direct these resources towards their objectives. Stephan and Ulhaner (2010) have shown that a socially supportive culture positively affects commercial entrepreneurship and Stephan *et al.* (2015) concluded that the same happens for social entrepreneurship. For all of these reasons, we propose the following:

Proposition 1: Action resources drive social entrepreneurship at a societal level.

Previous research has highlighted the importance of culture as a determinant of economic behaviour (North, 1990; Williamson, 2000). Different studies have analysed, particularly, the relationship between entrepreneurship and culture (Acs, 1992; Thomas and Mueller, 2000; Hayton *et al.*, 2002). For example, Thomas and Mueller (2000) built over Hofstede's (1980) extensive cultural studies and concluded that some cultures are more conducive for entrepreneurship than others. Uhlaner and Thurik (2007) find that certain cultural values (self-expression values) hinder commercial entrepreneurship. Specifically, in Social Entrepreneurship research, according to GEM (2009), differences in the variation of the phenomenon are attributed to regional variations in economic development and to social, geographic and institutional backgrounds. Variations in social entrepreneurial activity cannot be attributed exclusively to economic factors (Griffiths *et al.*, 2013). Hoogendoorn (2016) affirms that societies with a higher prevalence of self-expression values will generate more social entrepreneurial projects, *vis-à-vis* commercial projects. According to Inglehart, self-expression values are the consequence of a process of individualism. Heated and historical disputes regarding the "nature" of individualism are still open. Some authors consider individualism to be a selfish process (Hofstede, 2001) that causes people to focus on their well-being to the detriment of collectivistic values, in which members of a group might expect their relatives to look after and to favour them. Individuals become self-centred and decrease their concern for others. Other authors view individualism as a source of autonomy and independence from closely knit groups (Schwartz, 2004) but not, necessarily, of selfishness. In the social entrepreneurship literature, Hoogendoorn and Hartog (2011) observed that individualism can be considered as a driver of the phenomenon. The selfish–unselfish debate is relevant for social entrepreneurship since social entrepreneurs have been highlighted for their "strong ethical fibre" (Drayton, 2002), for being "concerned with caring and helping more than with making money" (Thompson, 2002) and for their "social mission" (Dees, 2001). Social entrepreneurship is theoretically founded over the assumption that people are driven by intrinsic motivations that imply helping others and including them. This is one of the reasons they are considered "change agents" (Sullivan Mort *et al*., 2003; Barendsen and Gardner, 2004). Further, Miller *et al*. (2012), intending to show how compassion turns into social entrepreneurship, built a model that included three mechanisms, one of which was the commitment to alleviating others' suffering.

Emancipative values are a byproduct of individualisation. The apparent paradox between individualisation and social entrepreneurship is theoretically interesting since a process that supposedly favours selfishness moves people to start ventures that solve social and environmental problems. Additionally, Welzel (2013) affirms that these values tie individualism to a pro-social orientation, turning it into a benign form of individualism. This definition might shed light on this apparent paradox since it might synthesise the opposition between "other-regarding and caring" and "individualism". Welzel claims that the social prevalence of emancipative values unleashes and amplifies the unselfish impulse of an individual and that more prevalent emancipative values raise a society's mean levels of both individualism and unselfishness. This pro-civic orientation of emancipative values favours openness towards diverse people, bridging upon group boundaries and orienting interest and resources towards others and the environment. By voicing claims of those that are excluded and mobilising resources towards their active integration and empowerment, people might be, in fact, acting as many social entrepreneurs do. Particularly, the egalitarian orientation of emancipative values is directly linked to the type of objectives that social entrepreneurs usually pursue, as it initiates an exogenous process that focuses attention on "others". Several traits that have been related to social entrepreneurs are coincident with emancipative values, such as pursuing well-being over material or financial priorities, commitment towards environmental sustainability, supporting social issues that go from gender equality to integration and voicing of ethnic minorities and immigrants, among others. Emancipative values favour generalised trust and humanistic orientations, vitalising civil society and generating collective action and social movement activity. Following this idea, among the many ways in which the umbrella construct of social entrepreneurship has been defined, one conceptualisation (Sena, Rocha and Martí, 2018) implies defining the concept as "collective action" and/or community-based enterprise (Hulgard and Spear, 2006; Peredo and Christman, 2006). For all of these reasons, we propose the following:

Proposition 2a: Emancipative values drive social entrepreneurship at a societal level.

As Maslow (1954), Levie and Bosma (2010) affirm, only when a person's own needs are already satisfied will that person be able to attend to other people's needs. Extreme deprivation hinders people from attending to "higher demands". This is coincident with Welzel's sequence thesis of the emancipation theory, where values arise if people are relatively capable. "Emancipative values" are understood as a theoretical construct comprising four different components or domains that were clustered into two main orientations, one related to freedom and the other related to equality of opportunities. Although we have asserted that at a societal level more emancipative values will display more social entrepreneurial activity, the emancipative values constituting components might have a different impact on driving social entrepreneurship. On the one hand, the liberating orientation of emancipative values is focused on the value given to the possibility of making autonomous and free choices. The two domains that constitute the liberating orientation are Autonomy and Choice. On the other hand, the egalitarian orientation of emancipative values emphasises equality of opportunities and its two constituting domains are Equality and Voice. Prima facie, social entrepreneurship seems to be better theoretically founded in the egalitarian orientation than in the liberating orientation. As Prabhu (1999) notes, the term "social" refers to initiatives aimed at helping others, and social entrepreneurs are people who create organisations whose primary mission is the development of their client group. Social Entrepreneurship is generally associated with an "other" (a given community or group; a disadvantaged person; a minority; or even the environment) that is, in a way, excluded from society by not being able to access a service or exercise a right. This pro-social interest (Zahra *et al.*, 2009) inherently pushes entrepreneurs to "others". Mair and Martí (2006), for example cite three cases while distinguishing the distinctive domain of social entrepreneurship and all three of them are related to the inclusion and integration of a collective and the alteration of existing social structures by combining resources. The Grameen Bank gave financial accessibility to the poor; Aravind Eye Hospital cured thousands of blind people who were unable to pay for surgery; and Sekem generated sustainable development by including people in value chains while respecting ecological principles. Several papers use different examples because most of the empirical literature in social entrepreneurship is qualitative and case-centred (Short *et al.*, 2009). However, the commonality among them is that the studied organisations and individuals are attempting to generate an impact, considered "social", by promoting the development of either an "other" or of the environment. *Helping society* is one of the themes that motivate social entrepreneurs (Germak and Robinson, 2014) and Miller *et al.* (2012) highlight the commitment to alleviating others' suffering as a mechanism to turn compassion into social entrepreneurship. The attention is always centred on others. Is precisely the intention of giving autonomy and freedom of choice *to others* what moves social entrepreneurs? Combating malaria, AID/AIDS, or other diseases; promoting gender equality; fighting against poverty and hunger; or generating labour inclusion, are all other-centred or collective-centred activities. Undeniably, entrepreneurs emphasise freedom of choice. Autonomy is an important dimension of entrepreneurial orientation (Lumpkin and Dess, 1996; Lumpkin *et al.*, 2009). That is the reason why it has been proposed as the guiding aim of entrepreneurship education (Van Gelderen, 2010). Business starters want autonomy (also labelled as independence or freedom) (Van Gelderen and Jansen, 2006). Rindova *et al.* (2009) highlighted three aspects of *entrepreneuring*, one of which is "seeking autonomy". Emancipative values are an emancipative force and both its orientations possess emancipative compounds. The liberating orientation of emancipative values is adequately framed in an emancipation theory. However, although the locus of control (Rotter, 1966; Brockhaus, 1980b) and the desire of autonomy (Caird, 1991; Cromie and O′Donaghue, 1992) have been identified as entrepreneurial traits, and that the domain of Autonomy is framed in the "*entrepreneuring*-as-emancipation" perspective (Rindova *et al.*, 2009), the specific difference of social entrepreneurship or the "social" in social entrepreneurship is the exogenous force that funnels attention, resources and energy towards others. The egalitarian orientation of emancipative values, or the focus on equality of opportunities, is the motivational incentive that pushes entrepreneurs into action, more than the liberating orientation that is centred mainly on the individual. For these reasons, we propose the following:

Proposition 2b: The egalitarian orientation of emancipative values drives social entrepreneurship more than the liberating orientation, at a societal level.

The two domains in the egalitarian orientation, Equality and Voice, have already been cited in social entrepreneurial literature as drivers for social entrepreneurs. The other-regarding tendency, inherent to social entrepreneurship, assumes that everybody needs to meet a minimum living standard, under which it would be not acceptable to live. Giving every person the same opportunities is what drives social entrepreneurs into action. This process assumes that every person, particularly within those collectives that are excluded, have the same rights as everybody else. Social entrepreneurs assume that people are equal and that, as a consequence, they should be recipient of social initiatives that will promote them in whatever dimension they are excluded from. To cite an example, in 2007, Martin & Osberg defined social entrepreneurship in the following terms: "We define social entrepreneurship as having the following three components: (1) identifying a stable but inherently unjust equilibrium that causes the exclusion, marginalization, or suffering of a segment of humanity that lacks the financial means or political clout to achieve any transformative benefit on its own; (2) identifying an opportunity in this unjust equilibrium, developing a social value proposition, and bringing to bear inspiration, creativity, direct action, courage, and fortitude, thereby challenging the stable state's hegemony; and (3) forging a new, stable equilibrium that releases trapped potential or alleviates the suffering of the targeted group, and through imitation and the creation of a stable ecosystem around the new equilibrium ensuring a better future for the targeted group and even society at large". Definitions of social entrepreneurship abound. Zahra *et al.* (2009) identified twenty different definitions and Dacin *et al.* included 37 in their 2010 paper. However, no matter how many, a vast array of definitions identifies the objective of generating a long-lasting solution to a given social problem: inequality, poverty, some kind of exclusion suffered by a collective or group. The literature of the field is clear in the point that social entrepreneurs intend to include the deprived. Following Welzel, what the domain of equality represents is the assertion that everybody is equal. And, therefore, everyone's rights should be equally granted. Social entrepreneurs intend to grant these basic rights among those that are excluded, either because of poverty or because they are part of a minority that suffers particularly. Welzel considers that the most basic area of equality is gender equality. From a theoretical perspective, this does not entail a particular problem since "equality" as a domain reflects how much people value egalitarian treatment of human beings. It would be conceptually contradictory to defend equality in a particular context (e.g. gender) but to give unequal treatment to people because of their race, ethnicity or sexual orientation. Such an approach, closer to an Orwellian "Animal Farm" (1945) definition of equality, would be theoretically and logically invalid. Seemingly tautological, if a person believes that people are equal, he believes that they are equal no matter what differentiates them from others. Valuing equality translates into a certain axiological-ladder preference that implies that everybody deserves the same treatment, for the sole reason of being a human being. Without people valuing equality, there should be no foundation nor motivation for social entrepreneurial activity, since entrepreneurs would not be moved towards "others" or to their inclusion. For these reasons, we propose the following:

Proposition 2c: The domain of Equity drives social entrepreneurship at a societal level.

The second domain of the egalitarian orientation of emancipative values is Voice. Voice is not only "freedom of speech" but also voicing for those that could not participate in relevant decision-making processes, regarding both government and intermediate/commun–ty-level affairs. This domain of emancipative values is more widely known as *postmaterialism*. Under conditions of insecurity and of material scarcity and deprivation, people will expectedly give priority to the satisfaction of these essential and basic human needs (Maslow, 1954). Once these primary needs are satisfied, people might engage in activities related to the satisfaction of "higher" demands. Inglehart and Baker (2000) argue that when societies reach a given point of economic development, there is a transformation in the prevalent values that guide the persons living in it, from a society based on survival values into one where self-expression values and postmaterialism are prominent. Individuals turn to problems "outside" themselves and their groups when basic needs are satisfied. Previous research (Hoogendoorn and Hartog, 2011; Puumalainen *et al.*, 2015; Stephan *et al.*, 2015; Hoogendoorn, 2016) has already identified postmaterialism as a driver of social entrepreneurial activity. As Puumalainen *et al.* (2015) note, self-expressive values are linked with a growing emphasis on environmental protection, men's movement and rising demands for participation in economic and political life. All of these demands are coincident with the priorities of societies where emancipative values are prevalent (Welzel, 2013). Promoting those "without a voice", providing them the tools and resources to actively participate in society as equals, is the objective of many social entrepreneurs. For these reasons, we propose the following:

Proposition 2d: The domain of Voice drives social entrepreneurship at a societal level.

Finally, following the sequence thesis of Welzel's emancipation theory, the completing element of the human empowerment process is civic entitlements. Civic entitlements are guarantees for private and public action, for both personal and civic agency. By increasing personal autonomy rights and political participation rights, people are able to shape their private lives as they prefer and make their preferences heard and considered in the public sphere. Institutions are humanly devised constraints that structure political, economic and social interactions (North, 1991). Formal institutions assume the form of laws, property rights and rules. Welzel (2013) considers that institutions that guarantee universal freedoms are the result, and not the cause, of the empowerment process. Institutions complete the human empowerment process but do not initiate it. When freedoms grow, people gain control over their lives and their society's agenda. Emancipative values emerge as the psychological link between the growing utilities of these freedoms and their guarantees. The quality of these guarantees, e.g. a strong legal system, works as an incentive that guides the decisions of entrepreneurs (Estrin *et al.*, 2013), and a good regulatory framework is positively related to both commercial and social entrepreneurship entry (Estrin *et al.*, 2013). A supportive institutional context enhances social entrepreneurial activity (Stephan *et al.*, 2015) and countries with stronger rules of law and lower levels of perception of corruption have more social entrepreneurs (Méndez Picazzo *et al.*, 2015). Moreover, according to Sullivan (2007), governments can even support and promote social entrepreneurship within communities. For these reasons, we propose the following:

Proposition 3: Societies with stronger guarantees for personal agency and civic agency will display more social entrepreneurial activity.

Discussion and Conclusion

In this section, we specify the contributions to the emancipation theory and to both social entrepreneurship and IE literature. We conclude by pointing out the study's limitations and future research opportunities.

Contributions to the Emancipation Theory

We incorporate a novel element within the empowerment framework of Welzel's evolutionary theory of emancipation: the phenomenon of social entrepreneurship. Empowered and emancipated people intend to emancipate others by improving their existential conditions by, among other means, starting social ventures. Social entrepreneurship is part of the cycle of the human empowerment process proposed by Welzel's emancipation theory: empowered people start social businesses to address social and environmental challenges, and, additionally, social businesses and entrepreneurs modify the existential living conditions of excluded groups, allowing them to start the empowerment cycle process. We embedded the phenomenon of social entrepreneurship in the explanatory power of the emancipation theory.

First, social entrepreneurship is a consequence of the initiative of emancipated people. As previously affirmed, emancipative values tie individualism to a pro-social orientation, turning it into a benign form of individualism that is oriented towards others. Clearly, social entrepreneurship is one possible concretion of this pro-social behaviour that emancipative values encourage. Benign individualism moves individualistic people towards others, by providing them a voice and equalling their opportunities. Contrary to a culture of selfishness and greed (Mintzberg *et al*., 2002; Hemingway, 2005), social entrepreneurship is an inherently other-oriented activity by which entrepreneurs propose solutions to neglected social problems. Gender equality, poverty alleviation and the inclusion of minorities are among the type of objectives that social entrepreneurs usually pursue. The egalitarian orientation of emancipative values moves people to address these problems since gender or income inequality and exclusion make it impossible for people to be capable of exercising freedoms at their fullest. Social entrepreneurship is a byproduct of emancipated individuals and societies.

Second, according to Welzel (2013), empowered societies are ecologically aware and translate their environmental consciousness into activism. Social entrepreneurship addresses both social and environmental objectives. People activate their environmental consciousness through social ventures and businesses. Social entrepreneurship works as a means through which empowered individuals address environmental challenges towards sustainability.

Finally, another important insight is that social entrepreneurship tackles the conditions and contexts of people living under existential stress. Therefore, social entrepreneurship is part of the cycle of empowerment described by Welzel. Following his theory, empowered individuals and groups address oppressive living conditions so as to enable other (disadvantaged) members of the society to fully develop their capabilities and action resources. By improving their living conditions and promoting their welfare, the excluded individuals and groups are able to increase their actions resources, and the emancipation cycle grows in traction with the flow of people that starts the empowering process. Valuing their newly acquired freedoms, emancipative values among these individuals grow. Following the cross-fertilisation proposition, a person's emancipative values have a stronger impulse when these values are more prevalent in the society where this person lives. The more people value freedoms, the more prevalent the values are and the more each individual defends these values. Social entrepreneurship is a pro-social behaviour that waxes this virtuous cycle constantly. Coherent with the idea of being a cycle, social entrepreneurship is not only a consequence but also a cause of the empowerment process: empowered people that affirm emancipative values are moved by "benign individualism" to promote the living conditions of disadvantaged groups through, among other means, social entrepreneurship; these groups are able to exercise freedoms and value them, developing emancipative values; these newly empowered individuals help values to be more prevalent in the society and, therefore, every individual reinforces its preferences for these values (cross-fertilisation); and finally, empowered individuals develop benign individualism and start social businesses and ventures to promote the lives of others.

Contributions to Social Entrepreneurship

The contributions of this paper for social entrepreneurship literature are twofold: (a) first, we harmonise social entrepreneurship with individualism by building upon the concept of benign individualism and, (b) second, following Rindova *et al.*'s (2009) call, we relate social entrepreneurship with emancipation theory, providing a theoretical foundation and an explanatory framework for the phenomenon.

First, social entrepreneurship literature is clear about the "nature" of social entrepreneurs: they possess a "strong ethical fibre" (Catford, 1998; Drayton, 2002) and a "powerful desire for social change" (Schuyler, 1998); they intend to "make a difference" (Thompson *et al.*, 2000); and are driven by a "social mission" (Sullivan Mort *et al.*, 2003) and a "socio-moral motivation" (Nicholls, 2008). Their objective is "the creation of social value" (Mair and Schoen, 2007) and they are considered "change agents" (Chell, 2007; Sharir and Lerner, 2006). Social entrepreneurs address social problems by "mobilising resources to places that offer higher returns for society" (Dees and Battle Anderson, 2006, p. 60) and "crave social justice" (Johnson, 2000). Social entrepreneurs possess a strong empathetic attitude (Mair and Noboa, 2006; Hockerts, 2015) and focus their efforts on generating an impact on others (Miller *et al.*, 2012).

This characterisation of social entrepreneurs as "other-regarding" is seemingly contradictory with the conceptualisation of individualism of classical liberal economics (Santos, 2012). Self-interest might be driving many charitable initiatives in the corporate world, as strategic management literature has proven by showing that firms many times initiate philanthropic initiatives to gain legitimacy and, therefore, run operations more effectively (Wang and Qian, 2011; Orlitzky *et al.*, 2003). Additionally, this paradox might be interesting for the social entrepreneurship literature that has profoundly analysed the tensions between profit maximisation and mission within social businesses (Agafonow, 2015; McMullen and Bergman, 2017; Tracey *et al.*, 2011). Economic development facilitates a shift towards a culture associated with individualism (and a way of collectivism), resulting in an increased emphasis on individual freedom values (Inglehart and Oyserman, 2004). Moreover, emancipative values are a byproduct of a massive process of individualisation that happens when societies develop freedoms and evolve. While collectivistic values orient groups into caring for others, individualistic individuals are supposedly selfish and self-centred (Hofstede, 2001). Our theoretical framework suggests a causal effect of emancipative values on social entrepreneurship. Therefore, a byproduct of individualism might be the cause of an "other-regarding" paradigm. According to Inglehart and Baker (2001), self-expression values are also a consequence of individualisation.

Previous literature in social entrepreneurship showed that societies with high self-expression values experience higher shares of social entrepreneurial entry relative to societies with low self-expression values (Hoogendoorn, 2016) and that a secular-rational orientation and self-expressive values significantly explained social entrepreneurship, but only in established stages of the activity (Puumalainen *et al.*, 2015). How is it, then, that selfish and self-centred people start businesses to impact positively in society, aiming to create social value, alleviate poverty and promote the life of those living under existential constraints and stress?

Without denying the individualisation process occurring in modern societies, our contribution is to theoretically harmonise this apparent paradox between individualism and social entrepreneurship by building over the concept of "benign individualism" proposed by Welzel (2013). Emancipative values encourage a pro-social and pro-civic form of individualism that favours unselfishness and other-regarding initiatives, synthesising individualism and concern for others, the society and the environment. Economic theories — and, consequently, management theories — have failed to successfully integrate other paradigms than individual self-interest within their boundaries. Potent contributions to broaden the understanding of individual behaviour and to extend the possibilities of explaining economic action by considering other variables besides individual self-interest, such as social and relational motives (Rocha and Ghoshal, 2006), have been done in management literature. Undeniably, social entrepreneurship provides a clear example of economic actions motivated by others' interest (Santos, 2012). If our commitment towards the assumptions of classical liberal economics was of such a magnitude that it would prevent us from thinking otherwise, building upon the domain of equality, our theoretical contribution in this point is to question the scope of the "self" in "self-interest", by proposing that economic action — particularly in some cases, as in social entrepreneurship — might have broadened the scope of that "self" not towards an individual, a collectivity or a group, but to a species: humanity. Besides this, the benign form of individualism is theoretically relevant and coherent with previous empirical findings in social entrepreneurship literature, while providing a secure base for the conceptual development of the field.

Second, building upon the *entrepreneuring*-as-emancipation perspective (Rindova *et al.*, 2009), we presented an explanatory framework for the emergence of social entrepreneurship at a societal level. We identified the elements of the human empowerment process proposed by Welzel's evolutionary emancipation theory (action resources, emancipative values and civic entitlements, in this particular sequence) as the drivers of social entrepreneurship. Instead of pointing out isolated potential determinants, our study proposed a coherent theoretical framework to substantiate empirical testing. Therefore, this paper provides a broad theoretical frame which gives sense to different contributions in the literature of drivers of social entrepreneurship, shedding light on the reasons why some societies might be more socially entrepreneurial than others.

Besides this, the present work introduces a new theory of emancipation within the *entrepreneuring*-as-emancipation perspective. Rindova *et al.*'s (2009) paper opened the way by introducing the emancipation theory in entrepreneurship research. However, Welzel's (2013) emancipation theory remained absent from the debate, until now. There are many potential avenues of research that appear when integrating some of Welzel's contributions with the three core elements in the emancipatory process of *entrepreneuring*: seeking autonomy, authoring and making declarations.

Contributions to International Entrepreneurship

This study sheds light on the reasons why some societies are more socially entrepreneurial than others by proposing a consistent theoretical framework that gives sense and unifies different approaches and contributions in the field. The proposed theory is relevant since IE has been criticised for the absence of explanatory frameworks such as the one provided in this work to explain, among others, the emergence of the phenomenon of entrepreneurship in general (Keupp and Gaussmann, 2009; Coombs *et al.*, 2009). The same observation was applicable for social entrepreneurship since, as previously described, the existing contributions in the field derived hypotheses from different and not mutually aligned theories and conceptual frameworks, hindering the robustness of the findings. For this reason, a unifying theoretical framework which gives sense to data was urgent. At the same time, following various calls (Terjensen *et al.*, 2013; Jones *et al.*, 2011), we contributed to the foundations of cross-country, cross-cultural and combined cross-country and cross-cultural research. The international comparison of social entrepreneurship is relevant since it might help policymakers to understand the scope of the phenomenon and its capacity of tackling wicked social and environmental problems. This paper enables this comparability as Welzel's (2013) evolutionary emancipation theory is a unifying framework that the field lacked. We framed the phenomenon of social entrepreneurship in an integrative theoretical framework that coherently explained its emergence in an articulated manner. Now that the gap has been addressed, future research can empirically corroborate the potential hypotheses derived from the propositions by using the available international datasets on social entrepreneurship (mainly, GEM's 2009 and 2015 special editions) and those to be created in the future. We expect that such a framework will boost empirical research in social entrepreneurship from a "comparative international entrepreneurship" perspective.

Limitations and Future Research

An important limitation follows from the assumptions of Welzel's theory and restricts this study. By focusing mainly on the individual level of analysis and building from a methodological individualism approach, contextual, structural and institutional approaches to the phenomenon of social entrepreneurship and its emergence at a societal level might seem to be displaced. Moreover, the interactions among the micro, meso and macro levels of analysis are harder to identify and describe when assuming such a focus on the individual level. Prioritising agency over structure is a decision that has derivatives and that might hinder the possibility of further understanding the emergence of social entrepreneurship building over the contributions of other perspectives.

Future research must operationalise the theoretical propositions into hypotheses using the available datasets to methodologically corroborate or refute the presented theory. Additionally, an interesting avenue of research is related to differences in social entrepreneurship within countries. The proposed theoretical framework is consistent with the idea of entrepreneurial activities undertaken by a relatively more emancipated segment of the population with impact on the rest of the society. We think that there are several dynamics among individuals within countries that could be studied under the same theoretical framework. Moreover, as Zahra *et al.* (2008) observe, many entrepreneurs are addressing social problems on a worldwide scale, an element that country-centred data do not adequately show and that are relevant to consider from an "international opportunity" perspective (Mainela *et al.*, 2014). Our theory should also be contrasted to previous literature on this topic, such as Reuber *et al.* (2018), and although at another level of analysis, is coherent with previous findings (Knight and Cavusgil, 2004) regarding the capability of born global firms.

Following the proposed theory in this paper, empowered individuals or groups are those promoting the lives of others. It is necessary to further study this conclusion with the literature in social entrepreneurship, in empowerment and in social movement theory, including resistance and collective mobilisation, that focuses on self-managed groups or on grass-roots groups that commence emancipative initiatives without "external" interventions, such as, to provide a prominent example, the case presented by Fernández *et al.* (2017).

Finally, it would also be relevant to continue discussing the concept of benign individualism and its applicability in Management theories in general.

References

Acemoglu, D. and J. Robinson (2012). *Why Nations Fail: The Origins of Power, Prosperity, and Poverty.* Random House Digital, Inc.

Acs, Z. J. (1992). Small business economics: A global perspective. *Challenge*, 35(6), 38–44.

Agafonow, A. (2014). Toward a positive theory of social entrepreneurship. On maximizing versus satisficing value capture. *Journal of Business Ethics*, 125(4), 709–713.

Agafonow, A. (2015). Value creation, value capture, and value devolution: Where do social enterprises stand? *Administration & Society*, 47(8), 1038–1060.

Al Dajani, H., S. Carter, E. Shaw, and S. Marlow (2015). Entrepreneurship among the displaced and dispossessed: Exploring the limits of emancipatory entrepreneuring. *British Journal of Management*, 26(4), 713–730.

Alter, K. (2007). Social enterprise typology. *Virtue Ventures LLC*, 12, 1–124.

Alvesson, M. and H. Willmott (1992). On the idea of emancipation in management and organization studies. *Academy of Management Review*, 17(3), 432–464.

Alvord S. H., L. D. Brown, and Letts. (2004). Social entrepreneurship and societal transformation. *The Journal of Applied Behavioral Science*, 40(3), 260–282.

Austin, J., H. Stevenson, and J. Wei-Skillern (2006). Social and commercial entrepreneurship: Same, different, or both? *Entrepreneurship Theory & Practice*, 30(1), 1–22.

Bacq, S., and F. Janssen (2011). The multiple faces of social entrepreneurship: A review of definitional issues based on geographical and thematic criteria. *Entrepreneurship & Regional Development*, Vol. 23 (Nos. 5–6): 373–403.

Barendsen, L. and H. Gardner (2004). Is the social entrepreneur a new type of leader? *Leader to Leader*, *2004*(34), 43–50.

Barro, R. and J. W. Lee (2013). A new data set of educational attainment in the World, 1950–2010. *Journal of Development Economics*, Vol. 104, 184–198.

Beck, U. (2002). The cosmopolitan society and its enemies. *Theory, Culture & Society*, 19(1–2), 17–44.

Bosma, N. S. and J. Levie (2010). Global Entrepreneurship Monitor (GEM) 2009 Executive Report.

Bosma, N. S., T. Schøtt, S. A. Terjesen, and P. Kew (2016). Global Entrepreneurship Monitor 2015 to 2016: Special Topic Report on Social Entrepreneurship.

Brockhaus Sr., R. H. (1980). Risk taking propensity of entrepreneurs. *Academy of Management Journal*, 23(3), 509–520.

Busenitz, L. W., C. Gomez, and J. W. Spencer (2000). Country institutional profiles: Unlocking entrepreneurial phenomena. *Academy of Management Journal*, 43(5), 994–1003.

Caird, S. (1991). The enterprising tendency of occupational groups. *International Small Business Journal*, 9(4), 75–81.

Catford, J. (1998). Social entrepreneurs are vital for health promotion — but they need supportive environments too. *Health Promotion International*, 13(2), 95–97.

Chandra, Y. (2017). Social entrepreneurship as emancipatory work. *Journal of Business Venturing*, 32(6), 657–673.

Chell, E. (2007). Social enterprise and entrepreneurship. *International Small Business Journal*, 25(1), 5–26.

Choi, N. and S. Majumdar (2014). Social entrepreneurship as an essentially contested concept: Opening a new avenue for systematic future research. *Journal of Business Venturing*, 29(3), 363–376.

Cromie, S. and J. O'Donaghue (1992). Assessing entrepreneurial inclinations. *International Small Business Journal*, 10(2), 66–73.

Cukier, W., S. Trenholm, A. Carl, and G. Gekas (2011). Social entrepreneurship: A content analysis. *Journal of Strategic Innovation and Sustainability*, 7(1), 99–119.

Dacin, M. T. and P. A. Dacin (2011). Social entrepreneurship: A critique and future directions. *Organization Science*, 22(5), 1203–1213.

Dacin, P. A., M. T. Dacin, and M. Matear (2010). Social entrepreneurship: Why we don't need a new theory and how we move forward from here. *Academy of Management Perspectives*, 24(3), 37–57.

Datta, P. B. and R. Gailey (2012). Empowering women through social entrepreneurship: Case study of a women's co-operative in India. *Entrepreneurship, Theory & Practice*, 36(3), 569–587.

Dees, J. G. (1998). The meaning of social entrepreneurship. Durham, NC: Center for the Advancement of Social Entrepreneurship, Fuqua School of Business, Duke University. Available at https://centers.fuqua.duke.edu/case/wp-content/uploads/sites/7/2015/03/Article_Dees_MeaningofSocialEntrepreneurship_2001.pdf.

Dees, J. G. and B. B. Anderson (2006). Framing a theory of social entrepreneurship: Building on two schools of practice and thought. *Research on Social*

Entrepreneurship: Understanding and Contributing to an Emerging Field, 1(3), 39–66.

Defourny, J. and M. Nyssens (2010). Conceptions of social enterprise and social entrepreneurship in Europe and the United States: Convergences and divergences. *Journal of Social Entrepreneurship*, 1(1), 32–53.

Donnelly, J. (1984). Cultural relativism and universal human rights. *Human Rights Quarterly*, 6(4), 400–419.

Drayton, B. (2002). The citizen sector: Becoming as entrepreneurial and competitive as business. *California Management Review*, 44(3), 120–132.

Drucker, P. F. (1993). The rise of the knowledge society. *Wilson Quarterly*, 17(2), 52–71.

Estrin, S., J. Korosteleva, and T. Mickiewicz (2013). Which institutions encourage entrepreneurial growth aspirations? *Journal of Business Venturing*, 28(4), 564–580.

Estrin, S, T. Mickiewicz, and U. Stephan (2013). Entrepreneurship, social capital, and institutions: Social and commercial entrepreneurship across nations. *Entrepreneurship Theory and Practice*, 37(3), 479–504.

Fernández, P. D., I. Martí, and T. Farchi (2017). Mundane and everyday politics for and from the neighborhood. *Organization Studies*, 38(2), 201–223.

Fukuyama, F. (2011). *The Origins of Political Order: From Pre-human Times to the French Revolution*. Farrar, Straus and Giroux, New York: Farrar.

Galor, O. (2011). *Unified Growth Theory*. Princeton University Press.

Germak, A. J. and J. A. Robinson (2014). Exploring the motivation of nascent social entrepreneurs. *Journal of Social Entrepreneurship*, 5(1), 5–21.

Gras, D., E. Mosakowski, and G. T. Lumpkin (2011). Gaining insights from future research topics in social entrepreneurship: A content-analytic approach. In *Social and Sustainable Entrepreneurship*. Emerald Group Publishing Limited, (pp. 25–50).

Griffiths, M. D., L. K. Gundry, and J. R. Kickul (2013). The socio-political, economic, and cultural determinants of social entrepreneurship activity: An empirical examination. *Journal of Small Business and Enterprise Development*, 20(2), 341–357.

Hartog, C. and B. Hoogendoorn (2011). Prevalence and Determinants of Social Entrepreneurship at the Macro-level (No. H201022). EIM Business and Policy Research.

Hayton, J. C., G. George, and S. A. Zahra (2002). National culture and entrepreneurship: A review of behavioral research. *Entrepreneurship Theory and Practice*, 26(4), 33–52.

Hemingway, C. A. (2005). Personal values as a catalyst for corporate social entrepreneurship. *Journal of Business Ethics*, 60(3), 233–249.

Hockerts, K. (2006). Entrepreneurial opportunity in social purpose business ventures, In Mair, J., Robinson, J., and J. Hockerts, *Social Entrepreneurship*. New York: Palgrave MacMillan.

Hofstede, G. (1980a). Motivation, leadership, and organization: do American theories apply abroad? *Organizational Dynamics*, 9(1), 42–63.

Hofstede, G. (1980b). Culture and organizations. *International Studies of Management & Organization*, 10(4), 15–41.

Hoogendoorn, B. (2016). The prevalence and determinants of social entrepreneurship at the macro level. *Journal of Small Business Management*, 54(S1), 278–296.

Hoogendoorn, B., E. Pennings, and R. Thurik (2010). What do we know about social entrepreneurship: An analysis of empirical research.

Human Security Report Project (2006). Center for Security Studies, School of International Studies, Simon Fraser University (SFU), Vancouver, Canada, https://www.files.ethz.ch/isn/27140/HSC_Brief_2006_fulltext.pdf.

Huybrechts, B. and A. Nicholls (2012). Social entrepreneurship: Definitions, drivers and challenges. In *Social Entrepreneurship and Social Business.* Gabler Verlag, pp. 31–48.

Inglehart, R. F. (2008). Changing values among western publics from 1970 to 2006. *West European Politics*, 31(1–2), 130–146.

Inglehart, R. F. and W. E. Baker (2000). Modernization, cultural change, and the persistence of traditional values. *American Sociological Review*, 19–51.

Inglehart, R. F. and D. Oyserman (2004). Individualism, autonomy and self-expression: The human development syndrome.

Inglehart, R. F. and C. Welzel (2005). *Modernization, Cultural Change, and Democracy: The Human Development Sequence.* Cambridge University Press.

Jennings, J. E., P. D. Jennings, and M. Sharifian (2016). Living the dream? Assessing the 'entrepreneurship as emancipation' perspective in a developed region. *Entrepreneurship: Theory and Practice*, 40(1), 81–110.

Johnson, S. (2000). Literature review on social entrepreneurship. *Canadian Centre for Social Entrepreneurship*, 16, 23.

Lumpkin, G. T. and G. G. Dess (1996). Clarifying the entrepreneurial orientation construct and linking it to performance. *Academy of Management Review*, 21(1), 135–172.

Lumpkin, G. T., C. C. Cogliser, and D. R. Schneider (2009). Understanding and measuring autonomy: An entrepreneurial orientation perspective. *Entrepreneurship: Theory and Practice*, 33(1), 47–69.

Lundström, A. and C. Zhou (2014). Rethinking social entrepreneurship and social enterprises: A three-dimensional perspective. In *Social Entrepreneurship.* Springer, Cham, pp. 71–89.

Maddison, A. (2007). The world economy volume 1: A millennial perspective. Academic Foundation.

Mair, J. and I. Marti (2006). Social entrepreneurship research: A source of explanation, prediction, and delight. *Journal of World Business*, 41(1), 36–44.

Mair, J. and E. Noboa (2006). Social entrepreneurship: How intentions to create a social venture are formed. In *Social Entrepreneurship*. Palgrave Macmillan, London, pp. 121–135.

Mair, J. and O. Schoen (2007). Successful social entrepreneurial business models in the context of developing economies: An explorative study. *International Journal of Emerging Markets*, 2(1), 54–68.

Mair, J., J. Battilana, and J. Cardenas (2012). Organizing for society: A typology of social entrepreneuring models. *Journal of Business Ethics*, 111(3): 353–373.

Marti, I., D. Courpasson, and S. D. Barbosa (2013). 'Living in the fishbowl'. Generating an entrepreneurial culture in a local community in Argentina. *Journal of Business Venturing*, 28(1), 10–29.

Martin, R. L. and S. Osberg (2007). Social entrepreneurship: The case for definition. *Stanford: Stanford Social Innovation Review*, 5(2), 28–39.

Maslow, A. H. (1954). The instinctoid nature of basic needs. *Journal of Personality*, 22(3), 326–347.

McMullen, J. S. and B. J. Bergman (2017). Social entrepreneurship and the development paradox of prosocial motivation: A cautionary tale. *Strategic Entrepreneurship Journal*, 11(3), 243–270.

Méndez-Picazo, M. T., D. Ribeiro-Soriano, and M. A. N. Galindo-Martín (2015). Drivers of social entrepreneurship. *European Journal of International Management*, 9(6), 766–779.

Meyskens, M., C. RobbPost, J. A. Stamp, A. L. Carsrud, and P. D. Reynolds (2010). Social ventures from a resource based perspective: An exploratory study assessing global Ashoka fellows. *Entrepreneurship: Theory and Practice*, 34(4), 661–680.

Miller, T. L., M. G. Grimes, J. S. McMullen, and T. J. Vogus (2012). Venturing for others with heart and head: How compassion encourages social entrepreneurship. *Academy of Management Review*, 37(4), 616–640.

Mintzberg, H., R. Simons, and K. Basu (2002). Beyond selfishness. *MIT Sloan Management Review*, 44(1), 67.

Monge, C. B. (2018). Identifying cross-country key drivers of social entrepreneurial activity. *Journal of Social Entrepreneurship*, 1–19.

Montesano Montessori, N. (2016). A theoretical and methodological approach to social entrepreneurship as world-making and emancipation: Social change as a projection in space and time. *Entrepreneurship & Regional Development*, 28(7–8), 536–562.

Nga, J. K. H. and G. Shamuganathan (2010). The influence of personality traits and demographic factors on social entrepreneurship start up intentions. *Journal of Business Ethics*, 95(2), 259–282.

Nicholls, A. (2010). The legitimacy of social entrepreneurship: Reflexive isomorphism in a pre-paradigmatic field. *Entrepreneurship: Theory and Practice*, 34(4), 611–633.

Nolan, P. and G. Lenski (1999). Human Societies: An Introduction to Macrosociology. 8th ed. New York: McGraw-Hill.

North, D. C. (1991). Institutions. *Journal of Economic Perspectives*, 5(1), 97–112.

Nussbaum, M. C. (2006). Education and democratic citizenship: Capabilities and quality education. *Journal of Human Development*, 7(3), 385–395.

Nussbaum, M. C. (2006). Poverty and human functioning: Capabilities as fundamental entitlements. *Poverty and inequality*, 1990, 47–75.

Nussbaum, M. C. and A. Sen (eds.) (1993). *The Quality of Life*. Oxford University Press.

Orlitzky, M., F. L. Schmidt, and S. L. Rynes (2003). Corporate social and financial performance: A meta-analysis. *Organization Studies*, 24(3), 403–441.

Orwell, G. (2010). Animal farm (Vol. 31). Random House.

Peredo, A. M. and J. J. Chrisman (2006). Toward a theory of community-based enterprise. *Academy of Management Review*, 31(2), 309–328.

Peredo, A. M. and M. McLean (2006). Social entrepreneurship: A critical review of the concept. *Journal of World Business*, 41(1), 56–65.

Pless, N. M. and J. Appel (2012). In pursuit of dignity and social justice: Changing lives through 100% inclusion — How Gram Vikas fosters sustainable rural development. *Journal of Business Ethics*, 111(3), 389–411.

Popper, K. R. (1972). Objective knowledge: An evolutionary approach.

Popper, K. R. (2012). *The Open Society and Its Enemies*. Routledge.

Prabhu, G. N. (1999). Social entrepreneurial leadership. *Career Development International*, 4(3), 140–145.

Rindova, V., D. Barry, and D. J. Ketchen Jr. (2009). Entrepreneuring as emancipation. *Academy of Management Review*, 34(3), 477–491.

Roberts, D. and C. Woods (2005). Changing the world on a shoestring: The concept of social entrepreneurship. *University of Auckland Business Review*, 7(1), 45–51.

Rocha, H. O. and S. Ghoshal (2006). Beyond self-interest revisited. *Journal of Management Studies*, 43(3), 585–619.

Rotter, J. B. (1966). Generalized expectancies for internal versus external control of reinforcement. *Psychological Monographs: General and Applied*, 80(1), 1.

Santos, F. M. (2012). A positive theory of social entrepreneurship. *Journal of Business Ethics*, 111, 335–351.

Sachs, J. (2005). *The End of Poverty: How We can Make It Happen in Our Lifetime*. Penguin UK.

Schuyler, G. (1998). Social entrepreneurship: Profit as means, not an end. Digest 98–7. Ewing Marion Kauffman Foundation, Kansas City, MO. Center.

Shaw, E. and S. Carter (2007). Social entrepreneurship: Theoretical antecedents and empirical analysis of entrepreneurial processes and outcomes. *Journal of Small Business and Enterprise Development*, 14(3), 418–434.

Sharir, M. and M. Lerner (2006). Gauging the success of social ventures initiated by individual social entrepreneurs. *Journal of World Business*, 41, 6–20.

Short, J. C, Moss, T. W. and G. T. Lumpkin (2009). Research in social entrepreneurship: Past contributions and future opportunities. *Strategic Entrepreneurship Journal*, 3(2), 161–194.

SEN, A. K. (1999). *Development as Freedom*. Oxford: Oxford University Press, New York: Alfred Knopf.

Sena, S. A., Rocha, H. O. and I. Martí (2020). Social entrepreneurship: Exploring the nature of an analogous concept. Working paper.

Spear, R. and L. Hulgard (2007). Social entrepreneurship and the mobilization of social capital in European social enterprises. In *Social Enterprise*. Routledge, pp. 101–124.

Stephan, U. and L. M. Uhlaner (2010). Performance-based vs. socially supportive culture: A cross-national study of descriptive norms and entrepreneurship. *Journal of International Business Studies*, 41(8), 1347–1364.

Stephan, U., L. M. Uhlaner, and C. Stride (2015). Institutions and social entrepreneurship: The role of institutional voids, institutional support, and institutional configurations. *Journal of International Business Studies*, 46(3), 308–331.

Sullivan, D. M. (2007). Stimulating social entrepreneurship: Can support from cities make a difference? *The Academy of Management Perspectives*, 21(1), 77–78.

Sullivan Mort, G., J. Weerawardena, and K. Carnegie (2003). Social entrepreneurship: Towards conceptualization. *International Journal of Nonprofit and Voluntary Sector Marketing*, 8(1), 76–88.

Thomas, A. S. and S. L. Mueller (2000). A case for comparative entrepreneurship: Assessing the relevance of culture. *Journal of International Business Studies*, 31(2), 287–301.

Thompson, J. (2002). The world of the social entrepreneur. *International Journal of Public Sector Management*, 15(5), 412–432.

Thompson, J., G. Alvy, and A. Lees (2000). Social entrepreneurship — a new look at the people and the potential. *Management Decision*, 38(5), 328–338.

Tracey, P., N. Phillips, and O. Jarvis, (2011). Bridging institutional entrepreneurship and the creation of new organizational forms: A multilevel model. *Organization Science*, 22(1), 60–80.

Uhlaner, L. and R. Thurik (2007). Postmaterialism influencing total entrepreneurial activity across nations. *Journal of Evolutionary Economics*, 17(2), 161–185.

Van Gelderen, M. (2010). Autonomy as the guiding aim of entrepreneurship education. *Education and Training*, 52(8/9), 710–721.

Van Gelderen, M. and P. Jansen (2006). Autonomy as a start-up motive. *Journal of Small Business and Enterprise Development*, 13(1), 23–32.

Wang, H. and C. Qian (2011). Corporate philanthropy and corporate financial performance: The roles of stakeholder response and political access. *Academy of Management Journal*, 54(6), 1159–1181.

Weerawardena, J. and G. Sullivan-Mort (2006). *Investigating Social Entrepreneurship: A Multidimensional Model. Journal of World Business*, 41(1), 21–35.

Welzel, C. (2013). *Freedom Rising*. Cambridge University Press.

Williamson, O. E. (2000). The new institutional economics: Taking stock, looking ahead. *Journal of Economic Literature*, 38(3), 595–613.

Wilson, F. and J. Kickul (2006). For what, for whom? Examining the diverse motives of future female and male entrepreneurs. In *US Association for Small Business and Entrepreneurship 2006 Conference, Tucson, AZ, January*, pp. 12–16.

Zahra, S. A. and M. Wright (2016). Understanding the social role of entrepreneurship. *Journal of Management Studies*, 53(4), 610–629.

Zahra, S. A., E. Gedajlovic, D. O. Neubaum, and J. M. Shulman (2009). A typology of social entrepreneurs: Motives, search processes and ethical challenges. *Journal of Business Venturing*, 24(5), 519–532.

Zahra, S. A., H. N. Rawhouser, N. Bhawe, D. O. Neubaum, and J. C. Hayton (2008). Globalization of social entrepreneurship opportunities. *Strategic Entrepreneurship Journal*, 2(2), 117–131.

https://doi.org/10.1142/9789811228445_bmatter

Index

I

K

L

M

N

O

P

Lightning Source UK Ltd.
Milton Keynes UK
UKHW020627090321
380030UK00001B/47

9 789811 228438